Experiences in
Movement
& Music

Birth to Age 8

FIFTH EDITION

Experiences in
Movement
& Music

Birth to Age 8

RAE PICA

WADSWORTH
CENGAGE Learning·

Australia · Brazil · Japan · Korea · Mexico · Singapore · Spain · United Kingdom · United States

**Experiences in Movement and Music:
Birth to Age 8, Fifth Edition**
Rae Pica

Publisher: Linda Schreiber-Ganster

Acquisitions Editor: Mark Kerr

Assistant Editor: Joshua Taylor

Editorial Assistant: Greta Lindquist

Media Editor: Elizabeth Momb

Marketing Manager: Kara Kindstrom Parsons

Marketing Communications Manager:
Heather L. Baxley

Art and Cover Direction, Production
Management, and Composition:
PreMediaGlobal

Manufacturing Planner: Rebecca Cross

Rights Acquisition Specialist:
Thomas McDonough

Text Researcher: Pablo D'Stair

Cover Designer: CMB Design Partners

Cover Image: Photodisc; Larry Williams;
© Perkmeup/Dreamstime.com

For product information and technology assistance, contact us at
Cengage Learning Customer & Sales Support, 1-800-354-9706.

For permission to use material from this text or product,
submit all requests online at **www.cengage.com/permissions.**
Further permissions questions can be e-mailed to
permissionrequest@cengage.com.

Library of Congress Control Number: 2011945033

Student Edition:

ISBN-13: 978-1-111-83805-8

ISBN-10: 1-111-83805-4

Loose-Leaf Edition:

ISBN-13: 978-1-133-58976-1

ISBN-10: 1-133-58976-6

Wadsworth
20 Davis Drive
Belmont, CA 94002-3098
USA

Cengage Learning is a leading provider of customized learning solutions with office locations around the globe, including Singapore, the United Kingdom, Australia, Mexico, Brazil, and Japan. Locate your local office at **www.cengage.com/global.**

Cengage Learning products are represented in Canada by Nelson Education, Ltd.

To learn more about Wadsworth, visit **www.cengage.com/wadsworth.**

Purchase any of our products at your local college store or at our preferred online store **www.cengagebrain.com.**

Printed in the United States of America
1 2 3 4 5 6 7 16 15 14 13 12

Contents

PREFACE   ix
ABOUT THE AUTHOR   xiii
INTRODUCTION   xv

PART ONE   **The Basics of Movement Education   1**

Chapter 1   **Movement's Role in Child Development   2**
The Physical Domain   3
The Social/Emotional Domain   9
The Cognitive Domain   12
Assignments   18
Field Observations   18
References   19
Relevant Websites   20
Key Terms & Definitions   20

Chapter 2   **Movement's Role in Musical and Creative Development   22**
Music and the Young Child   23
Creativity and the Young Child   29
Assignments   35
Field Observation   35
References   35
Relevant Websites   35
Key Terms & Definitions   36

Chapter 3   **Child Development Characteristics and Their Impact on the Movement Program   37**
Infants   38
Toddlers   44
Preschoolers   54

Early-Elementary Children   61

Children with Special Needs   68

Assignments   73

Field Observations   74

References   74

Relevant Websites   75

Key Terms & Definitions   75

Chapter 4   Content of the Movement Program   76

The Elements of Movement   77

Locomotor Skills   81

Nonlocomotor Skills   88

Manipulative Skills   94

Educational Gymnastic Skills   100

Assignments   104

Field Observation   104

References   104

Relevant Websites   104

Key Terms & Definitions   104

PART TWO   Planning for Movement and Music   107

Chapter 5   Lesson Planning   108

Creating Lesson Plans   109

Developmental Progressions   113

Using a Variety of Movement Themes   114

Using a Single Movement Theme   117

Using a Single Unit Theme   119

Assignments   122

Field Observation   122

References   122

Relevant Websites   122

Key Terms & Definitions   122

Chapter 6   The When, Where, and What of Movement Sessions   123

Scheduling   124

Space   126

Group Size   128

Attire   129

Equipment and Props   130

Assignments   139

Field Observations   139

References   139

Relevant Websites   140

Key Terms & Definitions   140

Chapter 7 **Choosing and Using Music** **141**

Choosing Music   142

Using Music   145

Assignments   157

Field Observations   157

References   157

Relevant Websites   157

Key Terms & Definitions   157

PART THREE **Facilitating Movement Experiences** **159**

Chapter 8 **Teaching Methods** **160**

The Direct Approach   161

Guided Discovery   163

Exploration   167

Assignments   171

Field Observation   171

References   171

Relevant Websites   171

Key Terms & Definitions   171

Chapter 9 **Creating and Maintaining a Positive Learning Environment** **172**

Tried and Tested Teaching Tips   173

What about the Nonparticipant?   178

What about Disruptive Behavior?   179

The Role of Relaxation   181

Assignments   182

Field Observation   182

References   183

Relevant Websites   183

Key Terms & Definitions   183

PART FOUR **Movement and Music Through the Day** **185**

Chapter 10 **Movement Across the Curriculum** **186**

Art   188

Language Arts   192

Mathematics   193

Science   198

Social Studies   202

Putting It All Together   205

Assignments   208

Field Observation   208

References   208

Relevant Websites   209
Key Terms & Definitions   209

Chapter 11   Using Movement and Music for Transitions   210

Arrival   212
Transitions within the Classroom   216
Transitions to Outside the Classroom   217
Cleanup   218
Nap Time   219
Departure   221
Assignments   221
Field Observation   221
References   222
Relevant Websites   222
Key Terms & Definitions   222

Chapter 12   Bringing Movement Education Outdoors   223

Playground Space   226
Climbing Structures   227
Balance Beams   228
Tunnels   229
Platforms   229
Tires   230
Sand   231
Riding Toys   231
Slides   232
Swings   232
The Playground: A Place of Learning   234
Assignments   236
Field Observations   236
References   236
Relevant Websites   236
Key Terms & Definitions   236

APPENDIX   237
GLOSSARY   241
INDEX   243

I am pleased to present the fifth edition of *Experiences in Movement & Music*, and I'm grateful that it continues to be a useful resource to many pre- and in-service early-childhood professionals. The book has not changed substantially, as my reviewers did not request major revisions. *Experiences in Movement & Music* still offers both theory and practice for anyone who realizes the potential value of movement and music in young children's lives and who wishes to know more—and do more—about the subjects. It has been written for those who are (or plan to be) the following:

- early-childhood professionals in public or private preschools, kindergartens, or child care facilities
- physical education specialists, whose job descriptions now include preschoolers as well as kindergarten through third-grade students
- movement specialists working with young children in a wide variety of settings, including schools, recreation and gymnastic centers, YMCAs and YWCAs, and dance studios
- early-childhood and early-elementary music educators
- primary-grade classroom teachers

Chapter Material

The purpose of each section and chapter remains the same. Chapters 1 and 2 look at the role of movement—specifically in the child's physical, social/emotional, cognitive, musical, and creative growth. Chapter 3 looks at general milestones in cognitive, affective, and motor development of children from birth to age 8; at children with special needs; and at how movement experiences can be affected by the ages and stages of development. Chapter 4 defines the ingredients that should be part of an early-childhood movement curriculum. Together with the first three chapters, it makes up Part One, "The Basics of Movement Education."

Part Two, "Planning for Movement and Music," deals with such practical considerations as planning and scheduling lessons, group size, and the use of space and available equipment. Because music makes such a significant contribution to movement experiences, Chapter 7 offers detailed suggestions for choosing and using music.

Part Three, "Facilitating Movement Experiences," offers recommendations to help ensure success for both teachers and children. Chapter 8 focuses on the three teaching methods most often used in movement education, while Chapter 9 covers the topic that is frequently the teacher's primary concern: managing a room full of moving children.

Finally, because movement should not be a segregated part of the curriculum, Part Four, "Movement and Music Through the Day," explores some of the ways in which movement experiences can be used to enrich other content areas: art, language arts, math, science, and social studies. Chapter 11, "Using Movement and Music for Transitions," explains how to make daily transitions more manageable and more relevant to the curriculum as a whole. Chapter 12 explores how movement exploration can contribute to playground experiences.

At the end of each chapter, suggestions are made for assignments that will elicit answers to thought-provoking questions and that require students to conduct additional research and to gain hands-on experience. Throughout the book, numerous sample activities clarify points made, provide examples for children to enjoy, and stimulate the reader's own ideas. In addition, anecdotes—my own and those of others with stories to share—highlight some of the humor, frustrations, and joys related to simultaneously working in two exciting, rewarding, and important fields: early-childhood and movement education.

New to This Edition

The first two editions of this book were written for all of the professionals mentioned above, as well as others who work with children ages 2 to 8 and who know that children of this age need to move in order to develop physically, emotionally, socially, and cognitively. With the third edition, at the request of my reviewers, I addressed those people who work with infants. The inclusion of experiences in movement for infants was a reflection of the increasing number of infants being enrolled in child care centers. The fourth edition reflected the growing problem of sedentary children and its specific impact on their weight and health. This edition gives a nod to the growing influence of technology in our lives. As such, I've included call-outs to applicable videos and podcasts. At the request of reviewers, I included additional information about music, specifically the making of musical instruments, the classifications of instruments, and sources for multicultural music. Learning objectives have replaced the key points in every chapter. Finally, field observations have been added to the assignments at the end of each chapter.

Updated References and Resources

Once again, I have updated the resources cited throughout and at the end of the book. New websites have been added and those no longer relevant or active have been deleted.

Ancilliary Materials

Instructor's Manual

Available with this edition is an updated instructor's manual. In addition to chapter outlines, summaries, and key questions and answers, this edition's manual includes key terms and transparency masters by chapter, as well as instructions and ideas for using the online resource.

Book Companion Website

As with the fourth edition, the fifth edition of *Experiences in Movement & Music* includes a book companion website, which integrates Internet technology and early childhood education. The book companion website contains additional information and activities including Internet exercises, Web links, quizzes, and more. The online resources can be found at www.cengagebrain.com.

Acknowledgments

I want to offer my sincere thanks to everyone who helped make this book possible: my developmental editor, Joshua Taylor, for being so easy and enjoyable to work with; Mark Kerr, for the same; Dawn Bates, my friend and illustrator through numerous books; and to all the teachers and children with whom I've worked for over 30 years. My deepest appreciation, also, to the children and teachers who appear in the photos throughout the book.

I thank my reviewers for their time, effort, and contributions: Deb Ahola, Schenectady County Community College; Jill E. Fox, University of Texas at Arlington; Dennis M. Holt, University of North Florida; Jennifer M. Johnson, Vance-Granville Community College; Dina Rosen, Kean University; and Herman E. Walston, Kentucky State University.

The 5th edition of this textbook is dedicated to my business partner and kindred spirit, Errol St. Clair Smith, who has opened new worlds to me.

Finally, I am always glad to hear from my readers. If you want to share comments or ask questions—or if you want to schedule me for a keynote address, conference workshops, or staff development training—contact me through Wadsworth Cengage Learning, 10 Davis Drive, Belmont, CA 94002, or at raepica@bamradionetwork.com.

About the Author

RAE PICA is an internationally recognized education consultant specializing in early-childhood physical activity. Known for her lively and informative presentations, she has also consulted for such groups as the *Sesame Street* Research Department, the Head Start Bureau, the Centers for Disease Control, the President's Council on Physical Fitness and Sports, Nickelodeon's *Blue's Clues*, and state health departments throughout the country. As founder and director of Moving & Learning, Pica has been spreading the "movement message" since 1980.

Pica served on the original task force of the National Association for Sport and Physical Education (NASPE) that created *Active Start: A Statement of Physical Activity Guidelines for Children Birth to Five Years*. She is the author of 18 books, including the three-book *Moving & Learning Series; Physical Education for Young Children*; and the award-winning *Great Games for Young Children* and *Jump into Literacy: Active Learning for Preschoolers*. Rae also is co-founder of BAM Radio Network (www.bamradionetwork.com), where she hosts the syndicated Internet radio program *Body, Mind, and Child*, interviewing experts in the fields of early-childhood education, child development, play research, the neurosciences, and more, and is co-host, along with executive director Jerlean Daniel, of NAEYC Radio.

Introduction

In the first edition of this text, I mentioned the dilemma I often face when asked what I do for a living. Whether I'm on an airplane en route to a presentation or at a social gathering, this seemingly innocent question has thrown me for a loop for years.

"I'm a movement education consultant," I would formerly respond. And that would be where the trouble began—because people have absolutely no idea what movement education is, and I've never been very good at explaining it—despite the fact that I've been involved in movement education since 1980!

If you are reading this text, I of course have the advantage of your time, attention, and interest. For one thing, you want to understand what movement education is—otherwise you would not be reading this book. For you, I can look back at movement education's historical origins to provide some insight into what it is.

Rudolf Laban is generally considered to be the father of movement education. A dancer, choreographer, dance educator, and director of modern dance and ballet companies, Laban studied movement in its many forms. But it was not until Adolf Hitler's regime made it impossible for Laban to remain in Germany, forcing him to immigrate to England, that his work began to gain recognition. In England, he developed a system of analyzing movement through what he termed the elements of time, weight, space, and flow. (The elements described in Chapter 4 are adapted from Laban's ideas.) He also determined that experimentation should be used as a teaching method, which is the origin of the indirect teaching styles described in Chapter 8. Laban and his associates developed his work in the English schools. Gradually, his methods extended to Western Europe and then to the United States, where movement education has had its highs and lows but has never stopped evolving.

Of course, movement education's ever-changing state is one reason that it is difficult to nail down a definition. Indeed, sometimes it seems easier to describe what movement education is not.

Movement education incorporates creative movement and even creative dance, but it cannot accurately be called by either name. Both are concerned primarily with expressive movement, or the communication of ideas. Although Laban's work dealt more with the expressive than the functional—movement that "fulfills a purpose in work, sports, or activities of life" (Brown & Sommer,

1969, p. 44)—movement education today values both the expressive *and* the functional.

Although movement education is physical education in that learning takes place primarily through the physical domain, it is not physical education as many of us remember it. In other words, it is not the subject in which any of the following are true:

- The teacher stands in front of the students and tells them exactly what to do and how to do it. (Jumping jacks and sit-ups always surface in my recollections.)
- There is a right way and a wrong way to do everything. (Remember trying to climb the rope or staring down at the "horse" waiting to be jumped?)
- Only the physical domain is considered. (My repeated physical failures wreaked havoc with my affective domain.)

Instead, movement education

- often uses less direct and more child-centered approaches to instruction.
- allows children to experience success almost every time.
- involves the whole child.

In fairness, many physical education programs also do the same these days. But they also include activities that do not fall under the heading of movement education, such as soccer and square dancing.

So what is movement education? One of the best definitions I have ever read is from Moran and Kalakian (1974). They describe it as basic movement, which "is the foundation upon which the complex movements for all activity areas of physical education are built" (p. 111), and implementing movement exploration, which they call "the problem-solving approach to the teaching of physical education" (p. 111). Although many of us take movement a bit beyond the basics and use more than one instructional method, basic movement and exploration are indeed the essence of movement education. But Moran and Kalakian's description of the purpose of movement education hits the proverbial nail on the head:

> The intent of the program is to help the child become aware of his own potentials for moving efficiently and effectively in all aspects of living, including motor tasks involved in daily activities for play, work, and creative expression. Through movement education the child develops his general capacity for movement and learns the fundamentals necessary to facilitate his subsequent skill development ... Movement education incorporates the child's natural inclination to move freely, to be creative, and to test his own abilities. (p. 112)

Of course, after studying this text and facilitating movement experiences with children, you will probably find your own definition. And as the years pass and you find yourself adapting your movement activities to suit varying situations and different children, your definition will probably change, too. And that is as it should be.

As I continually attempt to describe movement education, my definition also keeps evolving. In a previous edition, I characterized it as a success-oriented, child-centered, noncompetitive form of physical education emphasizing fundamental movements and the discovery of their variations, which can later be used in games, sports, dance, gymnastics, and life itself. That is all still true; it is just a bit of a mouthful when addressing a stranger on a plane or a new acquaintance at a social gathering who has asked about my work only to be polite. And I've realized that perhaps this is the principal reason why I have such difficulty in explaining what I do. The person to whom I'm speaking would like a quick and easy response, and while I'd like to provide one, it is also critical that it be exactly the right one.

It was on yet another plane trip that the appropriate words actually—finally—did tumble out. I was talking to the grandfather of a 4-year-old girl, so it was especially important that I get it right. I told him that movement education is basic physical education that emphasizes fundamental motor skills and such concepts as body and spatial awareness, but that it is also a philosophy of physical education in that it is success-oriented, child-centered, and noncompetitive. And, you know, I think he got it.

Finally, as I mentioned in a previous edition, there is one thing I hope you will soon discover as you read the following chapters—and that will never change: Not only is movement education important, it is also fun.

By the way, just to simplify things, I now call myself a children's physical activity specialist.

References

Brown, M. C., & Sommer, B. K. (1969). *Movement education: Its evolution and a modern approach*. Reading, MA: Addison-Wesley.

Moran, J. M., & Kalakian, L. H. (1977). *Movement experiences for the mentally retarded or emotionally disturbed child*. Minneapolis: Burgess.

Credits

This page constitutes an extension of the copyright page. We have made every effort to trace the ownership of all copyrighted material and to secure permission from copyright holders. In the event of any question arising as to the use of any material, we will be pleased to make the necessary corrections in future printings. Thanks are due to the following authors, publishers, and agents for permission to use the material indicated.

Chapter 3: Reprinted from *Active Start: A Statement of Physical Activity Guidelines for Children Birth to Five Years* (2009) with permission from the National Association for Sport and Physical Education (NASPE), 1900 Association Drive, Reston, VA 20191-1599 (http://www.naspeinfo.org) From *Moving & Learning Series: Toddlers* (p. 70) by R. Pica, Belmont, CA: Cengage Learning. Copyright 2000 by Rae Pica. Reprinted by permission. From Rae Pica, *Wiggle, Giggle, & Shake: 200 Ways to Move and Learn*, p. 19. Reprinted with permission from Gryphon House, 10770 Columbia Pike, Suite 201, Silver Spring, MD 20901. (800) 638-0928.

PART ONE

The Basics of Movement Education

1 Movement's Role in Child Development

2 Movement's Role in Musical and Creative Development

3 Child Development Characteristics and Their Impact on the Movement Program

4 Content of the Movement Program

© Cengage Learning 2013.

Movement's Role in Child Development

Learning Objectives

After completing this chapter, the student will be able to:

1 Describe the role of movement in the child's physical domain.

2 Define the health-related components of physical fitness.

3 Describe the role of movement in the child's social/emotional and cognitive domains.

4 Explain the theory of multiple intelligences and how multiple intelligences differ from learning styles.

TERMS TO KNOW

physical fitness

health-related fitness

social development

emotional development

modalities of knowledge acquisition

intelligence

bodily/kinesthetic intelligence

cross-lateral movements

Typically, when considering children and movement, most people tend to think in terms of physical benefits only. Although movement contributes in numerous ways to the physical domain, it is also critical to social and emotional (affective), as well as cognitive, development.

The Physical Domain

Perhaps the simplest and most important reason children should be allowed and encouraged to move is to develop their movement skills. Although it is commonly believed that children automatically acquire motor skills as their bodies develop, maturation only means that they will be able to execute most movement skills at a low performance level. Continuous practice and instruction are required if a child's performance level and movement repertoire are to increase (Gallahue & Cleland-Donnelly, 2003). In other words, once a child is able to creep and walk, gross motor skills should be taught just as other abilities are taught. Furthermore, special attention should be paid to children demonstrating delays in gross motor skills, as such delays will not simply go away over time.

Standard 1a

According to Carson (2001), engaging in unplanned, self-selected physical activities—or even a movement learning center—is not enough for young children to gain movement skills. Carson explained that families and teachers "would not advocate learning to read or communicate by having their children enter a 'gross cognitive area' where children could engage in self-selected 'reading play' with a variety of books" (p. 9).

A developmentally appropriate movement curriculum can give children the practice and instruction necessary to refine their movement skills and expand their movement vocabularies. This curriculum is critical, because the ability to move well promotes feelings of self-confidence and will benefit children socially, emotionally, and physically (Bunker, 1991; Goodway & Rudisill, 1996). One study (Goodway & Rudisill, 1996) suggested that children who are enrolled in a motor skills program have higher perceptions of their mental abilities.

Standard 1a

When children feel good about their movement abilities, they are more likely to make physical activity part of their lives. Although children love to move—and adults tend to think of children as constantly being in motion—children today are leading much more sedentary lives than did their predecessors. Young

Development of movement skills is perhaps the most important reason children should be encouraged to move.

© Cengage Learning 2013.

children are watching television an average of four hours a day (American Academy of Pediatrics, 2006). In fact, watching television is the predominant sedentary behavior in children, second only to sleeping (Kaur, 2003). The advent of computers and video games has also contributed to the decline in activity. A study from the Kaiser Family Foundation determined that children ages 8 to 18 are spending more than seven and a half hours a day with electronic devices (Lewin, 2010)—the same number of hours some people spend at full-time jobs.

According to Bar-Or et al. (1998), there is one consistent observation that stands out among the studies of energy expenditure in young children: Children under the age of seven seem to expend about 20 to 30 percent less energy in physical activity than the level recommended by the World Health Organization. The Children's Activity and Movement in Preschools Study (CHAMPS) determined that children enrolled in preschools were engaged in moderate to vigorous physical activity (MVPA) during only 3.4 percent of the preschool day (NIEER, 2010). Pate et al. (2008) observed 2,000 children and found that "children attending preschools were engaged in MVPA during only 2.6% of observation intervals. During over 85% of intervals, children were engaged in either very light activity or sedentary behaviors" (p. 443).

To further compound the problem, Westerners have yet to completely accept the unity of mind and body, so we insist on training minds in classrooms and bodies in physical education classes, which are typically unavailable in preschools and child care centers and are increasingly disappearing from elementary schools due to budget cuts and an emphasis on high-stakes testing. When available, these classes too often stress competition and elimination. Under that emphasis, what happens to a child's love of movement?

Considered together, these factors provide cause for concern regarding children's fitness levels. Statistics indicate that 40 percent of 5- to 8-year-olds show at least one heart disease risk factor, including hypertension and obesity. The latter, which is on the rise, particularly among children, has been linked to television viewing (Bar-Or et al., 1998). A Canadian study (Science Daily, 2010) determined that the blood vessels of obese children have a stiffness normally seen in much older adults who have cardiovascular disease. Furthermore, the Centers for Disease Control (CDC) estimates that American children born in the year 2000 face a one-in-three chance of developing type 2 diabetes, previously known as adult-onset diabetes because it was rarely seen in children (Centers for Disease Control, 2005).

MORE ABOUT CHILDHOOD OBESITY

The issue of childhood obesity is of such concern that, in February 2010, First Lady Michelle Obama launched a campaign called *Let's Move!*, which is intended to combat the epidemic of childhood obesity through a comprehensive approach that engages every sector impacting the health of children by providing schools, families and communities simple tools to help kids be more active, eat better, and get healthy. As part of this effort, President Barack Obama established the Task Force on Childhood Obesity to develop and implement an interagency plan that details a coordinated strategy, identifies key benchmarks, and outlines an action plan to end the problem of childhood obesity within a generation. The action plan defines the goal of ending childhood obesity in a generation as returning to a childhood obesity rate of just 5 percent by 2030, which was the rate before childhood obesity first began to rise in the late 1970s.

More information about *Let's Move!* can be found at http://www.letsmove.gov.

Individuals who are physically active as children are likely to remain physically active in adulthood. Therefore, physical activity in childhood can have an impact on adult health (Blair, 1992; Blair, Clark, Cureton, & Powell, 1989). A sedentary lifestyle among adults is a major health problem in the United States: an estimated 300,000 deaths a year are due to low levels of activity and fitness (Cooper, 1999), placing sedentary living in the same risk category as smoking cigarettes or driving drunk.

Future Implications

The implications are clear—and frightening. One study determined that only 2 percent of adults who were inactive as children became active as adults (Activity and Health Research, 1992). Furthermore, once established in childhood, poor diet and physical inactivity (the two primary causes of obesity) tend to carry over into adulthood (Bar-Or et al., 1998; Moore, Nguyen, Rothman, Cupples, & Ellison, 1995). Heart disease is the leading killer of adults in the United States, accounting for more than half of all deaths every year (U.S. Department of Health and Human Services [U.S. DHHS], 1990). With risk factors appearing in children as young as five, cardiovascular disease may become an even greater threat in future generations.

Physical Best, developed by the American Alliance for Health, Physical Education, Recreation, and Dance (AAHPERD, 2005), defines physical fitness as "a physical state of well-being that allows people to (1) perform daily activities with vigor, (2) reduce their risk of health problems relative to lack of exercise, and (3) establish a fitness base for participation in a variety of physical activities." If this definition of *physical fitness* is to become a reality for the children of today, children must be taught that physical activity is just as important as good hygiene and a proper diet (Taras, 1992). Parents and teachers must encourage, praise, and validate physical activity at every opportunity. They must also serve as role models. Because Americans now burn fewer calories in the course of their daily lives than ever before, physical activity must be programmed back into our lifestyles.

naeyc
Standard 4b

The competition with television and video games is steep, but children will never be as motivated to be physically active as they are during the early years. Because children are "hardwired" to move, parents and early-childhood professionals are not without weapons in their war against sedentary lifestyles.

The Role of Movement

The role of movement is evident. Physical activity promotes fitness, which consists of two components: health-related fitness and skill-related fitness. The latter includes balance, agility, coordination, power, speed, and reaction time. However, it is the former that is relevant to a discussion about young children. Health-related fitness incorporates cardiovascular endurance, muscular strength, muscular endurance, flexibility, and body composition.

Cardiovascular Endurance. This is the ability of the heart and lungs to supply oxygen and nutrients to the muscles. Someone with great cardiovascular endurance has a strong heart, which means a larger heart that pumps more blood per beat than the heart of an individual who is not fit. Good cardiovascular endurance results when an individual exercises regularly. Typically, aerobic exercise improves cardiovascular fitness. However, for children, we must think of aerobics in a different way than we do for adults.

Young children, particularly before the age of six, are not ready for long, uninterrupted periods of strenuous activity. Not only is it unrealistic to expect children to perform organized exercises for 30 continuous minutes, as an adult does, it could also be physically damaging. At the very least, such exercise could instill an intense dislike for physical activity.

BAM! radio

PODCAST: *Go to www. bamradionetwork.com and search for the podcast "Solving the Growing Physical Inactivity Crisis".*

- *Adults tend to think of young children as constantly in motion, but Dr. Pate's research found that this is not true in preschool settings. What did the research show, and what are your thoughts relative to it?*
- *What, according to Dr. Pate's research, is one of the strongest predictors of whether or not a child is physically active?*
- *Cite two impediments to physical activity in preschool settings.*

Pumping on a swing contributes to muscle strength.

© Cengage Learning 2013.

Developmentally appropriate aerobic activities for children include moderate to vigorous play and movement. Moderately intense physical activity, like walking, increases the heart rate and breathing somewhat; vigorously intense movement, such as pretending to be an Olympic sprinter, takes much more effort and results in a noticeable increase in breathing. Playing tag, marching, riding a tricycle, dancing to moderate- to fast-paced music, and jumping rope are other forms of moderate- to vigorous-intensity exercise (known as MVPA) for children.

Muscular Strength. Muscular strength is described as the ability to exert force with a single maximum effort. Strong muscles are necessary not only for performing certain tasks, such as throwing for distance, hanging and swinging, climbing, and carrying heavy books and groceries, but also for preventing injury and maintaining proper posture. An added bonus is that increasing muscle strength also increases strength in tendons, ligaments, and bones.

Strength training, also known as resistance or weight training, is the best way to build muscular strength. However, again we must view things differently than if we were discussing adults. For adults, strength training usually means working with weights and equipment. For children, such a regimen is not appropriate. It is never a good idea to modify an adult strength-training program for use by children. Adults' bodies are fully developed; children's are not. Adults have long attention spans and the motivation to endure the monotony of repetitive exercises; children do not. Adults can follow specific instructions for proper form and understand the risks in handling strength-training equipment; children cannot. For these reasons, the best strength training for children uses their own weight in physical activities they typically enjoy, like jumping, playing tug-of-war, and pumping their legs to go higher on a swing.

Muscular Endurance. Muscular endurance, which is related to stamina, is the muscles' ability to continue contracting over an extended period of time. Children's muscular endurance is important because "a child who has good muscular endurance will enjoy and have greater success in his/her daily work activities, in play, and in sporting and athletic competitions" (Landy & Burridge, 1997, p. 8).

Flexibility. Flexibility is the range of motion around joints. People with good flexibility can bend and stretch without effort or pain. They can also take part in physical activities with less likelihood of muscle strain, sprain, or spasm.

In general, girls tend to be more flexible than boys. Boys start to lose their flexibility at around age 10. Girls begin to lose flexibility around age 12. However, if children are physically active, they will be more flexible than those who are sedentary.

Adults should encourage children to work specifically on their flexibility. Holding gentle, static stretches that take a muscle just beyond its usual length (without pain) for at least 10 seconds will help improve or maintain flexibility. Activities such as hanging and swinging from monkey bars also help increase flexibility.

It is important to keep in mind two cautions regarding stretching. First, children should work their own limbs through their ranges of motion rather than having an adult or someone else move them. An adult can easily stretch a child's muscles and joints too far. Second, children should be warned against ballistic stretching—bouncing while stretching—as this can cause small tears in the muscle fibers and is not as effective as static stretching.

Body Composition. The final component of health-related fitness is the body's makeup in terms of fat, muscles, tissue, and bone, or the percentage of lean body tissue to fat. Due to the escalating childhood obesity crisis, much attention is currently focused on body weight. However, weight alone is not a good indicator of fitness. For example, some children are simply largeboned and thus heavier than other children. In addition, muscle weighs more than fat, so two children may have the same weight but very different body composition, with one having muscle and very little fat and the other having too much fat.

Physical activity—particularly cardiovascular and muscle-strengthening activities—is the key to combating body fat. The significance of this information for teachers is that they must do more to ensure that their students are not experiencing extended periods of inactivity, which are considered inappropriate for normal, healthy children. If children are to experience lifelong fitness, teachers need to include movement as a regular part of each day beyond physical education and the playground. In other words, movement should take place in the classroom, too. Teachers can also make a meaningful impression by encouraging exercise outside school and by providing developmentally appropriate information regarding fitness and exercise. The activity itself is only one of the important facets of fitness education (Pangrazi & Corbin, 1993).

Finally, if a child's early encounters with movement are successful and fun while also building confidence, then that child is much more likely to want to keep moving throughout her or his life. Therefore, the early-childhood professional's most vital role in creating physically fit adults may simply be ensuring that children do not lose their natural love for movement.

Active Start

Physical Activity Guidelines for Children: Birth to Five Years

The following guidelines support the position of the National Association for Sport and Physical Education (NASPE) that all children from birth to age five should engage in daily physical activity that promotes health-related fitness and movement skills.

● **Infants (birth to 12 months)**

1. Infants should interact with parents and/or caregivers in daily physical activities dedicated to exploring movement and the environment.

(Continued)

2. Caregivers should place infants in settings that encourage and stimulate movement experiences and active play for short periods of time several times a day.
3. Infants' physical activity should promote skill development in movement.
4. Infants should be placed in an environment that meets or exceeds recommended safety standards for performing large-muscle activities.
5. Those in charge of infants' well-being are responsible for understanding the importance of physical activity and should promote movement skills by providing opportunities for structured and unstructured physical activity.

• **Toddlers (12 to 36 months)**

1. Toddlers should engage in a total of at least 30 minutes of structured physical activity each day.
2. Toddlers should engage in at least 60 minutes—and up to several hours—per day of unstructured physical activity and should not be sedentary for more than 60 minutes at a time, except when sleeping.
3. Toddlers should be given ample opportunities to develop movement skills that will serve as the building blocks for future motor skillfulness and physical activity.
4. Toddlers should have access to indoor and outdoor areas that meet or exceed recommended safety standards for performing large-muscle activities.

5. Those in charge of toddlers' well-being are responsible for understanding the importance of physical activity and promoting movement skills by providing opportunities for structured and unstructured physical activity and movement experiences.

• **Preschoolers (3 to 5 years)**

1. Preschoolers should accumulate at least 60 minutes of structured physical activity each day.
2. Preschoolers should engage in at least 60 minutes—and up to several hours—of unstructured physical activity each day and should not be sedentary for more than 60 minutes at a time, except when sleeping.
3. Preschoolers should be encouraged to develop competence in fundamental motor skills that will serve as the building blocks for future motor skillfulness and physical activity.
4. Preschoolers should have access to indoor and outdoor areas that meet or exceed recommended safety standards for performing large-muscle activities.
5. Caregivers and parents in charge of preschoolers' health and well-being are responsible for understanding the importance of physical activity and for promoting movement skills by providing opportunities for structured and unstructured physical activity.

Excerpted with permission from the National Association for Sport and Physical Education, an association of the American Alliance for Health, Physical Education, Recreation, and Dance, *Active Start: A Statement of Physical Activity Guidelines for Children Birth to Five Years* (Reston, VA: NASPE, 2009, 23–24).

Sample Activities

Physical activity, like everything else in children's lives, should be appropriate for their level of development. Calisthenics and structured exercise regimens are not developmentally appropriate for young children (Poest & Leszynski, 1988) and are not likely to contribute to a lifelong desire to keep moving. In fact, the "no pain, no gain" approach to exercise so often adopted by adults is not only incomprehensible to young children but can also create an early dislike for any movement.

Teachers need not be overly concerned with the type or intensity of an activity, as long as regular activity remains a part of children's lives. As evidenced by the activities listed here, the promotion of motor skill development and fitness do not have to be mutually exclusive; children can reap fitness benefits as they practice and refine their motor skills. If

fitness activities are not naturally occurring or if more are desired, teachers can incorporate into the program a daily walk or creative movement activities performed to moderate- to fast-paced music.

The following are more specific suggestions:

Marching. An energetic march around the room is a great fitness activity. You can provide an accompanying drumbeat or play a recording of a John Philip Sousa composition or a march from Hap Palmer's *Mod Marches* or *Patriotic and Morning Time Songs* or from Dennis Buck's *Patriotic Songs and Marches* (available from both Kimbo Educational and Educational Record Center, see Appendix 2). Challenge children to swing their arms and raise their knees while keeping the rest of their bodies straight and tall. What role do they want to play in the parade? Flag bearer? Baton twirler? Perhaps they would like to pretend to play a musical instrument found in a marching band. Which instrument do they want to play?

The Track Meet. Running is great aerobic exercise. A lively piece of music in a steady 4/4 meter can help motivate children to run. Ask them to pretend they are in an Olympic long-distance race. That means they must pace themselves if they are to make it to the finish line (the end of the song or a predetermined number of times around the room or playground). You can challenge primary-grade children to race across the country, plotting their daily progress on a U.S. map, thereby integrating physical fitness with geography and math lessons. For instance, once around the room might equal a mile on the map. With preschoolers, you might use a puzzle map instead. Every day that they run around the gym or playground or for the length of a favorite recording, another state is placed on the puzzle to show their progress.

Rabbits and 'Roos. Children love to pretend to be animals. Ask them to jump like rabbits and kangaroos, alternating from one to the other. Which is the larger of the two animals? Which would have a heavier jump? This activity is excellent for promoting muscular strength. If performed often, each time for a little longer, it will also contribute to muscular and cardiovascular endurance.

"Pop Goes the Weasel." Ask children to walk to this familiar melody, jumping into the air each time they hear the *pop*. You can hum or sing the song or play a recording of it. This popular piece can be found in Rae Pica's *Moving & Learning Series* (2000b, 2000c); on *Children's All-Star Rhythm Hits* by Jack Capon and Rosemary Hallum, available from Educational Activities (see Appendix 2); on Ella Jenkins's *Early Early Childhood Songs*; and on *The Hokey Pokey, Rhythm Band Time* and *Froggy Went a' Courtin'*, which are all available from Melody House (see Appendix 2). Once children have mastered the challenge to jump on the *pop*, ask them to jump and change direction at the same time.

Giddy-Up. If children in your group cannot yet gallop, challenge the class to move like horses. Those children who can gallop will likely do so, and those who cannot will simply pretend to be horses, still meeting your challenge and thus experiencing success.

In essence, any locomotor skill can be an aerobic activity if it is performed continuously. Begin slowly and gradually increase the length of the activities, challenging children to push themselves a bit further each time (Poest et al., 1990).

The Social/Emotional Domain

The term social development can encompass many interpretations, meaning different things to different people. To some early-childhood professionals, the term brings to mind social play, or the ability of children to interact with each other (Isenberg & Jalongo, 2000). To others, it connotes social studies, which Mayesky (2008) stated "are designed to develop intelligent, responsible, self-directing individuals who can function as members of groups—family, community, and world—with which they become identified." Erik Erikson used the term *psychosocial development* to refer to development of the personality, including one's self-concept. And Benard (1995) said social competence includes such qualities as "responsiveness, flexibility, empathy, communication skills, and a sense of humor" (p. 1). Emotional development, or how children feel about other people and things and the way in which they express their feelings, is closely associated with all of these interpretations of social development.

In the context of this book, social/emotional development will encompass all these meanings and include the development of a sense of personal and social responsibility, which Greenberg (1992) said,

- is activated by an urge to contribute something to someone—a person, a group, or one's own best "self";
- is an outgrowth of self-esteem, which in turn is an outgrowth of independence, competence, and initiative; and
- grows out of an ability to see other people's viewpoints and feel concern for them (empathy). (p. 17)

Regardless of how the term is specifically interpreted, social development is a long and continuous process that begins with self-discovery and results in the ability to interact with others. How well individuals learn to function with others can greatly depend on their early childhood experiences, especially in light of Bloom's (1964) contention that 90 percent of a person's habits and attitudes are established by age 12.

Early-childhood professionals must ensure that children do not lose their love of movement.

© Cengage Learning 2013

Future Implications

Imagine a world in which cooperation is valued more highly than competition, a world in which all people have such healthy self-concepts that they are able to respect one another's differences. Can you envision a world in which everyone is able to feel empathy with everyone (and everything) else? A world in which everyone demonstrates both self-responsibility and a social conscience?

In such a world, there would be fewer crimes and fewer wars (and possibly even no crime or war). There would be greater respect for all the world's creatures and for the planet itself. When a problem does arise, people would know how to work together to solve it. Such a world might well be considered utopia and beyond the range of possibility. But is not a perfect world what everyone wishes for the children of the future? If that is what we truly desire, then we must believe in its possibility. We must do our part to help make it a reality—beginning with the social development of children in our care. According to Jewett (1992),

Standard 1a

"Children who demonstrate a number of cooperative strategies and can attend to the needs of others while also asserting and defending their own rights are more likely to be socially successful and to establish reciprocal, mutually satisfying friendships than are other children."

The Role of Movement

Frostig (1970) wrote:

> Movement education can help a child to adjust socially and emotionally because it can provide him with successful experiences and permit interrelationships with other children in groups and with a partner. Movement education requires that a child be aware of others in [activities] in which he shares space … he has to take turns and to cooperate. He thus develops social awareness and achieves satisfaction through peer relationships and group play. (pp. 9–10)

Standard 5c

Frostig pointed out fairly obvious ways in which movement can affect children socially. But educators can also make important choices with regard to curriculum content and teaching methods that can help ensure that the movement curriculum has a positive impact on children's social development. First, educators can choose to incorporate activities that specifically emphasize cooperation (cooperative activity books are listed on page 11). Too many of the physical activities currently in children's lives pit them against one another, supposedly in

How well children learn to interact with others depends in great part on their early childhood experiences.

© Cengage Learning 2013.

preparation for a dog-eat-dog world. But when children are given opportunities to work together toward a solution or common goal—achieving a balance, creating a shape, planning a movement sequence, or crowding together on the one remaining seat in a game of cooperative musical chairs—they know they

each contribute to the success of the venture. Each child knows she or he plays a vital role in the outcome, and each accepts the responsibility of fulfilling that role. Children also learn to become tolerant of others' ideas and to accept one another's similarities and differences.

Second, curriculum planners can choose a balance between child-directed and teacher-directed learning experiences. Child-directed activities automatically place more responsibility on children. As a result, they learn to account for their own behavior and performance. In addition, a creative problem-solving approach to instruction (discussed in Chapter 8) lends itself to success because it allows students to respond to challenges at their own developmental levels and rates. This approach increases children's self-confidence (and, thus, their self-esteem), as they see their choices being accepted and validated. In addition, according to Mosston and Ashworth (1990), two important results of problem solving are the "development of patience with peers and the enhancement of respect for other people's ideas" (p. 259).

Although facilitating the development of social skills is indeed a goal of most early-childhood professionals, social skills are not achieved naturally on the playground or in other play situations. Therefore, teachers and caregivers must plan

MORE ABOUT
COOPERATION

Sports psychologist Terry Orlick's *Cooperative Sports and Games Book: Challenge Without Competition* is probably the best-known collection of cooperative activities. The newest edition from Human Kinetics (2006) is based on the premise that people should play together, not against each other. A similar idea is put forth in *Everyone Wins! Cooperative Games and Activities,* by Josette and Ba Luvmour (New Society Publishers, 2007).

Supporting the argument for cooperation is Alfie Kohn's *No Contest: The Case Against Competition* (Mariner Books, 1992), which is described as the first comprehensive book to show why competition is often damaging. Kohn refutes the myths that competition builds character and is an instinctive part of human nature.

experiences that promote social development and help facilitate it. They must also provide ample opportunity for physical activity, as the research shows that children who feel good about their physical abilities have a better overall view of themselves (Strickland, n.d.) and that "directed play and physical education programs contribute to the development of self-esteem in elementary children" and "may be the prime determiner of future behavior" (Gruber, 1985, p. 42).

The Cognitive Domain

Confucius said, "What I hear, I forget. What I see, I remember. What I do, I know." Since the time of Confucius, we have discovered that the majority of people are more likely to really know what they have a chance to do. In fact, the more senses involved in the learning process, the greater the impression it makes and the longer it stays with us. According to Fauth (1990), we retain

- 10 percent of what we read;
- 20 percent of what we hear;
- 30 percent of what we see;
- 50 percent of what we hear and see at the same time;
- 70 percent of what we hear, see, and say; and
- 90 percent of what we hear, see, say, and do (acting out, dramatizing, dancing, painting, drawing, constructing). (p. 160)

naeyc
Standard 1a

Studies of how young children learn have proven that they often acquire knowledge experientially through play, experimentation, exploration, and discovery. More recently, a great deal of research has been done on learning styles, with studies showing that children acquire knowledge by using different modalities and that individuals possess varying degrees of strength in each of those modalities.

The four modalities of knowledge acquisition are

- visual—information is obtained through the sense of sight,
- auditory—learning takes place primarily through what is heard,
- tactile (sometimes called *tactual*)—the sense of touch provides the greatest amount of information,
- kinesthetic—doing and moving stimulate learning.

naeyc
Standard 1a

Reiff (1992) reported a Barbe and Milone study concluding that approximately 25 to 30 percent of students in a classroom are visual learners, 25 to 30 percent are auditory, and 15 percent are tactile/kinesthetic. Flaherty (1992) reported that about 40 percent of K–12 students consider themselves visual learners, 20 percent believe they are auditory, and 40 percent say they are tactile or kinesthetic learners. Whatever the exact numbers, increasing evidence indicates that although some students have strengths and weaknesses in certain modalities, most students learn with all their modalities, and many who are doing poorly in school are primarily tactile or kinesthetic learners (Reiff, 1992).

In addition, the work of Howard Gardner (1993), a developmental psychologist at Harvard, has helped us understand that children (all individuals, in fact) are intelligent in different ways—that is, they have different ways of learning and knowing. Gardner contended that intelligence is not a singular entity that can be tested only with paper and pencil. Rather, he defined intelligence as the capacity to solve problems or make things that are valued in a culture. He also determined that we each possess at least nine major intelligences, to greater or lesser degrees and in various combinations. Based on strict criteria, Gardner determined these intelligences to be the following:

- Linguistic intelligence: Individuals strong in linguistic intelligence are "word smart." They may have been early talkers and/or readers as children, and

BAM! radio

PODCAST: *Go to www. bamradionetwork.com and search for the podcast "Is the Concept of Multiple Learning Styles Bogus?".*

- *What new ways of processing information did you learn about while listening to this segment?*
- *After listening to this interview, do you believe that the concept of learning styles is bogus? Do you think that the theory of learning styles has limited children? Explain why, or why not.*

Sample Activities

Activities that emphasize diversity, such as using the music or learning the dances of other cultures and countries, or that enhance a respect for the environment or the world's creatures can have a significant impact on young children. For such activities to do so, the imagination must play a large role. To feel empathy, one must be able to imagine what it is like to be someone or something else.

The first three activities encourage children to pretend. Whether or not they realize it, children will be putting themselves in someone (or something) else's shoes. The final activity, "It Takes Two," is performed most successfully with kindergartners and early-elementary children who are developmentally ready to handle the respect and cooperation involved.

"It's Their World, Too." Poems and songs about animals lend themselves to movement experiences that help develop empathy. By giving children opportunities to imagine what it is like to be animals, we are perhaps ensuring they will never be able to imagine a world without animals. After reading the following poem to the children, discuss the characteristics of the animals mentioned. Then select some of the images for the children to depict through movement.

© Cengage Learning 2013

> Can you imagine
> A world without dogs
> Or rabbits or horses or sheep?
> A world that had no playful kittens
> Or singing birds
> Or baby chickens that peep?
> Can you imagine
> What life would be like
> If we knew we never would see
> A groundhog poking up from his hole
> A dolphin swim
> Or a squirrel in a tree?
> How quiet, how still
> The forests would grow
> And the jungles and barnyards, too
> If, by chance, we had no animals
> To share the world
> With humans like me and you.
> How sad it would be
> If the day should come
> When the eagles no longer soared
> When elephants ceased swinging their trunks
> Seals didn't play
> And lions no longer roared
> The world is theirs, too
> And it's up to us
> To see that they always will be
> Allowed to live their lives as they should
> Life without fear
> Safe and happy and free
> Oh, it's their world, too
> Yes, it's their world, too
> It's a world large enough to share
> With all creatures great and small
> Living in peace, living in peace
> It can happen if we care!*

More Nature Activities. A similar activity is one in which children explore movements related to various aspects of weather (e.g., rain and wind of varying forces, lightning, thunder, snow, heat, and cold). Or children might be asked to move like a spider weaving a web, a bee flying from flower to flower, an ant carrying food to the nest, a caterpillar crawling, or a butterfly floating through the air (Pica, 2000a). Not only will children explore a variety of movement skills and concepts through such activities, they will also develop a greater awareness of nature. For example, by pretending to be insects, the children will develop a heightened awareness of insects and will be less inclined to take them for granted. Chances are that these children will later be more responsive to lessons learned in science class and will give greater consideration to insects' role in the environment.

Occupations. Ask children to demonstrate movements associated with the work of people in various occupations. Possibilities might include a police officer, a fire fighter, a chef, a hairstylist, a teacher, a musician, a secretary, and a homemaker. This activity allows children to consider the important societal roles played by each of these occupations. Children will also be alerted that they have all these options available to them in life, regardless of gender. Thus, by simply exploring movement possibilities and having fun, children can be introduced to some images of a world in which men and women are equal.

It Takes Two. This activity (from Pica, 2001) challenges partners to connect various body parts, which you designate, and then to remain connected as they discover how many ways they can move. After children have selected partners, ask them to connect right or left hands, right or left elbows, one or both knees, right or left feet, or backs.

---

*Pica, Rae, & Richard Gardzina. *Wiggle, Giggle, & Shake*. CD. Educational Activities, 2005.

they grow up to be the poets, writers, disc jockeys, and public speakers in our society.

- Logical/mathematical intelligence: People strong in this intelligence are governed by reasoning. They are the scientists, mathematicians, engineers, computer programmers, and bookkeepers among us.
- Spatial intelligence: Individuals with a strong spatial intelligence understand how things orient in space. They are able to visualize and have a strong sense of direction, design, and/or color. They often become architects, artists, navigators, and such.
- Naturalist intelligence: This intelligence is, according to Gardner, built into the human nervous system. It is the intelligence that determines sensitivity to one's environment. In natural surroundings, it allows individuals to recognize and discriminate among flora and fauna. In urban settings, someone with a well-developed naturalist intelligence would be adept at identifying such things as car models and sneaker brands.
- Existentialist intelligence: People who question why they are "here" and what their role is in the world have a highly developed existentialist intelligence. The most recent intelligence to be identified by Gardner, it is closely related to the field of philosophy.
- Interpersonal intelligence: This intelligence allows us to understand and relate well to others. Psychologists, counselors, nurses, and child care providers are examples of people strong in interpersonal intelligence.
- Intrapersonal intelligence: Individuals strong in this intelligence know themselves well—both their strengths and their weaknesses. They are usually self-reliant, independent, and goal-directed. Many entrepreneurs fall into this category.
- Musical intelligence: A fascination with sound and with the patterns created by sound indicate a strong musical intelligence. Gardner believed that this is the first intelligence to develop and that, if fostered, it will lead to a lifelong affinity with music.
- Bodily/kinesthetic intelligence: Individuals strong in this intelligence solve problems or create with their bodies or body parts. Actors, dancers, and athletes possess strength in bodily/kinesthetic intelligence, as do surgeons and craftspeople.

Reiff (1992) contended that understanding the various ways in which children learn is important for a number of reasons, including preventing discipline problems, communicating with parents, reducing teacher burnout and parent frustration, and helping children reach their potential.

All this information may lead one to imagine a major revolution in the educational system. Sadly, that revolution has been slow in coming. Kinesthetic

BAM! radio

PODCAST: Go to www. bamradionetwork.com and search for the podcast "Identifying & Nurturing the Intelligence of Movement".

- Of which two elements does the bodily/kinesthetic intelligence consist?
- How can teachers recognize the bodily/kinesthetic intelligence in the classroom?
- How does the bodily/kinesthetic intelligence relate to symbolic thought?

MORE ABOUT WAYS OF LEARNING

Although the learning styles theory and the multiple intelligences theory are similar, there is a difference. The former implies that an individual learns mostly everything using one modality. For example, if a person is a visual learner, she acquires nearly all of her information through her sense of sight. The multiple intelligences theory, by contrast, contends that we use different intelligences for different tasks. For instance, when I am redecorating a room in my home and choosing fabrics, patterns, and colors, I am employing my spatial intelligence. When Richard Gardzina and I worked together on children's songs, I was using my musical intelligence. When learning to crochet a new afghan pattern, because I must physically practice the pattern as I read it, I am making use of my bodily/kinesthetic intelligence. And as I wrote this explanation, I used my linguistic intelligence.

learners are still too often labeled hyperactive. Most elementary school children are still expected to sit for long periods and to learn by memorization and rote. The recent clamor for accountability has resulted in increasing seat work even for kindergartners and preschoolers.

In early-childhood programs, many professionals are torn between what they know about how young children learn and what they need to do to prepare children for "academics." In elementary schools, even recess is in danger of extinction as administrators attempt to offer students more "learning" time. The American Association for the Child's Right to Play (the U.S. affiliate of the International Play Association [IPA/USA]) estimates that 40 percent of elementary schools have now eliminated recess.

Future Implications

There is an impressive body of research showing the body's role in the learning process, beginning in infancy and continuing through adulthood (Hannaford, 2005). When we remove the body from children's education, we limit the "potential for learning, thought and creativity" (Hannaford, 2005, p. 20). Or, as Alfred North Whitehead wrote eight decades ago in *The Aims of Education* (1967), "I lay it down as an educational axiom that in teaching you will come to grief as soon as you forget that your pupils have bodies."

With the information we now have about how children (in fact, how most people) learn, it is frightening to imagine how much potential has been lost due to methods aimed at teaching subject matter rather than children. But that trend need not continue. According to Klein (1990), teachers must think in terms of educating children for the future as well as for the present. Klein insisted,

> If we want them [children] to be healthy, active, creative, thinking citizens of a democratic society, who can make intelligent choices and decisions, then we have to have programs that encourage such behavior. We cannot just sit them down and talk at them. If we want children to be thinkers, problem solvers and decision makers, we have to give them opportunities to think, to identify and solve problems, and to make decisions. (p. 27)

This is just another way of saying what the ancients knew long ago: "If you give a man a fish, he eats for a day; if you teach a man to fish, he eats for a lifetime." If children learn how to learn, they will have the ability to acquire any knowledge or skill they seek to acquire—now and in the future.

The Role of Movement

Consider the following:

- Studies by Coghill (1929), Piaget (1952), Jersild (1954), and Strauss and Kephart (1955) suggest that because the child's earliest learning is based on motor development, so, too, is subsequent knowledge.
- Jaques-Dalcroze (1931) asserted that joy is the most powerful mental stimulus. For children, movement is most certainly joyous.
- After years of observing children, Montessori (1949) determined that mental functioning is related to bodily expression.
- Albert Einstein explained that he felt an idea first, through visual and kinesthetic images, before he was able to put it into words (National Dance Association, 1990).
- A California Department of Education study found considerably higher academic achievement associated with higher levels of fitness in fifth-, seventh-, and ninth-grade students (Kun, 2001–2002).
- In a study of more than 500 Canadian children, students who spent an extra hour each day in physical education class performed considerably better on exams than did less-active children (Hannaford, 2005).

- Body image influences a child's emotional health, learning ability, and intellectual performance.
- When children deal with the concepts of space and shape, they are learning to deal with abstract thought.
- Movement activates the neural wiring throughout the body, making the whole body the instrument of learning (Hannaford, 2005).

For several years, Corso (1993) conducted research on how body-space awareness transfers to paper-space awareness. For example, Corso found that when she asked 3- to 8-year-old children to touch their shoulders, some always touched only one shoulder. Similarly, when asked to jump and touch the ceiling, some children reached with only one hand. When requesting samples of the children's papers, Corso discovered the quadrant of paper not used in writing and coloring was the same quadrant of body space not used. Corso's other findings include the following:

- Children who cannot cross the body's vertical midline tend to focus on the vertical of the paper, sometimes writing or drawing down the vertical center of the page and sometimes changing the pencil to the other hand at the midpoint of the paper.
- Children who have trouble finding a personal space or who line up too closely to the person in front or back of them usually write their letters in a similar pattern.
- Children who cannot cross the midline tend to stop reading at the middle of the page.
- The omission of gross motor instruction may be especially devastating to children who are predominantly kinesthetic learners.

Hannaford (2005), a neurophysiologist and educator, explained that cross-lateral movements, such as creeping and crawling, not only help children cross the body's midline but also activate both hemispheres of the brain in a balanced way. Because these movements involve both of the eyes, ears, hands, and feet, as well as core muscles on both sides of the body, they activate both hemispheres

An example of perceptual-motor functioning

© Cengage Learning 2013.

Sample Activities

Movement is less likely to stimulate learning if it is taught the way other subjects often are: through demonstration and imitation, or rote. Rather, teachers must offer children opportunities to solve problems, invent their own solutions to challenges, and make the abstract concrete. This is the key to learning for the young child.

Exploring Up and Down. Pose the following questions and movement challenges (Pica, 2000b):

- Do you know what up and down mean? Show me with your body.
- Can you make your body go all the way down?
- Make your body go all the way up. How high can you get?
- Show me you can go halfway down.
- Make yourself so tiny I can hardly see you.
- Now become as huge as a giant.
- Pretend your feet are glued to the floor.
- How can you move your body up and down without your feet moving?

Bridges and Tunnels. Talk with children about the differences between bridges and tunnels. Then ask them to show you both with their bodies. To make the activity more challenging, ask them to show you how many body parts can create bridges and tunnels. Finally, if they are responsible enough to handle the challenge, have half the class act as tunnels and the other half act as trains or cars travelling through the tunnels.

Body Parts. Children work with a variety of body parts in relation to other body parts or the floor. This activity requires them to think a bit more about the sum of their parts and about the space they occupy. Ask children to sit; then present the following challenges:

- Place an elbow on the floor. Now move it as far from the floor as possible.
- Stretch a foot far away from you. Now bring it back without touching the floor until it is in its original position.
- Put a shoulder (the other shoulder; both shoulders) on the floor.
- Touch an elbow to a knee. Now take it as far away from that knee as possible.
- Touch an elbow to a foot.
- Can you touch your shoulder to your foot?
- Come up from the floor with your head leading and the rest of your body following.
- Go back down to the floor with your nose leading the way.
- Come back up with an elbow leading.

The American Flag. As will be discussed in Chapter 10, movement can be used to explore study units or classroom themes. The following is an example excerpted from Pica (2001) that can be used for a history lesson or for several different holidays, including Independence Day and Flag Day.

Show children the U.S. flag and discuss it with them. What colors is it? What shapes are on it? What do the 50 stars represent? Have the children ever seen a flag being raised on a flagpole? Discuss some of the reasons a flag might be lowered to half-mast, the proper way to fold a flag, and the respect our flag deserves.

Now tell the children they are going to pretend to be a lot of different things associated with the flag. Ask them to show you the shape of a flag, a star, a stripe, a flagpole, a flag being raised on a flagpole, a flag at half-mast, a flag waving proudly in the breeze, a flag being lowered on a flagpole, and a flag being folded.

Exploring Upside Down. When a teacher uses guided discovery (also known as convergent problem solving; refer to Chapter 8), the challenges are intended to produce specific outcomes. Here is an example of an activity involving guided discovery that is suitable for children at the preschool or early-elementary level.

The ultimate goal of the questions and challenges is a forward roll. However, because this approach allows students to respond to challenges at their own developmental levels and rates, even if the children do not manage to perform the desired forward roll, their responses should be accepted. Ultimately, all children can be led to the "correct" answer through guided discovery.

Specific questions and challenges will vary according to the responses elicited from the students, but the following is an example of the process:

- Show me an upside-down position with your weight on your hands and feet.
- Show me an upside-down position with your weight on your hands and feet and your tummy facing the floor.
- Can you put your bottom in the air?
- Can you look behind yourself from that position?
- Can you look at the ceiling? Try to look at even more of the ceiling.
- Show me you can roll yourself over from that position. Can you do it more than once?
- Show children the U.S. flag and discuss it with them

© Cengage Learning 2013.

and all four lobes of the brain. This means cognitive functioning is heightened and learning becomes easier.

Making movement part of the learning process does not serve only kinesthetic learners. Every child has the capability for multimodal learning; in fact, many children, including those thought to be low-achieving, retain more information when it is introduced through multiple senses (Fauth, 1990; Isenberg & Jalongo, 2000). When children are physically active, they are receiving sensory input from their tactile and kinesthetic senses, which means they are feeling as well as observing. Similarly, just as movement experiences obviously address the bodily/kinesthetic intelligence, they also enhance spatial intelligence. Activities requiring children to solve movement problems (for example, finding three ways to balance on four body parts) strengthen both intrapersonal and logical/mathematical intelligences. In addition, because music is often used in conjunction with movement, musical intelligence is further developed. Cooperative activities also foster interpersonal intelligence, while using themes from nature and poetry, stories, and songs to inspire movement address the naturalist and linguistic intelligences.

Thanks to brain research, it is now understood that, because a child's earliest learning is based on motor development, so is much of the knowledge that follows. The cerebellum, the part of the brain previously associated with motor control only, is now known to be involved in a great number of cognitive activities. Study after study has demonstrated a connection between the cerebellum and such cognitive functions as memory, spatial orientation, attention, language, and decision making, among others (Jensen, 2008).

We also now know that most of the brain is activated during physical activity—much more so than when doing seat work. In fact, according to Jensen, sitting for more than 10 minutes at a time "reduces our awareness of physical and emotional sensations and increases fatigue," which results in reduced concentration and, in children, discipline problems (2000, p. 30).

Movement, on the other hand, increases the capacity of blood vessels and possibly even their number, allowing for the delivery of oxygen, water, and glucose, otherwise known as "brain food," to the brain. This cannot help but optimize the brain's performance.

Unfortunately, the idea that the intellect is separate from our body has long been a part of Western culture. Somehow, we view the functions of the body as less important than the functions of the mind. The truth is, however, that thinking and learning do not take place only in our heads. Physical movement, from the beginning of and throughout our lives, plays a critical role in the creation of nerve cell networks that are essential to learning. Hannaford (2005) stated, "We have spent years and resources struggling to teach people to learn, and yet the standardized achievement test scores go down and illiteracy rises. Could it be that one of the key elements we've been missing is simply movement?" (p. 20).

ASSIGNMENTS

1. Create four or five imaginative activities that involve crawling and/or creeping and that make cross-lateral movement fun for children.

2. Determine a benefit of movement not cited in this chapter and justify it in writing.

FIELD OBSERVATIONS

1. Observe a group of children for a day. Note the ways you detect them learning kinesthetically.
2. Choose a preschool or early-elementary child as a subject. For one week, compare the time that the child spends in sedentary activity with time spent in physical activity. (You can simply observe the time spent in child care or school, or you can enlist the aid of the child's parents. If they are willing to keep a log of the child's activities at home, you can gain a more accurate view.)

REFERENCES

Activity and Health Research. (1992). *Allied Dunbar national fitness survey*. London: Sports Council and Health Education Authority.

American Academy of Pediatrics. (2006). Policy statement: Active healthy living: Prevention of childhood obesity through increased physical activity. Retrieved from: http://aappolicy.aappublications.org/cgi/reprint/pediatrics;117/5/1834.pdf.

American Alliance for Health, Physical Education, Recreation, and Dance (AAHPERD). (2005). *Physical best program*. Reston, VA: Author.

Bar-Or, O., Foreyt, J., Bouchard, C., Brownell, K. D., Dietz, W. H., Ravussin, E.; et al. (1998). Physical activity, genetic, and nutritional considerations in childhood weight management. *Medicine and Science in Sports and Exercise, 30*(1), 2–10.

Benard, B. (1995). Fostering resiliency in children. *ERIC/EECE Newsletter, 7*(2), 1–2.

Blair, S. N. (1992). Are American children and youth fit? The need for better data. *Research Quarterly for Exercise and Sport, 63*(2), 120–123.

Blair, S. N., Clark, D. G., Cureton, K. J., & Powell, K. E. (1989). In G. V. Gisolfi & D. R. Lamb (Eds.), *Perspectives in exercise science and sports medicine: Vol. 2. Youth, exercise, and sport* (pp. 401–430). Indianapolis: Benchmark.

Bloom, B. (1964). *Stability and change in human characteristics*. New York: Wiley.

Bunker, L. (1991). The role of play and motor skills development in building children's self-confidence and self-esteem. *Elementary School Journal, 91*(5), 467–471.

Carson, L. M. (2001). The "I am learning" curriculum: Developing a movement awareness in young children. *Teaching Elementary Physical Education, 12*(5), 9–13.

Centers for Disease Control and Prevention. (2005). *Preventing diabetes and its complications*. Retrieved from: http://www.cdc.gov/nccdphp/publications/factsheets/Prevention/diabetes.htm.

Coghill, G. E. (1929). *Anatomy and the problem of behavior*. Cambridge: Cambridge University Press.

Cooper, K. H. (1999). *Fit kids!* Nashville, TN: Broadman & Holman.

Corso, M. (1993). Is developmentally appropriate physical education the answer to children's school readiness? *Colorado Journal of Health, Physical Education, Recreation, and Dance, 19*(2), 6–7.

Department of Health and Human Services. (1990). *Health, United States, 1989, and prevention profile* (DHHS Publication No. [PHS] 90-1232). Washington, DC: U.S. Government Printing Office.

Fauth, B. (1990). Linking the visual arts with drama, movement, and dance for the young child. In W. J. Stinson (Ed.), *Moving and learning for the young child* (pp. 159–187). Reston, VA: AAHPERD.

Flaherty, G. (1992). The learning curve: Why textbook teaching doesn't work for all kids. *Teaching Today, 67*(6), 32–33, 56.

Frostig, M. (1970). *Movement education: Theory and practice*. Chicago: Follet.

Gallahue, D. L., & Cleland-Donnelly, F. (2003). *Developmental physical education for all children*. Champaign, IL: Human Kinetics.

Gardner, H. (1993). *Frames of mind: The theory of multiple intelligences*. New York: Basic Books.

Goodway, J. D., & Rudisill, M. E. (1996). Influence of a motor skill intervention program on perceived competence of at-risk African American preschoolers. *Adapted Physical Activity Quarterly, 13*(3), 288–300.

Greenberg, P. (1992). How to institute some simple democratic practices pertaining to respect, rights, roots, and responsibilities in any classroom (without losing your leadership position). *Young Children, 47*(5), 10–17.

Gruber, J. J. (1985). Physical activity and self-esteem development in children: A meta-analysis. *The Academy Papers, 19*, 30–48.

Hannaford, C. (2005). *Smart moves: Why learning is not all in your head*. Salt Lake City: Great River.

Isenberg, J. P., & Jalongo, M. R. (2000). *Creative expression and play in early childhood*. Upper Saddle River, NJ: Prentice Hall.

Jaques-Dalcroze, E. (1931). *Eurhythmics, art, and education* (F. Rothwell, Trans.; C. Cox, Ed.). New York: A. S. Barnes.

Jensen, E. (2000). *Learning with the body in mind*. Thousand Oaks, CA: Corwin.

Jensen, E. (2008). *Brain-based learning: The new paradigm of teaching*. Thousand Oaks, CA: Corwin.

Jersild, A. T. (1954). *Child psychology*. Englewood Cliffs, NJ: Prentice Hall.

Jewett, J. (1992). *Aggression and cooperation: Helping young children develop constructive strategies*. ERIC Digest No. ED351147.

Kaur, H. (2003). Duration of television watching is associated with body mass index. *Journal of Pediatrics, 143*(4), 506–511.

Klein, J. (1990). Young children and learning. In W. J. Stinson (Ed.), *Moving and learning for the young child* (pp. 23–30). Reston, VA: AAHPERD.

Kun, P. K. (2001–2002). *New study supports physically fit kids perform better academically*. 2001–2002 study by the California Department of Education. Retrieved from: http://www.cde.ca.gov/cyfsbranch/lsp/health/pecommunications.htm.

Landy, J., & Burridge, K. (1997). *Fifty simple things you can do to raise a child who is physically fit*. New York: Macmillan.

Lerch, H. A., Becker, J. E., Ward, B. M., & Nelson, J. A. (1974). *Perceptual-motor learning: Theory and practice*. Palo Alto, CA: Peek.

Lewin, T. (2010). If your kids are awake, they're probably online. Retrieved from: http://www.nytimes.com/2010/01/20/education/20wired.html.

Mayesky, M. (2008). *Creative activities for young children*. Belmont, CA: Cengage Learning.

Montessori, M. (1949). *The absorbent mind*. Madras, India: Kalakshetra.

Moore, L. L., Nguyen, U. D. T., Rothman, K. J., Cupples, L. A., & Ellison, R. C. (1995). Preschool physical activity level and change in body fatness in young children: The

Framingham children's study. *American Journal of Epidemiology, 142*(9), 982–988.

Mosston, M., & Ashworth, S. (1990). *The spectrum of teaching styles: From command to discovery.* New York: Longman.

National Association for Sport and Physical Education (NASPE). (2009). *Active start: A statement of physical activity guidelines for children birth to five years.* Reston, VA: Author.

National Dance Association. (1990). *Guide to creative dance for the young child.* Reston, VA: Author.

National Institute for Early Education Research. (2010). Preschool's role in fighting childhood obesity. *Preschool Matters, 8*(1).

Pangrazi, R. P., & Corbin, C. B. (1993). Physical fitness: Questions teachers ask. *Journal of Health, Physical Education, Recreation, and Dance, 64*(7), 14–19.

Pate, R. R., McIver, K., Dowda, M., Brown, W. H., & Addy, C. (2008). Directly observed physical activity levels in preschool children. *Journal of School Health, 78*(8), 438–444.

Piaget, J. (1952). *The origins of intelligence in children.* New York: International Universities Press.

Pica, R. (2000a). *Moving & learning series: Early elementary children.* Belmont, CA: Cengage Learning.

Pica, R. (2000b). *Moving & learning series: Preschoolers & kindergartners.* Belmont, CA: Cengage Learning.

Pica, R. (2000c). *Moving & learning series: Toddlers.* Belmont, CA: Cengage Learning.

Pica, R. (2001). *Wiggle, giggle, and shake: 200 ways to move and learn.* Silver Spring, MD: Gryphon House.

Poest, C. A., & Leszynski, L. (1988). *Kinderkicks: Preschool exercise and nutrition.* Unpublished manuscript.

Poest, C. A., Williams, J. R., Witt, D. D., & Atwood, M. E. (1990). Challenge me to move: Large muscle development in young children. *Young Children, 45*(5), 4–10.

Reiff, J. C. (1992). *Learning styles: What research says to the teacher series.* Washington, DC: National Education Association.

Science Daily (2010). Retrieved from: http://www.sciencedaily.com/releases/2010/10/101025005834.htm

Strauss, A. A., & Kephart, N. C. (1955). *Psychopathology and education of the brain-injured child: Vol. 2. Progress in theory and clinic.* New York: Grune and Stratton.

Strickland, E. (n.d.). *Why play outdoors?* Retrieved from: http://content.scholastic.com/browse/article.jsp?id=686&FullBreadCrumb=%3Ca+href%3D%22%2Fbrowse%2Fsearch.jsp%3Fquery%3DWhy+Play+Outdoors%3F%26c1%3DCONTENT30%26c17%3D0%26c2%3Dfalse%22%3EAll+Results+%3C%2Fa%3E.

Taras, H. L. (1992). Physical activity of young children in relation to physical and mental health. In C. M. Hendricks (Ed.), *Young children on the grow: Health, activity, and education in the preschool setting* (pp. 33–42). Washington, DC: Eric Clearinghouse.

Whitehead, A. N. (1967). *The aims of education and other essays.* New York: Free Press.

RELEVANT WEBSITES

For activities, resources, and more:

BAM! Radio Network – The Education Station:
www.bamradionetwork.com

PE Central:
www.pecentral.org

Centers for Disease Control and Prevention—Healthy Living:
www.cdc.gov/HealthyLiving

The Cooper Institute:
www.cooperinstitute.org

American Academy of Pediatrics:
www.aap.org

American Alliance for Health, Physical Education, Recreation, and Dance:
www.aahperd.org

American Association for the Child's Right to Play:
www.ipausa.org

National Association for Sport and Physical Education:
www.naspeinfo.org

Brains.org (for information on brain research)
www.brains.org

New Horizons for Learning:
http://education.jhu.edu/newhorizons

Dr. Thomas Armstrong:
www.thomasarmstrong.com

KEY TERMS & DEFINITIONS

bodily/kinesthetic intelligence Strongest in individuals able to solve problems or create with their bodies or body parts.

cross-lateral movement Movement, such as crawling and creeping, in which limbs move in opposition. This type of movement helps children cross the body's midline and activate both hemispheres of the brain in a balanced way.

emotional development How children feel about other people and things and the way they express their feelings.

health-related fitness One of the two components of physical fitness; consists of cardiovascular endurance, muscular strength, muscular endurance, flexibility, and body composition.

intelligence According to Howard Gardner, the capacity to solve problems or make things that are valued in a culture.

modalities of knowledge acquisition These are divided into four basic groups: visual, auditory, tactile, and kinesthetic.

physical fitness According to the American Alliance for Health, Physical Education, Recreation, and Dance, a physical state of well-being that allows people to perform daily activities with vigor, reduce their risk of health problems relative to lack of exercise, and establish a fitness base for participation in a variety of physical activities.

social development A long, continuous process that begins with self-discovery and results in the ability to interact with others.

© Cengage Learning 2013.

Movement's Role in Musical and Creative Development

Learning Objectives

After completing this chapter, the student will be able to:

1 Describe the role of music in the child's life and education.

2 Explain the role of movement in the child's music education.

3 Discuss the importance of creativity.

4 Explain the role of movement in the child's creative development.

TERMS TO KNOW

creativity

aesthetic sense

common meters

self-expression

Musical and creative growth are not traditionally associated with the domains of child development. Perhaps that is one reason these two areas are often considered "nonessential" and given little time and attention in a child's education. In fact, music and art—both of which foster **creativity**—are two of the three programs, along with physical education, most often eliminated from school systems when budget cuts are made.

However, music and creativity are much more than "frills." A child's musical and creative growth are vital to his or her development as an individual. Both music and creativity have much to contribute to children and adults—socially, emotionally, cognitively, and even physically.

Music and the Young Child

Why is music important to children? Although many teachers and caregivers remain unaware of why they make music part of the curriculum (other than the fact that young children often enjoy it), music is frequently an ingredient in early-childhood programs.

The reasons children should have many and varied musical experiences are numerous. Among those reasons is the belief that children exposed to music have a greater motivation to communicate with the world, perhaps because music provides them with their first exposure to the existence and richness of their own culture, as well as the heritage and cultures of other people and regions. Perhaps it is because music can be a nonverbal form of communication and, therefore, can bridge the gaps among people of different backgrounds.

Standard 5a

Music is also vital to the development of language and listening skills. Music and language arts both consist of symbols and ideas; when the two are used in combination, abstract concepts become more concrete. For example, the word *slow* has only so much meaning to a child when he reads or spells it. When he actually hears slow music, however, the meaning is expanded (Pica, 2007). Furthermore, music activities can improve attention span and memory and increase vocabulary (Edwards et al., 2008). According to Isenberg and Jalongo (2000),

> The child who learns to sing "This Old Man," for instance, has learned to focus on a task, sequence material, and link words … with actions. Musical experiences, such as creating a tune at a keyboard, can develop all the higher-level thinking skills of application, analysis, synthesis, and evaluation.

ABOUT MUSIC AND MOODS

More and more research is focusing on the power of music to alter moods and even to restore and maintain health. Hospitals are using music to hasten the healing process and supplement the use of anesthesia, as music has been found to stimulate the release of endorphins, the body's natural painkillers. Studies show that the body's rhythms—brain frequencies, heart rate, and respiration—work in greater harmony when tuned to music. But even without the benefit of research studies, most of us can state unequivocally that music does indeed have the ability to energize, soothe, and change moods.

Personally, I have all the evidence I require. Should I ever need the emotional release of a good cry and a sad movie is not on television, all I have to do is put on a recording of Samuel Barber's "Adagio for Strings." On the other hand, if my mood is in serious need of improving, in goes my CD of the Boston Pops performing Johann Strauss waltzes. It does not seem to matter how grumpy I was feeling; in a matter of moments, I'm pirouetting around the house. And should I need affirmation or inspiration, Josh Groban's music works like magic.

Many teachers have related stories to me about the effect of music on young children's painting techniques. These teachers have found that playing slow classical music during painting sessions results in long, smooth brushstrokes, while livelier pieces of music result in short, punctuated jabs.

Listening in on a staff meeting prior to a workshop one evening, I was fascinated by the teachers' discussion regarding behavior management. They talked about what was working, what was not, and what had been overused. They then turned to one teacher who had not contributed to the conversation.

"You!" one of them said, pointing at her. "You have the best-behaved class in the school—you and your Handel's *Water Music*!" They all laughed good-naturedly, but they did not seem to realize they had actually discovered the solution to their behavior management dilemma: the calming effect of certain music.

Music is also mood altering (see "About Music and Moods"). Whether a teacher or caregiver is trying to bring peace to overstimulated children, make routine activities more enjoyable, or provide a little extra energy to a low point in the day, music can be the key.

In addition, recent research continues to strengthen the argument that music does indeed contribute to the more traditional domains of child development. In one study, preschool children who studied piano performed better in tasks related to spatial and temporal reasoning than did preschool children who had spent the same amount of time with computers (Rauscher et al., 1997).

Bolduc's (2008) review of the literature determined that music education may effectively contribute to reading and writing skills in young children, even when there are learning difficulties present. Bolduc proposed that children who took part in musical and first-language interdisciplinary programs developed phonological awareness, word recognition, and invented spelling skills more efficiently than those classmates who did not participate in such programs.

Coulter (1995) maintained that songs, movement, and musical games are "brilliant neurological exercises" (p. 22) vital to intellectual development. She stated that by combining rhythmic movement with speech and song, we are giving young children the opportunity to further develop their minds, particularly in the areas of "inner speech" and "impulse control," which contribute to language development, self-management, and social skills.

A great deal of evidence shows that music activities engage the left, right, front, and back portions of the brain. In fact, studying music involves more right- and left-brain functions than any other activity measured (Habermeyer, 1999).

Finally, McDonald and Simons (1989) believed that the most important role of music in education may be what it offers children aesthetically—that is, "the development of sensitivity for the feelings, impressions, and images that music can convey" (p. 2). By helping children develop their aesthetic sense, we can significantly enrich their lives.

Video

VIDEO: *ECE/Child Development: "Infants & Toddlers: Communication Development" (Child Care in Action)*

Future Implications

Greek philosopher Plato once said,

> Music is a moral law. It gives a soul to the universe, wings to the mind, flight to the imagination, a charm to sadness, gaiety and life to everything. It is the essence of order and leads to all that is good, just, and beautiful, of which it is the invisible, but nevertheless dazzling, passionate, and eternal form.

Plato may have gotten a bit carried away with his estimation, but music does have much to offer humankind. Music is "the universal language, and it is part of every culture's identity and its celebrations" (Lazdauskas, 1996, p. 22). Imagine a Christmas with no carols, a birthday party without the traditional "Happy Birthday," or a patriotic parade with no marching bands. What would a wedding be without the couple dancing to that one special song? Would children enjoy memorizing their ABCs if not learned musically?

If children receive a rich variety of musical experiences, music will continue to serve them into and throughout adulthood. Although many will never become professional—or even amateur—musicians, they will know they can rely on music to offer peace, enjoyment, or a little extra energy. They can turn to music when they wish to learn more about a region or a culture. And if their early experiences with music have indeed heightened their sensitivities, how much better for the world in general. Greata (2006) wrote,

> When studies show that music does enhance children's ability to learn, it is tempting for music educators to use this information to boost their programs. However, others warn that we should not lose sight of the fact that music should not be taught just for its ability to enhance other subjects—in other words, as a means to an end. Rather, it should be taught for its own worth. If we want to educate the whole child, the arts, including music, must be part of her education. Although there is evidence that music can affect cognitive development, music is worth teaching and learning for its own sake. If other benefits are realized from our musical experiences, that's wonderful. (p. 29)

The Role of Movement

It is impossible to think of music and movement as completely separate entities. Music educator Carl Orff based his approach on the belief that music, movement,

BAM!radio

PODCAST: *Go to www. bamradionetwork.com and search for the podcast "The Value of Arts in Education".*

- *Why is it important to focus on process rather than product, even in the arts?*
- *Name a few different ways cited by Jennifer Stuart of bringing art into the classroom.*

For young children, experiencing music is not limited to the auditory sense.

© Cengage Learning 2013.

and speech are interrelated. Jaques-Dalcroze (1931) believed that traditional methods of training musicians concentrated too heavily on the intellect, thereby neglecting the senses. To him, "the most potent element in music and the nearest related to life is rhythmic movement" (p. 115).

Educators like Jaques-Dalcroze and Orff are not the only ones who consider music and movement inseparable; children do, too. For young children, experiencing music is simply not limited to the auditory sense (Edwards et al., 2008; Haines & Gerber, 1999; Isenberg & Jalongo, 2000), as evidenced even by infants' "whole-body" response to music.

Standard 5c

Unfortunately, a child's musical ability is too often judged by an ability to sing or play an instrument (Driver, 1936). Even if a child possesses such talent, if his exposure to music is limited to one of these two avenues, he is not experiencing music to the fullest. And what of the child who shows no interest in, or aptitude for, singing or playing an instrument?

If all children are to fully experience music, they should explore it as a whole, being given opportunities to listen, sing, play, create, and move. When a child tiptoes to soft music, stamps her feet to loud music, moves in slow motion to Johann Sebastian Bach's "Air on the G String" and then rapidly to Nikolai Rimsky-Korsakov's "Flight of the Bumblebee," sways to a 3/4 meter, and then skips to a piece in 6/8, she is experiencing music on many levels. Not only is she listening, but she is also using her body, mind, and spirit to express and create. Because she is using a multimodal approach, what she learns will make a lasting impression.

ABOUT DEVELOPMENTAL STAGES OF MUSICAL EXPERIENCES

As with motor development, every child progresses through the stages of musical development at his or her own pace. Although the sequence of developmental stages remains the same for all children, the ages at which they reach and pass through each stage can vary from child to child.

Infants
- **Birth to 8 months**   Display receptiveness to music with their eyes, eventually turning their heads toward its source
- **3 to 6 months**   Respond to sounds by vocalizing
- **10 to 18 months**   Indicate the types of music they like and dislike
- **10 to 18 months**   Rock, bounce, or clap hands to music, though not necessarily rhythmically
- **13 to 16 months**   Attempt to sing sounds to music
- **18 months**   Like to be rocked or swayed to music while being held
- **18 months**   Attempt to sing with words
- **All ages**   Enjoy having their names sung in songs

2-Year-Olds
- Continue to use their bodies in response to music
- Can learn short, simple songs
- Show an increasing ability to follow directions in songs
- Respond enthusiastically to favorite songs, often asking to hear them repeatedly
- May sing parts of songs (often not on pitch), but seldom sing with a group
- Enjoy experimenting with sounds, using everything from household objects to musical instruments
- Can discriminate among songs

3-Year-Olds
- Have greater rhythmic ability
- Can recognize and sing parts of familiar tunes, though usually not on pitch

- Make up their own songs
- Walk, run, and jump to music
- Enjoy dramatizing songs

4-Year-Olds

- Can grasp basic musical concepts, such as tempo, volume, and pitch
- Show a dramatic increase in vocal range and rhythmic ability
- Create new lyrics for songs
- Enjoy more complex songs
- Love silly songs
- Prefer "active" listening (singing, moving, doing fingerplays, accompanying music with instruments)

5- to 6-Year-Olds

- Can reproduce a melody
- Begin to synchronize movements with the music's rhythm
- Enjoy singing and moving with a group
- Enjoy call-and-response songs
- Have fairly established musical preferences
- Can perform two movements simultaneously (e.g., marching and playing a rhythm instrument)

7- to 8-Year-Olds

- Are learning to read lyrics
- Can learn simple folk dances
- Enjoy musical duets
- May display a desire to study dance or play an instrument
- Can synchronize movements to the beat of the music
- Can compare three or more sounds

ABOUT LEARNING BY DOING

Following a two-hour workshop that was part of a residency at a university in Maine, two music majors approached me to say thank you. During the workshop, we had moved to "Robots and Astronauts," in which we contrast a robot's motions with those of an astronaut floating weightlessly in outer space. It was not until the two students had actually moved to this song, which provided an example of staccato and legato, that they fully understood these two musical terms. Naturally, I was a bit taken aback by their gratitude. After all, these were music majors. They went on to explain, however, that not only had their professor never asked them to move to examples of staccato and legato (though I cannot imagine why not!), but also she had never even played examples. She had merely given them definitions of the terms.

I got over my initial surprise, and I, in turn, have been grateful to those two students ever since. What better testimony could I have received? I knew for certain that if physically experiencing a concept could make such an impression at the university level, then learning by doing was the only answer in early childhood.

Sample Activities

Although the information in Chapter 7 will provide more information—and, thus, more ideas—for choosing and using music, the following are several activities for exploring some music basics (excerpted from Pica, 2000).*

Clapping Rhythms. Explain to children that you will clap a small group of beats and then they will attempt to repeat those beats. You can choose any beat groupings you like. However, this would be a good time to introduce the most commonly used meters in Western music.

The first of these is 2/4—two quarter notes in each measure (or you count to two before beginning again). A quarter note can be likened to a walking step, as it takes approximately the same time to complete. Clap and count 1–2, 1–2, and so on, at a moderate tempo.

Next is 3/4, or three quarter notes to the measure—clap and count 1–2–3, 1–2–3, with the accent on the 1. In 4/4 time, there are four quarter notes to the measure—clap and count 1–2–3–4. In 6/8 time, there are six eighth notes to the measure (Figure 2.1). An eighth note is twice as fast as a quarter note—it's more like a running step—so you will clap 1–2–3–4–5–6 at a brisker pace, again with the accent on 1.

Once children are comfortable clapping these meters, ask them to stand and try stepping in place to each count. You may have to count more slowly here. You may also find that 6/8 is too difficult at first.

FIGURE **2.1** Sample measures.

Exploring Common Meters. After introducing children to the common meters, the next step is to select pieces of music in each of these four meters, encouraging children to try your suggested movements for each. The following are some possible movements:

- For pieces in 2/4 (clapping 1–2): marching, stamping feet, jumping, or hopping
- For pieces in 3/4 (clapping 1–2–3): swinging bodies or body parts, or swaying
- For pieces in 4/4 (clapping 1–2–3–4): jogging, stamping feet, or bouncing
- For pieces in 6/8 (clapping 1–2): marching, rocking, or moving head from side to side

Statues. Asking children to move in the way the music makes them feel is bound to be an intimidating request for many of them. But making a game out of putting movement to music can free children of inhibitions. Statues is a great game for this purpose. It also develops listening skills, helps children differentiate between sound and silence, and offers practice with starting and stopping, which, along with holding still, promotes self-regulation skills.

Instruct children to move in any way they like while the music is playing. When the music stops (when you press the pause button), they must freeze into statues and stay that way until the music begins again.

To take children by surprise and inspire a variety of responses, vary the time you allow them to move before stopping the music. Do not always stop it at the end of a musical phrase (unless, of course, the object is to teach them about musical phrases).

To expose children to a variety of musical styles and rhythms, use a different song with a different feel—a march, a waltz, rock and roll—each time you play Statues. (See Chapter 7 for more on providing musical variety.)

Props are also wonderful for alleviating self-consciousness, as the focus is on the prop and not the child. Give children lightweight scarves, streamers, hoops, foam balls, or rhythm sticks, depending on what you have available and the song you will be playing. Ask them to show you how the music makes the *prop* feel like moving.

Two-year-olds enjoy experimenting with sounds.

*From Pica, Rae (2000). *Moving & Learning Series: Preschoolers & Kindergartners,* 3rd ed. Cengage LearningBelmont, CA. Copyright 2000 by Rae Pica. Reprinted by permission.

Creativity and the Young Child

What is creativity? Answers can differ, depending on whom you ask. Various definitions tell us that creativity

- may be defined as the interpersonal and intrapersonal process through which original, high-quality, and genuinely significant products are developed (Tegano, Moran, & Sawyers, 1991);
- is a way of thinking and acting or making something original for the individual and valued by that person or others (Mayesky, 2006);
- describes ideas, behaviors, and products (not a person) that are appropriately novel (Amabile, 1992);
- is a way of using the mind and body to engage in a task that has no prescribed approach. In the creative process, ideas, feelings, skills, and knowledge work together in innovative ways, allowing an individual to make or learn something new (Doyle, 1998);
- is the sensing of problems or gaps in information, forming ideas or hypotheses, testing and modifying these hypotheses, and communicating the results. This process may lead to any one of many products—verbal and nonverbal, concrete and abstract (Torrance & Goff, 1989); and
- is the ability to think in unique ways, produce unusual ideas, or combine things in different ways (Isbell & Raines, 2007).

According to Torrance and Goff (1989, p. 142), the most extensive research in the field indicates a number of abilities are involved in creative thinking, including

- sensitivity to problems;
- fluency, or the ability to produce large numbers of ideas;
- flexibility, or the ability to produce a variety of ideas or use a variety of approaches;
- originality, or the ability to produce new, unusual, or innovative ideas;
- elaboration, or the ability to fill in details; and
- redefinition, or the ability to define or perceive in a way that differs from the usual, established, or intended way.

Amabile (1992) reported that the key personality traits of highly creative people, if not naturally occurring, can be developed in childhood. These traits include

- self-discipline about work,
- perseverance even when frustrated,
- independence,
- tolerance for unclear situations,
- nonconformity to society's stereotypes,
- ability to wait for rewards,
- self-motivation to do excellent work, and
- a willingness to take risks.

When considering creativity in early childhood, note that there is no one profile of the creative child. Creative expression is a developmental process, as are other facets of the child's development. In addition, educators and parents must focus on the process rather than on end products, because young children do not always have the skills necessary to make creative products (Tegano et al., 1991).

One point the experts appear to agree on is that creative potential exists to varying degrees in all young children. Unfortunately, that potential is greatly diminished for the majority of individuals on their way to adulthood. Why does this happen? Where does creativity go?

Dudek (1974) followed a group of children from first through sixth grade and found that creativity begins to "dry out" at just 5 years of age. It then suffers drastic reductions at about age 9 (fourth grade) and again at age 12 (seventh grade). School—with its "restrictive classroom environments" (Gilliom,

1970), insistence on conformity, academic accountability, and emphasis on competition—is often blamed for squelching creative potential.

Because each child is born with creative potential and because the ages between 3 and 5 are thought to be critical years for the development of creativity (Fauth, 1990; Schirrmacher, 2005), early-childhood professionals have a tremendous opportunity to encourage creativity and foster those personality traits that demonstrate creative potential. Early-childhood teachers can take advantage of this opportunity simply by implementing developmentally appropriate practices and allowing children to play, explore, and solve problems. In addition, they must value process over product, allow children to express themselves in their own individual ways, and recognize and nurture creative potential.

Standard 5c

According to Mayesky (2008),

> Adults who work with young children are in an especially crucial position to foster each child's creativity. In the day-to-day experiences in early childhood settings, as young children actively explore their world, adults' attitudes clearly transmit their feelings to the child. A child who meets with unquestionable acceptance of her unique approach to the world will feel safe in expressing her creativity, whatever the activity or situation. (p. 23)

Standard 5c

Future Implications

Unfortunately, a number of misconceptions related to creativity threaten its existence. First, people often believe that children who show high academic achievement are the most creative. Given this belief, adults tend to value correct answers more highly than original thought. Therefore, children find it "less rewarding to express interest in things, to be curious, to be creative in investigating their world" (Mayesky, 2008). In fact, a creative child may or may not be academically gifted; some children who struggle academically show tremendous creativity.

BAM! radio

PODCAST: *Go to www. bamradionetwork.com and search for the podcast "Right & Wrong Ways to Teach Creativity to Children".*

- *Why did creativity expert E. Paul Torrance consider 4-year-olds to be the most creative people in the world?*
- *Why is it important that children be given projects that are "open-ended?"*

Video

VIDEO: *"Ken Robinson Says Schools Kill Creativity":*

http://www.ted.com/talks/lang/eng/ken_robinson_says_schools_kill_creativity.html

ABOUT SELF-EXPRESSION

Self-expression is an integral part of the creative process. But many educators and parents knowingly and unknowingly discourage creative expression. An early-childhood professional once told me that he believed creative children were much more difficult to deal with, so he purposely tried to discourage creativity. Though the following anecdotes are all related to self-expression in art, they are typical of some of the ways in which creativity is discouraged—too often, very early in life.

- Witkin (1977) related the story of a young boy whose teacher assigned the class to draw horses and who then received a grade of F for turning in a blue horse. The teacher explained that horses are white, black, or brown. The little boy, who went home in tears, was confused. In his house was a painting by Franz Marc in which three blue horses roamed a brightly colored field.
- Amabile (1992) recollects her excitement in getting to the easel and clay table every day in kindergarten, where she had access to bright colors and big paintbrushes and many other art materials. Her excitement was such that when she returned home in the afternoons, she wanted only to play with crayons and paint. Although she did not completely understand, she was thrilled to one day overhear her kindergarten teacher tell her mother she had the potential for artistic creativity. The next year, however, art became "just another subject."

Gone was the free access to art materials. Even worse, in second grade, her class was given small reprints of painted masterworks and asked to reproduce them with their crayons. The children's reproductions were then graded by the art teacher.

- In Graham, Holt-Hale, and Parker (2009), James Smith described the wonder he felt when his young daughter, carrying easels, paintbrushes, and watercolors, accompanied him to a lake and, in moments, perfectly captured the essence of the September scene before them. His wonder turned to dismay, however, when she came to him for help in drawing a sailboat soon after she began school. Her teacher, it seems, did not care for interpretive artwork. Rather, the teacher insisted that the class create sailboats from dittoed triangles.

- I once heard a story about a first-grade girl who, when asked to draw a butterfly like the teacher had drawn on the chalkboard, happily put purple polka dots on her butterfly—and was promptly scolded. After all, the teacher's butterfly had no polka dots.

Are these isolated incidents, or are they typical of everyday occurrences in the lives of young children? Are adults who stifle children's self-expression merely guilty of not knowing any better, or are they trying to mold the children into conformity? I do not know the answers to these questions, but I do know kindergarten was the pinnacle of Amabile's artistic career. Smith's daughter, when planning her semester schedule years later, was appalled by her father's suggestion that she take creative writing or beginning painting. "Who, me?" she asked. "Paint or write? Good grief, Dad, you ought to know better than that!" And I would guess the artistic—and creative—inclinations of the little girl with the polka-dotted butterfly and the little boy with the blue horse were similarly dampened.

Why is conformity valued more highly than creativity? Certainly, people like Albert Einstein, Florence Nightingale, and George Washington Carver were nonconformists whose problem-solving abilities played an invaluable role in their achievements. If we wish to help create a generation of future Einsteins, Nightingales, and Carvers—not to mention Shakespeares, O'Keeffes, and Bachs—we must encourage the children in our care to express themselves, whether it be through art, movement, or whatever medium they wish.

Second, to many people, creativity is thought to be the domain of artists—painters, writers, composers, and so forth. Clearly, the world benefits from the creativity of its artists, but it also benefits from creativity in business and industry, science, medicine, education, and life itself. Goleman, Kaufman, and Ray (1992) asserted that daily life is "a major arena for innovation and problem solving—the largest but least honored realm of the creative spirit" (p. 29).

In addition, although society claims to value creativity, all indications are that society places far greater value on the one "right" answer, as evidenced by the perceived value and ever-increasing call for standardized testing. Although all children are naturally motivated toward creative thinking, they will not continue to think creatively if their ideas are discouraged and they are continually told there is only one correct answer to any question (Amabile, 1992).

Can you imagine a world without creativity and self-expression? Today, more than at any time in history, the ability to imagine may be in grave danger of disappearing. Current technology, including television, computers, and video, provides children with so many ready-made images, they have little need to create their

BAM! radio

PODCAST: *Go to www. bamradionetwork.com and search for the podcast "Is Standardized Testing Producing a Creativity Crisis?".*

- *What are the four key skills employers believe students need to be successful in the future?*
- *After listening to this segment, do you feel that standardized testing is having a negative impact on creativity? Explain why, or why not.*

own. Also, today, more than at any time in history, with the world changing so rapidly and incessantly, we may be more in *need* of creativity than ever.

Creative people are those who can imagine. This means they can imagine the solutions to problems and challenges faced. They can also imagine what it is like to be someone or something else—that is, they have empathy. They can imagine answers to the question, What if? They can plan full and satisfying futures.

Goff and Torrance (1991) contended that creative activities give people a chance to communicate with one another and with themselves. Creative expression brings satisfaction, "arouses the adventurous spirit within, and creates a zest for living" (Goff & Torrance, 1991, p. 302). According to Schirrmacher (2005), in addition to helping with personal development, "creativity advances civilization and society by addressing and attempting to solve the global problems of hunger, poverty, disease, war, and pollution."

For children, creative activities mean they will develop skills beneficial to them later in life. According to Doyle (1998), "[I]n school and beyond, [children] learn to make choices, take chances, see new possibilities, listen to their own voice—and let their imaginations soar" (p. 41).

The Role of Movement

Certainly, a movement program that requires children merely to imitate the instructor will do nothing to foster creativity. But a program using movement exploration (see Chapter 8), with its emphasis on divergent problem solving, discovery, and self-expression, can make a substantial contribution.

When you present children with a challenge, such as "Show me how crooked you can be," chances are that no two responses will be alike. Divergent thinking, one of the cognitive skills required for creativity, will be enhanced through problem-solving challenges that allow for various responses. In addition, when you validate the different types of responses, children realize that it is okay to find their own individual solutions and that they are not in competition with one another. Thus, their confidence will grow, and they will continue to take greater creative risks.

Creative movement activities also give children many opportunities to imagine. To replicate the movement of a turtle, they must imagine the slowness of that animal. They must call to mind a time when they were not happy to move as though they were sad. They must envision a partner balance or group shape in order to achieve that shape.

With divergent problem solving, a challenge to find a way to move across the balance beam results in many possible responses—all of which are "correct."

MORE ABOUT FOSTERING CREATIVITY

The important adults in children's lives have tremendous influence over their attitudes. We can either help or hinder creativity simply by paying careful attention to our words. Following are examples of both inappropriate and appropriate phrases, adapted from Doyle (1998, p. 39):

Standard 4b

Instead of Saying

- "There's no such thing as a blue horse."—Limiting what is possible dampens children's ideas.
- "I'll show you how to do it."—Focusing on the "right" way discourages experimentation.
- "That's not what pots and pans are for."—Limiting possible uses for materials makes children feel that new ideas are not acceptable.
- "What is this a picture of?"—Focusing on the product rather than on the process.

Try Saying

- "I see you made your horse blue!"—Validating their choices.
- "You try it; I'm sure you can."—Encouraging creative risk-taking.
- "You've made some musical instruments out of the pots and pans!"—Congratulations on the discovery are in order.
- "You used a lot of green in your painting!"—Describing and encouraging without judgment.

Goleman et al. (1992) explained that creativity does not happen only in the mind. Rather, the relationships "between thinking and feelings, between mind and body, are critical to unleashing creativity" (p. 27). What better medium for establishing relationships between thinking and feelings or between mind and body than creative movement?

Sample Activities

Self-expression is critical to creativity. The following activities, excerpted from Pica (2000), encourage self-expression because they allow children to find their own way of responding to challenges. Each activity, to a greater or lesser degree, also requires children to use their imaginations.

Make-Believe Walks. Incorporate imagery into the locomotor skill of walking by asking children to walk as if they are big and strong, fat and jolly like Santa Claus, really mad, really sad, looking for the towel with soap in their eyes, in a parade, on hot sand that is burning their feet, or trying to get through sticky mud.

"At the Zoo." Read the following poem in its entirety and then discuss it with children. Then read it again, as slowly as necessary, with children acting out the movements of each animal.

Let's visit a while at the local zoo
And see what we might see
A tall giraffe or a kangaroo

Even a chimpanzee!
See the elephant swinging his trunk
And hear the lion roar
Could that black-and-white creature be a skunk?
Do you want to see some more?
Why, there's a gorilla in that cage
And, my, it seems to me
The tiger is in a terrible rage
But the bear is as calm as can be.
Well, it's getting late; but don't you fret
We'll come back another day
You haven't seen the hippos yet
Or the slippery seals at play!

Make-Believe Striking. Before exploring the nonlocomotor skill of striking, explain to children that they are to hit only the air. Then ask them to strike as though playing a big bass drum, swinging a bat, hammering a nail, chopping wood, swatting at a mosquito, or hitting a ball.

(Continued)

Children need frequent opportunities to express themselves. This child is demonstrating his interpretation of a crooked shape.

Making Shapes. Shape is a movement element that is fun to explore in one's personal space. Make sure children have enough room to respond without touching one another. Then ask them the following:

- How round can you be?
- How flat can you be? Wide? Narrow? Long? Short? Crooked? Straight?
- Can you make your body look like a table? A chair?
- Can you look like a ball? A pencil with a point at the end?
- Can you look like a flower? A teapot? A rug?

"A Face Has Many Roles in Life." The lyrics to this song (from Pica, 2000) require children to express themselves with only their faces. For the chorus, you can have them point to or move the parts named. On the next-to-last line, they can cover their faces with their hands, uncovering them on the last line to display an expression or funny face of their choice. You can explore this song as a poem.

A face has many roles in life
I guess you know that's true
It smiles and frowns and even cries
When you are feeling blue
A face can show that you're angry
A face can show you're glad
A face can pout and sulk and whine
When you are feeling bad
A face can show that you're tired
With yawns or drooping eyes
A face can even show delight
When someone yells, "Surprise!"
A face has many roles in life
But most unique by far

An unhappy face.

A delighted face.

'Cause yours belongs to only you
I can tell who you are!
Chorus
A nose, a mouth, a couple of eyes
Two eyebrows that you raise
These belong to any face
But you use them in your own ways!

ASSIGNMENTS

1. Determine a benefit of music not cited in this chapter. Justify it in writing.
2. Experiment with music of varying moods and note the effects on a child or group of children.
3. Cite an example not given in this chapter of a way in which music and movement enhance each other.
4. Create a movement activity that requires children to use divergent problem solving, imagination, and/or self-expression.

FIELD OBSERVATION

1. Observe a group of children for a period of time. Note the number of incidents when creativity is either validated or invalidated. Explain each.

REFERENCES

Amabile, T. M. (1992). *Growing up creative: Nurturing a lifetime of creativity*. New York: Crown.

Bolduc, J. (2008). The effects of music instruction on emergent literacy capacities among preschool children: A literature review. *Early Childhood Research and Practice, 10*(1). Retrieved from: http://ecrp.uiuc.edu/v10n1/bolduc.html.

Coulter, D. J. (1995). Music and the making of the mind. *Early Childhood Connections: The Journal of Music- and Movement-Based Learning, 1*, 22–26.

Doyle, C. (1998). Creative minds at play. *Scholastic Parent & Child, 5*, 36–41.

Driver, A. (1936). *Music and movement*. London: Oxford University Press.

Dudek, S. (1974). Creativity in young children: Attitude or ability? *Journal of Creative Behavior, 8*, 282–292.

Edwards, L., Bayless, K. M., & Ramsey, M. E. (2008). *Music and movement: A way of life for the young child*. Upper Saddle River, NJ: Prentice Hall.

Fauth, B. (1990). Linking the visual arts with drama, movement, and dance for the young child. In W. J. Stinson (Ed.), *Moving and learning for the young child* (pp. 159–187). Reston, VA: AAHPERD.

Fox, J. E. & Schirrmacher, R. (2011). *Art and creative development for young children*. Belmont, CA: Cengage Learning.

Gilliom, B. C. (1970). *Basic movement education for children: Rationale and teaching units*. Reading, MA: Addison-Wesley.

Goff, K., & Torrance, E. P. (1991). Healing qualities of imagery and creativity. *Journal of Creative Behavior, 25*, 296–303.

Goleman, D., Kaufman, P., & Ray, M. (1992). *The creative spirit*. New York: Penguin.

Graham, G., Holt-Hale, S., & Parker, M. (2009). *Children moving: A reflective approach to teaching physical education*. New York: McGraw-Hill.

Greata, J. (2006). *An introduction to music in early childhood education*. Clifton Park, NY: Delmar Learning.

Habermeyer, S. (1999). *Good music, brighter children*. Roseville, CA: Prima.

Haines, B. J. E., & Gerber, L. L. (1999). *Leading young children to music*. New York: Merrill.

Isbell, R. T., & Raines, S .C. (2007). *Creativity and the arts with young children*. Clifton Park, NY: Delmar Learning.

Isenberg, J. P., & Jalongo, M. R. (2000). *Creative expression and play in early childhood*. Upper Saddle River, NJ: Prentice Hall.

Jaques-Dalcroze, E. (1931). *Eurhythmics, art, and education* (F. Rothwell, Trans.; C. Cox, Ed.). New York: A. S. Barnes.

Lazdauskas, H. (1996). Music makes the school go 'round. *Young Children, 51*, 22–23.

Mayesky, M. (2008). *Creative activities for young children*. Belmont, CA: Cengage Learning.

McDonald, D. T., & Simons, G. M. (1989). *Musical growth and development: Birth through six*. New York: Schirmer.

Pica, R. (2000). *Moving & learning series: Preschoolers & kindergartners*. Belmont, CA: Cengage Learning.

Pica, R. (2007). *Jump into literacy: Active learning for preschool children*. Silver Spring, MD: Gryphon House.

Rausher, F. H., Shaw, G. L., Levine, L. J., Wright, E. L., Dennis, W. R., & Newcomb, R. L. (1997). Music training causes long-term enhancement of preschool children's spatial-temporal reasoning. *Neurological Research, 19*, 2–8.

Tegano, D. W., Moran, J. D., & Sawyers, J. K. (1991). *Creativity in early childhood classrooms*. Washington, DC: National Education Association.

Torrance, E. P., & Goff, K. (1989). A quiet revolution. *Journal of Creative Behavior, 23*, 136–145.

Witkin, K. (1977). *To move, to learn*. Philadelphia: Temple University Press.

RELEVANT WEBSITES

Early Childhood Music & Movement Association:
www.ecmma.org

National Association for Music Education:
www.menc.org

Music Teachers National Association:
www.mtna.org

The Creative Classroom Project:
www.pzweb.harvard.edu/Research/CrClass.htm

Creativity Portal:
www.creativity-portal.com

Art and Creativity in Early Childhood Education:
http://artandcreativity.blogspot.com

KEY TERMS & DEFINITIONS

Creativity It is not necessarily related to academic intelligence. The potential for creativity exists in all people, but the greatest chance for its development exists in children between the ages of 3 and 5 years old.

aesthetic sense With regard to music, the development of sensitivity for the feelings, impressions, and images music can convey.

common meters The meters of 2/4, 3/4, 4/4, and 6/8 are the most commonly used in Western music. A meter indicates the distribution of beats in a measure of music.

self-expression The expression of one's personality. An integral part of the creative process.

© Cengage Learning 2013.

Child Development Characteristics and Their Impact on the Movement Program

TERMS TO KNOW

developmental
appropriateness

object permanence

social play

individual education plan (IEP)

physically challenged

hearing impairment

visually challenged

emotional disability

emotionally handicapped

limited understanding

learning disabled

mental retardation

Learning Objectives

After completing this chapter, the student will be able to:

1 Discuss the developmental milestones, as they pertain to movement experiences, for infants, toddlers, preschoolers, and early-elementary children.

2 Create appropriate movement experiences for infants, toddlers, preschoolers, and early-elementary children.

3 Describe general accommodations to be made for the inclusion of children with physical challenges, hearing impairments, visual impairments, emotional disabilities, and limited understanding.

Standard 1c

Although the benefits of movement education are usually reaped by all children, their impact can vary depending on the ages and developmental levels of participating children. Reinforcing concepts such as up and down, for example, has much greater cognitive value for toddlers than for kindergarteners, because toddlers are just beginning to understand spatial relationships. Kindergarteners, on the other hand, are at a higher level of cognitive development and require greater challenge. Thus, movement activities must be planned according to the developmental stages of children participating. This, in essence, is what a developmentally appropriate program is all about.

According to the National Association for the Education of Young Children (NAEYC), the concept of **developmental appropriateness** has three dimensions: age appropriateness, individual appropriateness, and social/cultural appropriateness. The first reminds us there are universal, predictable sequences of development in all domains: physical, social/emotional (affective), and cognitive. The second indicates that all children are unique individuals who develop according to their own timetables. The third tells us that learning experiences should be "meaningful, relevant, and respectful for the participating children and their families" (Bredekamp & Copple, 2009).

Infants

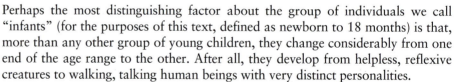

© Cengage Learning 2013.

Perhaps the most distinguishing factor about the group of individuals we call "infants" (for the purposes of this text, defined as newborn to 18 months) is that, more than any other group of young children, they change considerably from one end of the age range to the other. After all, they develop from helpless, reflexive creatures to walking, talking human beings with very distinct personalities.

Of course, their movement capabilities are extremely limited when compared with those of their older counterparts. In view of this—and the fact that infants spend more time sleeping than doing anything else—it comes as no surprise that the concept of movement education is markedly different for infants than it is for children 18 months and older.

Still, movement experiences may be more important for infants than for children of any other age group. Recent evidence indicates that today's babies are spending upward of 60 hours a week in things—high chairs, car seats, and the like. Not only does this have an impact on their personalities (babies need to be held), it also greatly affects their cognitive and motor development.

Thanks to new insights in brain research, we now know that "early movement experiences are beneficial to optimal brain development" (Gabbard, 1998, p. 54). In fact, early movement experiences are considered essential to the neural stimulation (the use-it-or-lose-it principle involved in keeping or pruning neurons) necessary for healthy brain development. In addition, the "prime time" for basic motor skill development appears to be from the prenatal period to about age 5 (Robert, 2001).

Despite all this, structured movement "programs," in which babies are run through patterned actions and their limbs are manipulated by adults, are not

Infants do well with the basics, including one-on-one time in which verbal and visual encouragement are offered.

© Cengage Learning 2013.

required or necessarily appropriate. Rather, infants do well with the basics: one-on-one time during which verbal and visual encouragement are offered, floor time that inspires them to test their developing capabilities, and both the time and space to (safely) move.

In this section, we look at some milestones in the cognitive, affective, and motor development of infants and the implications of those milestones for movement experiences. Also offered are sample activities to promote development in all of these domains.

Cognitive Development

In the first few months of life, everything is new to infants. Although their senses are present at birth, they are still developing. Between 1 and 4 months of age, the baby watches things closely—objects, her parents' faces, her own hands. At this point,

Standard 1a

she looks in the direction of a sound (she will be able to locate the sound between 4 and 8 months of age) and imitates such gestures as clapping hands and waving good-bye.

The most significant cognitive development during the next four months of life is the realization that something that has been hidden still exists—what Piaget termed **object permanence**. Depth perception, or the ability to figure out the approximate distance of an object, is also apparent during this stage, as the child displays fear of falling from high places.

In addition, during this time, speech and language development are evident as the infant responds to the sound of his own name, as well as to encouragement to perform simple tasks, such as waving "bye-bye." From 8 to 12 months, the infant can follow simple instructions and begins to babble single syllables, like "ma-ma-ma." Size and shape discrimination moves from a general sense (e.g., recognizing his own bottle) between 1 and 4 months to the ability to put a few large pieces into a foam puzzle by the time he is 2 years old.

Infants need opportunities to explore and discover, watch and imitate, move and learn. Being "containerized" does not lend itself to these opportunities.

© Cengage Learning 2013.

As the child enters her second year of life, she is able to name commonplace objects, identify body parts upon request ("Where's baby's nose?"), and pass an object from one hand to another (crossing the midline) when handed a second object. It is also during this period that she uses from 5 to 50 words, which are 25 to 50 percent intelligible.

Implications for Movement Experiences. As mentioned, current brain research indicates that movement plays a valuable role in an infant's cognitive development. However, it has long been known that a child's earliest learning experiences are based on motor development and motor learning, with subsequent learning suspected to be dependent upon it as well.

Although nature provides infants with the necessary ingredients for brain development, optimal development relies upon experiences. Albrecht and Miller (2001) contend,

> Children gain coordination of fine and gross motor skills by repeating the patterns of those skills over and over again, strengthening the communication and coordination between neurons. Babies who do not have experiences on the floor, moving their bodies, reaching and batting at objects, picking up many different objects, etc., may not receive enough stimulating experiences to increase synaptic coordination and communication. (p. 255)

Standard 1c

Infants also need to receive cues from the adults around them. When a baby interacts with her environment, she elicits certain reactions from adults. When those reactions are positive (e.g., exclamations of pride and wonder), the child is much more likely to repeat the actions, thus gaining valuable knowledge and strengthening neural pathways with the repetition. When the cues are verbal (e.g., "You're clapping your hands!"), language development is also promoted.

Sample Activities

Finger Puppets. To promote visual tracking, provide the infant with bright, colorful objects to watch. Finger puppets—or a brightly colored sock—placed on your hand can gain and keep the infant's attention. Slowly move your hand up and down, in circles, and to the right and left.

Blowing Bubbles. Blow bubbles for the baby to watch (making sure the bubbles are far enough away so they don't pop in the baby's face). When the baby is old enough, encourage him to reach for the bubbles—or any other object of desire you place above him. Always use language with the child, describing what you are doing and what he is doing or seeing.

Sound Games. Play sound games with the baby. Shake a rattle or other noise-producing object above the baby's head or to her side, encouraging her to locate the sound.

Concept Games. Play concept games with the baby. For example, ask, "How big is my big boy?" Then take his hands in yours, spread his arms wide, and exclaim, "This big!" Ask, "How high is the sky?" Then, lifting one or both hands overhead, proclaim, "This high!"

Object Permanence. To help develop object permanence, partially hide a favorite toy under a blanket or piece of material. The baby will learn to pull at the part of the toy that is visible and will eventually know to remove the blanket completely in order to find the toy.

Crossing the Midline. To encourage crossing the midline of the body, hand the baby desirable items in such a way that she has to reach across her body to retrieve them from you. Later, when the baby is crawling and creeping, place a favorite stuffed animal or other preferred object on the floor, just out of reach, encouraging her to go get it.

Affective Development

Babies need to be touched, cuddled, tickled, rocked, and held. But they are also very good at amusing themselves, discovering such body parts as fingers and toes. At about 6 weeks, an infant begins to smile. From about 4 to 8 months of age, the baby becomes aware of himself as a separate individual. During this stage, he imitates sounds, actions, and facial expressions and responds appropriately to the latter. As the child moves through the next four months, he displays a positive reaction to the sound of his own name.

naeyc
Standard 1a

Although very outgoing in nature from 4 to 8 months, from 8 months to 1 year, the baby begins to display both stranger anxiety (fear of strangers) and separation anxiety (resistance to being separated from a parent). As she progresses through her second year of life, she will once again become *less* distrusting of strangers and will greatly enjoy the attention of adults.

Babies need to be touched, cuddled, tickled, rocked, and held.

© Cengage Learning 2013.

It is also during the second year of life that the child begins to display independence and the onset of the temper associated with the "terrible twos." He is not yet able to play cooperatively with other children at this point, but he does enjoy their company. He is also perfectly capable of playing alone for short periods of time.

Implications for Movement Experiences. As with cognitive development, experience and repetition are critical to the child's developing self-concept and ability to relate to others. When the newborn is cuddled, tickled, rocked, and held, the result is a sense of security. Later, as she begins to realize she can have an impact on her environment (e.g., eliciting a smile in response to one of her own), she develops a sense of confidence and a belief that she can make things happen.

Standard 4b

Playing also contributes to this self-confidence. When an infant fits a small object into a larger one, he begins to discover cause and effect. As he pushes a toy ahead of him as he walks, he feels a sense of mastery. All of this affects emotional development.

Playing with or near others also promotes social development. Although not yet able to play together, babies are fascinated by other babies (and by children in general) and do enjoy playing in their company. However, caregivers should not expect them to share at this point. According to Albrecht and Miller (2001), caregivers should also be aware that very young children have "limited skills in controlling impulses, delaying gratification, using expressive language, entering play, reading social cues, and regulating emotions" (p. 129). Thus, much adult facilitation is required in social interactions between and among babies.

Motor Development

During the first month of life, motor activity is primarily reflexive, with such reflexes as sucking, swallowing, yawning, blinking, and eliminating being present at birth. As the central nervous system

Standard 1a

Sample Activities

Any activity in which you interact with the infant will foster affective development, simply because you are promoting both self-awareness and social interaction. The following activities, however, lend themselves specifically to these goals.

Peekaboo. There is nothing like the tried-and-true game of peekaboo to help a child begin to see herself as a separate individual. It also makes babies laugh! Once the baby is familiar with this game, you can move on to "Where's [teacher]?" Begin by placing your hands over your face, just as you would with peekaboo. Later, hide your whole self behind a piece of furniture, asking, "Where's [teacher]?" You then pop up, answering, "Here's [teacher]!"

Patty-Cake. Games like patty-cake have lasted through the years because they work so well with infants. These games offer opportunities for social interaction, imitation, touch, and rhythmic awareness—as well as yet another chance for baby to hear your voice. While playing, encourage the child to imitate your facial expressions, giving her labels such as sad and happy.

Dancing. Because babies love both music and being held, you should cradle the infant in your arms and dance at every opportunity. The baby will find this soothing and enjoyable. In addition, you will be creating rhythmic awareness and a sense of security.

© Cengage Learning 2013.

matures, intentional, purposeful behavior begins, and the infant becomes able to lift her head and upper body on her arms while lying facedown. While lying faceup, she can hold her head up at about 4 months of age. She also moves from reaching for objects with both arms (between 4 and 8 months) to reaching with one hand or the other (between 8 and 12 months). Other significant milestones between the ages of 4 and 8 months include the ability to sit with only the arms propped in front for support, getting into a creeping position by raising up on the arms and drawing the knees up under the body, and rolling over from front to back and the reverse.

Perhaps the most noteworthy development between 6 and 12 months is the onset of crawling and then creeping—the child's first real form of locomotion. Also during this period, the baby begins to pull himself up to a standing position and then standing alone while using the furniture for support. He can also "walk" with adult support.

Between 12 and 18 months comes that moment a parent waits for—when the baby finally walks unassisted. Once able to transport herself in this manner, she enjoys pushing, pulling, and carrying objects while walking.

Implications for Movement Experiences. The natural assumption is that until an infant is at least able to creep, movement experiences are severely limited. However, this assumption is not necessarily so. Babies can move in many ways (e.g., kicking, reaching, rolling over) without actually transporting themselves from place to place. Babies should also enjoy many physical experiences (e.g., visual tracking) in preparation for later movement activities.

Standard 1c

During this "premobile" period, babies should be offered many sensory experiences. Their environments should consist of objects of different colors, sizes, and shapes that they can see and feel. They also need the opportunity to hear different sounds, such as voices talking, whispering, and singing; noises created by themselves or others, such as keys being rattled or pots and pans being struck with wooden spoons; and music of varying textures and rhythms (see Chapter 7).

Since 1992, when the American Academy of Pediatrics (AAP) instituted its "Back to Sleep" campaign to reduce the incidence of sudden infant death syndrome (SIDS), babies have spent too much time on their backs. (Parents and providers seem to have forgotten that the second part of the campaign slogan is "Tummy to Play.") As a result, many children are experiencing "flat head syndrome"—weak arm, neck, shoulder, and trunk muscles—and delays in developmental milestones like rolling over, crawling, pulling up to stand, and walking. Therefore, perhaps of greatest importance for the developing infant is tummy

Placing a desired object just out of reach can encourage babies to work on their crawling or creeping skills.

© Cengage Learning 2013.

time. Being on his tummy will at first encourage experimentation with lifting his head and with rolling from his tummy to his back and the reverse. Later, tummy time will offer opportunities for crawling and creeping, which are both so essential to his ability to cross the midline of his body and to increase communication between the left and right hemispheres of his brain.

Of course, once the child is mobile—whether via creeping or toddling—the number one consideration is safety. Caregivers must do everything possible to prevent tumbles and falls and the exploration of such unsafe objects as cleaning materials, balloons, and items small enough to swallow.

Toddlers

When looking through books dealing with toddlers, one finds several definitions of these very young children. In some cases, toddlers are defined as those who have just acquired the ability to transport themselves in an upright position and are at the toddling stage, between creeping and true walking. Often, the toddler years are described as falling between certain ages, although these ages vary considerably. For the purposes of this text, toddlers will be defined as children between the ages of 18 and 36 months.

Those who work with toddlers already know that these children present a unique challenge—especially where movement is concerned. Although the motor abilities of toddlers are rapidly emerging, these children do not yet possess enough gross motor skills to succeed at a wide variety of movement activities. Toddlers seem to be in almost constant motion, but due to their extremely short attention spans, it can be difficult to channel that motion into organized movement activities. In addition, because of this short attention span, it is unrealistic to expect these young children to stay involved for longer than 20 to 30 minutes (at the most). However, because it usually takes longer for toddlers to organize as a group, it is impractical to set aside less than 20 minutes each day for a movement session.

Sample Activities

Body Awareness. As with older children, body awareness is where movement education begins with babies. Play games like "This Little Piggy" with the infant. Touch his nose, exclaiming, "I've got your nose!" Then proceed to play the game with such other body parts as toes, ears, fingers, and legs. When the baby is developmentally ready, ask him to find your nose, ears, mouth, and so on.

Reaching and Kicking. Not only should you offer the baby plenty of items to reach for, but you should also provide objects the baby can kick. Place a stuffed animal or a small pillow by her feet, close enough to touch, and encourage her to kick away. Give her soft objects to throw as well, retrieving them for her as long as she stays interested.

Rolling and Pushing a Ball. When the baby is able to sit unassisted, make him comfortable on the floor with his legs apart. Then sit opposite him in a similar manner and roll a large, brightly colored ball toward him. Describe what you're doing as you encourage him to push it back toward you.

Creeping and Crawling. Because a child can never get too much cross-lateral experience, do everything possible to encourage creeping and crawling, even if it means getting down on the floor and moving along with her. Make a game of it by moving both quickly and slowly.

Enjoying Music. Play music that infants can bounce to while they hold on to furniture. Rock them while they listen to lullabies.

Pushing and Pulling. Once the child is toddling, provide wheeled toys that she can push or pull as she walks. This will give her an incentive to keep practicing this important motor skill. It also brings about an awareness of cause and effect.

To make the most of a movement session for toddlers, you should, first and foremost, know what challenges they are capable of responding to. Plan more activities than you expect to use, to allow yourself to move quickly from one activity to another and to switch gears in case a particular activity is just not working. Whenever possible, plan movement sessions for morning, as this is the best time for toddlers to participate in movement experiences. If afternoon is your only option, wait until the children have been up from their naps for a while before expecting them to be creative. Toddlers thrive on individual attention, so the general rule for movement is to have no more than four toddlers per adult whenever possible. Miller (2001) offers some attention-getting techniques that include enticing children with a novelty factor as well as the "flop down and do" method. For the former, Miller suggests bringing out something children have not yet seen that day, such as a music box, to grab their undivided attention. For the latter, she recommends, "Instead of calling toddlers over and trying to get them all to sit down and pay attention at the same time, simply flop down on the floor and start doing whatever it was you wanted to present to them." Once a couple of children have joined you, others will want to "get in on the action." These children will "stay longer when it was their choice to come over in the first place."

Naturally, the better you understand toddlers, the easier it will be to plan and provide successful movement experiences for them. Excellent resources are cited in the References to contribute to your knowledge of children between the ages of 18 and 36 months.

Cognitive Development

The emerging intellectual development of very young children is truly a wonder to behold. Between the ages of 18 and 24 months, toddlers are speaking in just two- or three-word sentences, with only about 66 percent of their speech being intelligible. Within the next 12 months, however, their speech becomes about 90 percent intelligible. They also speak in longer sentences and are able to associate a word with an object.

Size, space, and shape become increasingly meaningful concepts to toddlers.

© Cengage Learning 2013.

Due to toddlers' short attention spans, directions must be kept brief.

Even though toddlers are not yet proficient verbal communicators, words are extremely important to them. According to Charlesworth (2010), language and concept development go hand in hand, with verbal cues that are accompanied by demonstrations playing a vital role in the learning process. Toddlers learn much through imitation. They learn even more when imitating behaviors accompanied by a verbal explanation.

Among the quantitative concepts toddlers are busy discovering are "some," "more," and "big," as well as spatial relationships like up, down, inside, outside, behind, over, and under. Understanding these location words is necessary for children to later "make sense of the order of letters and words on a page" (Miller, 2001). Size, space, and shape are becoming increasingly meaningful concepts to toddlers; between 30 and 36 months, these children are especially curious about how things work and what objects are made of. However, number concepts are too abstract for toddlers—even those who can count by rote—because the numbers do not yet represent quantities or sequences for them (Miller, 2001).

An exciting development during toddlerhood is the beginning of the ability to use the imagination. From 18 to 24 months, children are in the stage of symbolic representation—they can internally visualize events and objects. This development not only allows them a better understanding of cause and effect but also enables them to fantasize. They can now pretend to be something else, such as a cat, a dog, or something they saw on a field trip the day before, or they can imagine that one object is actually another—for example, a block of wood becomes a fire engine (Castle, 1991; Miller, 2001).

By the time children are 2 years old, they can learn—and often sing—short, simple songs and activities with short, simple directions. They enjoy the familiar, positively thrive on repetition, and are curious, information-seeking individuals. Toddlers can also identify at least six body parts.

Implications for the Movement Program. Because movement exploration does not emphasize right or wrong answers, it allows young children the opportunity to experience and discover and to learn by doing. In particular, movement exploration can help toddlers identify body parts, understand quantitative concepts and

Standard 4b

spatial relationships, and make greater use of the imagination. Specific teaching methods, however, must be employed with toddlers if you and the children are to enjoy the utmost success.

One important word to keep in mind is *brief*. Due to toddlers' short attention spans, activities—and their instructions—must be kept brief. This is especially true if you have more 18- to 24-month-old children than 2- to 3-year-olds in your class. If this is the case, you may find it takes these young children longer to complete a single lesson. Or you might discover that you cannot keep their attention long enough to complete much of anything.

Whenever possible, accompany your directions with gestures or demonstrations. Labeling children's actions is a multimodal form of instruction that promotes concept and language development. For instance, if children are creeping through a tunnel, you should say the word *through* as the children are experiencing it.

Although toddlers are learning to fantasize, their experiences are extremely limited. Therefore, using images they can easily relate to is especially important. If you are going to ask toddlers to move like certain animals or objects, they must be animals or objects the toddlers have personally experienced. Likewise, if you are going to ask toddlers to reproduce, for example, straight and round shapes, you must first show them straight and round objects.

In addition, although young children love music, you should use it sparingly as part of your movement program. The fewer things we ask them to concentrate on, the easier it will be for them. Moving without music also allows children to find and use their own personal rhythms. When you do use music, it should make a contribution to the learning experience involved in the activity. Use short, simple songs with basic melodies (nursery rhymes set to music and songs like "Row, Row, Row Your Boat" are among children's favorites). Be prepared to repeat those songs often!

Sample Activities

Body-part identification is the basis of any movement program, but it is especially important for toddlers, because their awareness and understanding of body parts is just developing.

Head, Belly, Toes. To help reinforce this growing awareness, perform activities like Head, Belly, Toes, in which you call out the names of these three body parts as the children touch the part on their bodies being called out. Start off slowly, saying the parts in the same order each time. As children gain experience, vary the tempo and the order. A bit more challenging is "Head, Shoulders, Knees, and Toes."

Simon Says. Simon Says is another appropriate body-parts activity if it is played without the elimination process. With toddlers, it should be performed at a very slow tempo. You should also model the actions as you say them. You might consider saying, "Simon says" prior to every challenge. If your toddlers are too young to grasp the concept of Simon, use the name of a favorite stuffed animal or character or substitute the phrase, "Show me."

Fingerplays. Toddlers love fingerplays, even if they cannot perform them from start to finish. "Where Is Thumbkin?" is a fingerplay that incorporates body-part identification, singing, echoing responses, and the positional concepts of in front and behind. If children are unable to hold up single fingers, they can simply point to the appropriate one.

Body Percussion. This activity uses body parts to create sounds and offers a basic introduction to rhythm. Begin by asking children to clap their hands—something they have been doing since patty-cake. Then challenge them to use their hands to pat other parts of their body. Ask, "Which parts make the most noise?" What else can they pat with their hands to create sounds? How can they use their feet to make noise? Can they make a lot of noise? Just a little noise? Are there other body parts they can make noise with?

Up and Down. In addition to reinforcing body-part identification, "Head, Shoulders, Knees, and Toes" and Head, Belly, Toes draw attention to the concepts of up and down, which are important spatial relationships for young children. You can specifically focus on up and down by doing gentle bending and stretching exercises with toddlers. Challenge them to show you how they can make their bodies go all the

(Continued)

way down and all the way up. Use the words *low* and *high* in connection with their actions.

Blast Off! Count down from 10 and have children "launch" themselves at the command to blast off. This is another activity that reinforces the concepts of up, down, low, and high. (Until your toddlers become familiar with this activity, you will have to model.) Then ask children to make themselves very small and very big.

"Ring Around the Rosie." This traditional favorite focuses on the spatial relationships of around and down and can serve as children's first introduction to group participation.

Obstacle Courses. Simple obstacle courses or learning centers can also play a critical role in introducing and reinforcing spatial relationships. Tunnels (purchased from catalogs or created from desks or large boxes), balance beams (purchased or homemade), ropes, hoops, and the like can all be used to develop greater understanding of important positional concepts.

© Cengage Learning 2013.

"Ring Around the Rosie" can serve as toddlers' introduction to group participation and reinforces the spatial relationships of around and down.

Affective Development

Standard 1a

During the first two years of life, a child's personality is forming. He is rapidly developing a sense of himself as an individual. This sense is referred to as the self-concept.

According to Castle (1991), the self-concept "includes what the child thinks about himself in terms of his capabilities, physical characteristics, and self-worth … A child's self-concept affects everything he does. Children who have positive views of themselves are more successful in everyday life and later in school. Children who have negative views tend to do less well" (p. 5).

Self-concept is greatly influenced by feedback from the important people in a child's life. Toddlers, in particular, tend to seek approval from and act to please adults. Thus, caregivers can play an enormous role in helping toddlers develop positive self-concepts.

Of course, when toddlers are not acting to please adults, they are acting to assert their increasing independence and to gain some control over their world. They frequently display defiant, contrary behavior, with *no* being one of their favorite words. They occasionally throw tantrums and can be physically aggressive—perhaps because their limited verbal skills make it difficult for them to express themselves (Essa, 2010; Miller, 2001). Especially between 30 and 36 months, children feel a need to express their emotions strongly.

Though unable to adequately indicate what they want, toddlers are becoming increasingly aware of what they do and do not want and what they do and do not like. They like routine and derive much comfort and security from the familiar. They do not like having to wait for something they want.

From 18 to 24 months, toddlers are in the stage of solitary play (see "Categories of Social Play"). Two-year-olds, however, become increasingly aware of one another; though there is still little interaction, they move on to the stage of parallel play and tend to imitate what others are doing. During this time, they also begin to understand that others have feelings, too—the beginnings of empathy.

Implications for the Movement Program. As mentioned, a toddler's emerging self-concept is greatly influenced by feedback received from the important adults in his life. Therefore, not only is it essential for toddlers to have the successful experiences offered by movement education, but also caregivers must complement each success with positive feedback to advance the development of healthy self-concepts.

naeyc
Standard 4b

Charlesworth (2010) explained that adults who use positive suggestions are much more likely to receive compliance from toddlers. Therefore, "show me you can" introductions to challenges—as opposed to "can you … ?" questions (see Chapter 9)—are especially useful when working with toddlers. Presenting challenges that assume that children can do what you ask addresses their desire to please you and helps offset that ever-present urge to say "no."

Video

VIDEO: *ECE/Play 2.5 Years: Play in Early Childhood (Development Videos); Also: Young Children's Stages of Play: An Illustrated Guide (Teach Source)*

ABOUT SOCIAL PLAY

Although play researchers continue to refine Parten's (1932) categories of **social play**, the six categories are still being used today. The following definitions of these categories are reprinted with permission from Frost (1992, pp. 85–86):

1. *Unoccupied Behavior*   The child is not playing but occupies him- or herself with watching anything that happens to be of momentary interest. When there is nothing exciting taking place, he plays with his own body, gets on and off chairs, just stands around, follows the teacher, or sits in one spot glancing around the room (or playground).

2. *Onlooker Behavior*   The child spends most of his time watching the other children play. He often talks to the children being observed, asks questions or gives suggestions, but does not overtly enter into the play. This type differs from unoccupied in that the onlooker is definitely observing particular groups of children rather than anything that happens to be exciting. The child stands or sits within speaking distance from other children.

3. *Solitary Play*   The child plays alone and independently with toys that are different from those used by the children within speaking distance and makes no effort to get close to other children. He pursues his own activity without reference to what others are doing.

4. *Parallel Play*   The child plays independently, but the activity chosen naturally brings him among other children. He plays with toys that are like those the children around him are using but he plays with the toys as he sees fit, and does not try to influence or modify the activity of the children near him. He plays beside rather than with the other children.

5. *Associative Play*   The child plays with other children. The communication concerns the common activity; there is borrowing and loaning of play materials; following one another with trains or wagons; mild attempts to control which children may or may not play in the group. All the members engage in similar activity; there is no division of labor and no organization of the activity around materials, goal, or product. The children do not subordinate their individual interests to that of the group.

6. *Cooperative Play*   The child plays in a group that is organized for the purpose of making some material product, striving to attain some competitive goal, dramatizing situations of adult and group life, or playing formal games.

Although Parten (1932) found that the play categories demonstrate a hierarchy related to children's increasing age (i.e., children ages 2 to 2 1/2 years old engaged mostly in solitary play; 2 1/2 to 3 1/2, in parallel play; 3 1/2 to 4 1/2, in associative play; and 4 1/2 on, in cooperative play), later studies did not

(Continued)

completely support these findings. For example, preschoolers today are less skilled in associative and cooperative play than were preschoolers in the late 1920s. Most researchers agree, however, that children do advance from playing alone to playing cooperatively with others, though children do not necessarily outgrow their need for solitary activity (Frost, 1992).

In parallel play, the child plays independently while among other children.

© Cengage Learning 2013.

Waiting for turns is never a good idea for children participating in movement activities. However, it is especially critical that toddlers—with their short attention spans and inability to delay gratification—spend no time waiting. Your challenges should allow all children to respond at the same time, each in his or her own way.

Finally, because toddlers derive comfort from routine, you may attract greater interest and participation from them by opening and closing your movement sessions the same way every time. By doing so, you will be addressing their need for repetition, while ensuring success and providing special satisfaction.

Sample Activities

As previously stated, self-concept involves children's views of their capabilities, physical characteristics, and self-worth (Castle, 1991). Movement exploration contributes to self-concept precisely because it makes children aware of many of their capabilities and physical characteristics. When movement exploration offers numerous opportunities for success, it enhances self-worth as well. Therefore, any developmentally appropriate movement activities you perform with toddlers will promote the me-and-I-am-great part of affective development.

"If You're Happy and You Know It." To take advantage of toddlers' increasing interest in one another and to help promote their budding feelings of empathy, you can perform activities that specifically focus on the concept of feelings. "If You're Happy and You Know It" is a simple, repetitive song that toddlers enjoy. Once you have experienced the "happy" verse, you can make up your own verses based on other emotions—for example, "If you're grumpy and you know it, stamp your feet."

See My Face. This game (taken from Pica, 2000a) challenges children to display angry, surprised, sad, and happy faces, among others (see Figure 3.1). Once children become familiar and comfortable with these challenges, you can ask them to show these same emotions, and more, with their hands and with their whole bodies. For instance, how would they walk if they were very mad? These activities not only give

toddlers a much-needed outlet for their emotions, but also, when they begin to see similar responses among their peers, they begin to realize they share similar feelings.

Moving Like Animals. Asking children to move like familiar animals can also help develop empathy. Although they are too young to really imagine what it is like to be the animals, they can become more aware of animals through movement activities—an important first step.

Of course, one of the wonderful things about moving with toddlers is they are probably the most uninhibited beings in the world. They, unlike their older counterparts, will gladly move in the way the music makes them feel—and you do not even have to ask. All you need to do is put on the music, and they will be dancing before you know it—especially if you start dancing yourself or if you provide bright, colorful scarves for them to dance with. Simply by participating in this group activity, young children experience not only the joy of movement but also the joy of moving together.

FIGURE 3.1 Ask children to demonstrate various emotions with their faces only.
From Pica, Rae (2000a), Moving & Learning Series: Toddlers, Clifton Park, NY: Delmar Learning, p. 70. Copyright 2000 by Rae Pica. Reprinted by permission.

Motor Development

Control over the body occurs from top (head) to bottom (toes) and from the middle (trunk) to the outside (extremities) (see Figure 3.2). This control is one development area caregivers can actually see occurring during the toddler stage (Castle, 1991). Not only do children grow quite a bit during the first three years of life, but they also gain considerable mastery over their bodies. They become more coordinated, more stable, and more determined to explore every bit of space available to them. This determination, combined with their drive toward independence and their inexhaustible energy, makes motor development one of the most important aspects of their young lives.

Standard 1a

FIGURE **3.2** The pattern of development.
From M. Mayesky, Creative Activities for Young Children, 8th ed. Copyright 2006 by Delmar Learning.

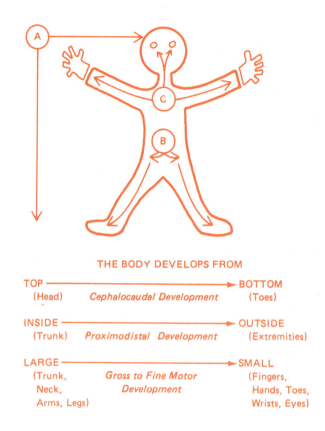

THE BODY DEVELOPS FROM

TOP ⟶ BOTTOM
(Head) *Cephalocaudal Development* (Toes)

INSIDE ⟶ OUTSIDE
(Trunk) *Proximodistal Development* (Extremities)

LARGE ⟶ SMALL
(Trunk, *Gross to Fine Motor* (Fingers,
Neck, *Development* Hands, Toes,
Arms, Legs) Wrists, Eyes)

By the time children are 2 years old, they are walking more confidently and have lost most or all of the wobble. They are also running, but not with as much control—their ability to balance and to start and stop quickly needs improving. Still, these minor inconveniences do not keep them from wanting to run. Essa (2010) said that running is a "pleasure in itself rather than means of getting somewhere fast."

Jumping is another newfound skill. It often begins with jumping off a low object, such as a bottom step. Toddlers tend to land with their knees straight, with one foot landing before the other. Later, when they begin to jump with both feet together, they will most likely jump from a flat-footed stance, with the body weight shifted backward. It is only after children become more proficient at the flat-footed jump that they can begin a jump from the balls of their feet, swinging their arms forward and upward before they finally shift the body weight forward.

Climbing is one of the great adventures in the life of a toddler—and she will try to climb everything. Toddlers enjoy throwing and kicking, too, but will require another few years of practice and maturation before they approach a mature pattern in these skills. Two-year-olds can also roll a ball. Hand dominance is generally evident by 3 to 4 years old and established by age 6.

Implications for the Movement Program. Anyone who lives or works with toddlers will tell you that movement is a way of life for them. If toddlers are going to be constantly on the move, however, we must also ensure that they come to no harm during their activity. Safety is a key factor in working with toddlers.

Standard 1c

Because they are going to walk, run, and jump with a certain degree of instability, they are also going to fall. Thus, caregivers must take every precaution to ensure that the falls are injury free (see Chapter 6). If toddlers are going to practice throwing, lots of soft objects should be available for them to throw. If they are going to climb, Miller (2001) strongly advises providing a stable, toddler-sized climbing structure (with mats or padding beneath) so that caregivers can redirect them from climbing on inappropriate and perhaps unsafe objects, such as tables and chairs.

Success is also especially important for toddlers, whose emerging self-concepts depend so much on early experiences. If they are going to practice kicking, their feet are more likely to actually strike something if very large balls, like beach balls, are made available. Caregivers must also remember that these young children are still capable of performing only a few movement skills. Thus, caregivers must avoid asking toddlers to attempt skills for which they are not yet developmentally ready.

Sample Activities

Follow the Leader and mirroring activities appeal to toddlers' knack for imitation.

The Mirror Game. Described in Chapter 4, this game is played in place and is therefore appropriate for experimenting with nonlocomotor movement. Although the only nonlocomotor skills with which toddlers are experiencing adequate amounts of success are bending and stretching, you can use this game to further explore the concepts of up, down, high, low, big, and small. Demonstrate simple shapes that the children must replicate. Two-year-olds are also capable of imitating clapping, patting, raising their arms overhead, and other such simple actions.

Follow the Leader. Toddlers love Follow the Leader, which can be used to provide children with practice time for their newly acquired locomotor skills. Though this game involves only walking, running, and jumping skills, you can use the elements of movement to vary how children perform them (see Chapters 4 and 8). Children 30 to 36 months of age have usually acquired the ability to walk on tiptoe, so be sure to include this skill with your older toddlers.

Tossing Games. Toddlers love to throw things. You can give them opportunity to safely practice the manipulative skill of throwing by providing lots of soft objects for them to toss—stuffed socks, foam balls, yarn balls, and so on. Striking at stationary objects with their hands or simple rackets provides an introduction to yet another manipulative skill.

Rolling a Ball. To help toddlers develop the skill of rolling a ball, provide playground balls, large foam balls, or beach balls and large, lightweight targets so they can practice "bowling." Targets can include objects large enough to hit and light enough to knock over, such as empty plastic soft drink and dish or laundry detergent bottles (see Figure 3.3).

An additional benefit of practicing rolling and throwing is that it further familiarizes toddlers with the idea of cause and effect.

Jack Be Nimble. Hammett (1992) suggested that children practice jumping and landing with an activity called "Jack Be Nimble." For this game, each child needs a "candlestick" made from a bathroom tissue roll. You—and the children, if they know the rhyme—then recite the nursery rhyme "Jack Be Nimble." At "Jack jump over the candlestick," the children jump over their candles. Be sure to repeat this often so that children get a chance to do lots of jumping and landing—of course, the children will insist on it as well!

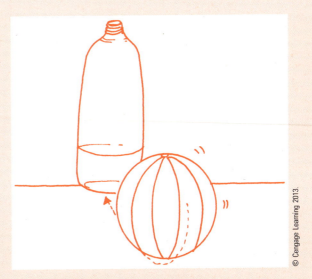

FIGURE **3.3** Small beach balls and empty soda bottles can make "bowling" a successful experience for toddlers.

© Cengage Learning 2013.

Preschoolers

Possibilities abound for exploring movement with preschoolers. (Within the scope of this book, children ages 3 to about 5 1/2 are considered preschoolers.) These children are acquiring more and more motor skills, their cognitive abilities are increasing by leaps and bounds, and their social skills are rapidly improving. In general, all of this translates into fewer restrictions on the movement program. However, it does not translate into "anything goes." Preschoolers still have special needs, including movement activities that are specifically designed with their capabilities and limitations in mind.

The following general points bear consideration in planning a movement program for preschoolers:

Standard 4b

- The younger the preschoolers, the more time they will need to organize themselves as a group—an essential fact if you are planning movement sessions as short as 15 minutes.
- In general, 45 minutes is the longest amount of time you can expect to keep preschoolers interested and involved in movement activities.
- If you are working with mixed-age groups of children 3 to 5, you can expect the youngest children—at least initially—to respond by imitating the older children. This is a natural developmental stage and does not mean the younger preschoolers are not gaining anything from the experience; much is learned from imitation. As the movement program continues and individual responses are positively reinforced, the children's self-confidence will increase, and all the participants will eventually respond in their own ways.
- Preschoolers run into objects and each other because depth perception is a learned ability. Therefore, their paths must be kept clear. Children must also be allowed enough time to change directions.
- When verbal instructions are given, the initial motor response of a preschooler will be toward the sound of your voice.

As mentioned earlier, children acquire gross motor skills according to their own, individual timetables. They do not, however, instantly acquire the ability to perform these skills perfectly. Preschoolers will first execute each new skill in imperfect, individual ways; you should be concerned only if, after practicing the skill for a long time, a child shows no progress toward mastering it.

In planning and providing movement experiences for your preschoolers, keep in mind Sinclair's (1973) advice:

> The preschooler up to the age of 5 is very busy learning new ways to move and practicing those he already knows. He can be helped best by being provided opportunity, motivation, encouragement, and a certain degree of protection, and by being allowed full rein for his creativity and discovery. (p. 64)

Cognitive Development

As with motor development in toddlers, teachers and caregivers can almost literally see cognitive development taking place between the ages of 3 and 5. Speech goes from about 80 percent intelligible at age 3 to nearly 100 percent intelligible at age 5, with children's interest in words and their ability to express themselves growing annually. Four-year-olds in particular have a fascination with words—especially silly ones.

Standard 1a

Attention span increases significantly during the preschool years. Three-year-olds begin to follow simple storylines, with 4-year-olds being able to repeat stories, songs, and fingerplays. At age 5, children are able to retell a story in the correct sequence (Feldman, 1991).

Curiosity increases, too. Four-year-olds ask many questions beginning with the words *why* and *how*. They enjoy stories about how things work and grow.

And although they are not yet ready to sit still and learn, they do show interest in such academic subjects as letters and numbers. In fact, these symbols are becoming more and more recognizable for them. Between the ages of 3 and 5, children also learn to recognize shapes, sizes, and colors.

Three-year-olds understand more spatial concepts than do toddlers, including such positional words as *between, in back of,* and *on top of.* Four year-olds understand many concepts related to space and time, whereas 5-year-olds comprehend most of those concepts, including the days of the week, months, and seasons.

Implications for the Movement Program. Obviously, the increasing attention spans of preschoolers will allow you to plan and provide longer movement sessions. Forty-five-minute sessions are possible with 5-year-olds and even 4-year-olds, as

long as those sessions are fast-paced. Keep in mind that this does not mean that all activities should be fast-paced; rather, the activities should flow easily from one to the next. With 5-year-olds, you can even extend individual activities longer, providing extra experience with the movement skills and elements being explored. Five-year-olds are also able to handle combinations of movement elements (see "Sample Activities").

The preschooler's lengthening attention span also translates into greater powers of concentration. Children from ages 3 to 5 become increasingly able to physically replicate what their eyes are seeing—for example, accurately imitating the movement or shape of something or someone else. In addition, they become better able to respond to what they are hearing in a piece of music—for example, physically demonstrating changes in the music's tempo, volume, or pitch (see Chapter 7).

The preschool years are the perfect opportunity to take advantage of children's fascination with words in order to encourage an appreciation for the language arts. Use nursery rhymes to inspire movement with 3-year-olds and, with preschoolers in general, use lots of fingerplays, stories, poems, and songs (for 4-year-olds, the sillier the better!). Using descriptive words as the children move and pose will ensure their ability to provide their own descriptions of their actions, positions, and shapes by the time they are 5. Preschoolers, with their growing vocabulary and ability to express themselves, will also be glad to offer suggestions and ideas for movement activities.

Perhaps the most important opportunity is being able to validate and develop children's creative abilities. Preschoolers have a powerful curiosity and active imaginations. We can encourage and stretch these valuable tools by giving children chances, through movement, to imagine, explore, and discover.

Sample Activities

Bodily and spatial awareness continue to require emphasis during the preschool years. For bodily awareness, games like Simon Says can be played faster, with more body parts involved. (Elbows and shoulders can be particularly difficult for many preschoolers to find, so be sure to include them in your challenges.)

"The Body Poem." This poem (from Rae Pica, *Wiggle, Giggle, and Shake: 200 Ways to Move and Learn,* p. 19. Reprinted with permission from Gryphon House, PO Box 207, Beltsville, MD, 20704–0207. (800) 638–0928.) uses rhyme and simple numerical concepts to reinforce body awareness. It also appeals to the 4-year-old's fondness for silliness.

I have two feet,
Two ears, two legs
Ten fingers and ten toes;
I have two knees,
Two lips, two hands,
And even two elbows;
I have two eyes
And four eyelids.
So why, do you suppose,
With all these parts
On my body
I only have one nose?!

(Continued)

Read the poem slowly at first, asking children to touch or display the appropriate body parts as you name them. For the third segment, they should shrug on "So why, do you suppose." Then, for the next two lines, they should move their hands from top to bottom the length of their bodies. As the children become familiar with the poem, they will have fun if you do it faster each time.

As children begin to master basic body-part activities, you can present them with greater challenges, such as the body-part activity described under "Cognitive Development" in Chapter 1. Eventually, you can introduce the concept of laterality, asking children to perform actions on only one side of their bodies. Later, you can ask them to perform opposite tasks with the opposite halves of their bodies (Figure 3.4). For example, you might challenge them to stretch the top half of the body while bending the lower half or to make a slow movement with one arm followed by a fast movement with the other.

Space and Shape. As children mature, you can provide greater challenges related to spatial concepts. Use imagery to explore up and down, asking them to move like a yo-yo, popcorn popping, seeds growing, or ice cubes melting. Ask them to take on geometric shapes, beginning with vertical and horizontal lines, as described in Chapter 10. Obstacle courses and learning centers should also become continually more complex.

Moving with Limitations. Asking preschoolers to move with limitations enhances their critical-thinking skills. You could, for example, challenge them to move while being very small, tall, round, or narrow. Can they move with the body very close to the ground? Is there another way? Can they move without using their feet at all?

Combining Movement Elements. As mentioned earlier, older preschoolers can demonstrate success with combinations of movement elements. For instance, instead of merely asking them to move slowly, you can ask them to move slowly and backward. You might challenge them to walk backward while bending forward or to walk quickly with a great deal of force.

© Cengage Learning 2013.

FIGURE **3.4** Exploring the opposition of body halves can be as simple as stretching the top half of the body while bending the lower half.

Affective Development

Standard 1a

Each year of growth during the preschool stage shows a corresponding growth in self-awareness, self-confidence, and self-control, all of which are areas of affective development. Similarly, preschoolers show increasing interest and concern for one another, learning to take turns, share, and collaborate. Three-year-olds move from the parallel to the associative phase of play, with children ages 4 and 5 most often playing cooperatively.

Whether preschoolers are 3, 4, or 5, they show an eagerness to please adults and are susceptible to praise. Four-year-olds often seek adult approval, and 5-year-olds show a special fondness for their teachers.

Rules begin to take on greater meaning throughout the preschool years. Three-year-olds will learn some simple rules, though they usually follow those rules according to their own interpretations (Harris, 1999). Four-year-olds are interested in rules and need to have limits set for them. However, if the rules are within reason and consistently enforced, they often have few problems with them (Miller, 2001). By the time children are 5, they have enough self-control so as not to require many rules, though they seem to enjoy having and following them (Allen & Marotz, 2000; Mayesky, 2008).

Preschoolers love to make believe. Although their experience is limited, 3-year-olds do engage in pretend play, alone and with others. At age 4, children's pretend play ranges from the silly to the adventurous. By 5, children's imaginary play has become quite elaborate (Allen & Marotz, 2000; Feldman, 1991).

BAM!radio

PODCAST: Go to www.bamradionetwork.com and search for the podcast "At What Age Should Children Be Introduced to Competition?".

- Why does Marc Warnke believe that being driven by competition provides children with the skills they need for their future success as an adult? Do you agree with him? Why or why not?

- What are your thoughts on the commentary at the end of the segment? Do you agree that a child's education places too little emphasis on collaboration, cooperation, and being part of a society? Why or why not?

Research indicates that preschoolers prefer cooperative to competitive activities. Although it is generally believed that competition is human nature, Kohn (1992) asserted that competition is learned behavior and that preschoolers usually have not yet been indoctrinated into the competitive atmosphere so prevalent in American society.

One study indicates that gender identity, which is typically established by the age of 3, plays a role in whether children are naturally cooperative or competitive (Garcia, 1994). According to the study, preschool girls are cooperative, caring, and supportive of one another when learning new movement skills. They are not interested in competing or succeeding at someone else's expense and actually seem to learn less efficiently when competition is introduced.

Preschool boys, on the other hand, are interested in how well they perform and in how their abilities compare with those of their classmates. However, the study further indicates that the differences in the boys' and girls' behavior may indeed be dictated by society and culture, as Asian preschoolers of both genders tended to be cooperative and supportive.

A few final points: Children of 3 often develop fears—of the dark, animals, people, noises, and such. Four-year-olds display emotional extremes that change quite unpredictably, from one minute to the next. By the time children are 5, however, they usually have their act together.

Implications for the Movement Program. Not only do rules play a critical role in the lives of preschoolers, but they are also very important in the movement program. To ensure that your rules are considered reasonable—and are therefore followed—ask children to take part in making the rules. Children will be less

Standard 4b

Sample Activities

As mentioned, preschoolers are able to display a greater range of emotions than their toddler counterparts. Clements and Schiemer (1993) suggested challenging children to use their bodies to demonstrate many emotions, including mighty, friendly, proud, playful, gloomy, lazy, worried, and brave.

Act Out Fears. Although 3-year-olds might not be able to relate to all the feelings suggested by Clements and Schiemer, they can identify with fearful things. Ask young preschoolers to act out their fears. If they are afraid of thunder, ask them to pretend to be thunder. If they are afraid of a certain animal, ask them to pretend to be that animal. Often, this role playing helps diminish the fear.

Silly Moves. Because 4-year-olds love to be silly, you should give them occasional opportunities to move in silly ways or to make silly faces. An activity like "Body Sounds" (Chapter 7) has special appeal to 4-year-olds.

Cooperative Activities. Cooperation should be the key factor in partner and group activities. It Takes Two (Chapter 1) and Footsie Rolls (Chapter 4) are examples of somewhat advanced cooperative partner activities. For simpler challenges, partners can be asked to mirror and shadow one another's movements and to create shapes and balances together. The Machine (Chapter 10) and Musical Hoops (Chapter 6) are examples of group cooperative activities.

© Cengage Learning 2013.

Children at ages 4 and 5 are ready to try simple partner activities.

likely to break rules they themselves have established. In addition, positive reinforcement is a powerful tool during the preschool years—use it to further ensure a smooth-running movement program.

Because preschoolers are so fond of pretending, offer them frequent opportunities for role playing through movement to help increase their creative potential while continuing to enhance their blossoming empathic feelings. As children mature, they can express a greater range of emotions and take on more complex roles. In addition, allowing them to assume roles that are important to them will add relevance to, and ensure greater interest in, the movement program.

For children who are 4 and 5, your program can include some activities that involve taking turns—on a limited basis, and only if children are not expected to wait very long. You can also incorporate some partner and simple group activities into the movement experiences. Of course, although children naturally develop greater self-confidence as they mature, this process could be seriously affected if their movement experiences are not positive and successful.

Motor Development

The preschool years are an exciting time for motor development. Three-year-olds begin simply by moving with greater ease and grace than their toddler counterparts; by the time they are 5, preschoolers are executing most, if not all, of the basic locomotor and nonlocomotor skills, as well as a number of manipulative and gymnastic skills.

naeyc
Standard 1a

Once 3-year-olds are walking and running comfortably, many begin to gallop. At about 3, children are even experimenting with brief hops on the preferred foot. Most preschoolers hop successfully on the dominant foot at age 4 and on the nondominant foot at about 4 1/2. Sliding and skipping, the two most challenging locomotor skills, are sometimes not acquired until children are older than 5. Many 4- and 5-year-olds first skip on one side only; this should be considered a normal developmental stage. Older preschoolers are capable of combining some of the movement skills (see "Sample Activities").

Balance shows tremendous improvement during the preschool years. Three-year-olds can balance briefly on the preferred foot and walk a low balance beam with adult assistance. By the time children are 5, they can manage the balance beam by themselves, hop on either foot for 15 feet, and stand on one foot, hands on hips, for 10 seconds or longer (Skinner, 1979).

Manipulative skills also develop significantly during this time. Children begin to throw with greater accuracy, for longer distances; their throwing pattern matures to the point where, at 5, they are stepping out with the foot opposite the throwing hand. Three-year-olds experience some success at catching a bounced ball. Four-year-olds begin bouncing a ball with control and can kick a ball with some accuracy toward a target. Five-year-olds are usually able to catch a medium-sized thrown ball and kick a rolling ball.

Although it is true that each child develops according to his or her own timetable, some general milestones normally take place by certain ages. Figure 3.5 highlights some of these milestones in gross motor development.

Implications for the Movement Program. Movement programs for preschoolers are tremendously exciting because there are always more movement skills to explore—and more ways to explore them. As children mature, they gain control over newly acquired skills and continue to acquire still others.

As this process unfolds, the focus gradually shifts from the elements of movement to the movements themselves (see Chapters 4 and 5). You will, of course, use the full array of movement elements to modify the ways movement skills are performed, providing children with greater practice, time, and experience with each skill. But during the preschool years, it is critical that you also begin evaluating how well children perform the movement skills.

naeyc
Standard 1c

FIGURE **3.5** Milestones in motor development.

Birth–6 Months

- Turns head side to side
- Holds head up while lying face down; later while lying face up
- Reaches for objects with both arms
- Sits with arms propped in front for support
- Rolls from back onto side

6–12 Months

- Rolls over from front to back and reverse
- Crawls and later creeps
- Pulls self up to standing position
- Walks with adult support
- Reaches for objects with one hand or the other

12–18 Months

- Walks without support
- Pushes, pulls, and carries objects while walking
- Able to roll and kick a large ball

18–24 Months

- Walks forward, backward, and sideways
- Runs with stops and starts, but unable to stop and start quickly
- Climbs stairs
- Jumps up and down, but often falls

24–30 Months

- Ascends and descends stairs alone
- Imitates simple actions like clapping, patting, and raising arms overhead
- Throws overhand
- Steps in place
- Rolls a ball
- Bends easily at the waist without toppling over

30–36 Months

- Walks on tiptoe
- Balances momentarily on one foot
- Jumps in place without falling; jumps forward; jumps off objects
- Kicks large ball

3 Years

- Changes speed, direction, or style of movement at signal
- Walks a straight line and a low balance beam
- Runs on tiptoes
- Throws ball without losing balance and can throw underhand
- Gallops
- Hops briefly
- Uses hands and feet simultaneously—for example, stamping feet while clapping
- Uses alternate feet to ascend stairs
- Catches a large or bounced ball with both arms extended
- Jumps to floor from approximately 12 inches

4 Years

- Starts, stops, turns, and moves easily around obstacles and others (well oriented in space)
- Hops on nondominant foot

(Continued)

- Crosses feet over midline of body
- Descends stairs with alternate feet
- Jumps over objects 5 to 6 inches high
- Leaps over objects 10 inches high
- Bounces and catches a ball
- May skip on one side only

5 Years

- Slides
- Skips using alternate feet
- Catches a thrown ball, though not always successfully
- Balances on either foot
- Shifts body weight to throw ("steps out" with foot opposite throwing hand)
- Executes simple dance steps
- Kicks a rolling ball

6–8 Years

- Has well-developed gross motor skills
- Executes two or more skills concurrently—for example, running and catching
- Learns simple folk and partner dances

If you are working with a mixed-age group of 3- to 5-year-olds, it is especially important that you be aware of the capabilities and limitations of each child. Knowing the developmental stages of your students will allow you to phrase challenges so they can all experience success. For instance, if some children in your group can gallop and others cannot, rather than issuing a challenge to gallop, you might simply ask the children to move like horses. Those preschoolers who can gallop most likely will; the others will still be able to meet your challenge by pretending to be horses. They may even learn to gallop through imitation.

Similarly, if you are working on throwing, you might guarantee failure for some if you insist that they all throw at a target from a specified distance. However, if you permit children to choose how far from the target they wish to stand, they will make choices that allow them to be successful. (Of course, these methods are part of the basic philosophy of movement education, but they are important enough to warrant reiterating here.)

Among preschoolers, 4-year-olds have the most energy and the greatest need to expend it. Plan your movement program for 4-year-olds accordingly, offering them the highest level of activity.

If you are working with 5-year-olds, possibilities truly abound. Not only can they manage many combinations of movement skills, but they can also learn some simple dances. They can even make up their own—and should be encouraged to do so!

Sample Activities

Most or all of the locomotor and nonlocomotor activities suggested in Chapter 4 can be explored with preschoolers. As mentioned, with 5-year-olds, you can even begin working on combinations of skills.

Combining Movements. Challenge children to jump (or hop) and turn at the same time. Then ask them to combine running and leaping. Can they execute several running steps followed by a leap? Can they run-run-leap? How about step-leap, step-leap, and so on?

With a Partner. Even simple locomotor skills become more challenging when performed with a partner. Ask pairs of preschoolers to move side by side, matching one another's movements. Challenge them to make one physical contact (e.g., holding hands, linking arms, placing inside hands on one another's shoulders) and to synchronize their movements. Can they smoothly change direction on signal? Can they find a way to execute the locomotor skill with one partner moving forward and the other backward?

Older preschoolers who have had adequate movement experience can also be asked to explore such nonlocomotor skills as pushing and pulling with partners. Sullivan (1982) even suggested having partners roll each other along the floor.

Hokey Pokey. This simple group dance is appropriate and fun for preschoolers. The song, "The Hokey Pokey," can be found on a number of recordings, including *The Hokey Pokey* (available from Melody House and Educational Record Center), *Kidding Around with Greg and Steve* (available from Kimbo), *Children's All-Time Rhythm Favorites* by Jack Capon and Rosemary Hallum and *Singing Action Games* (both available from Educational Activities), and *All-Time Favorite Dances* and *Around the World in Dance* (both available from Educational Record Center).

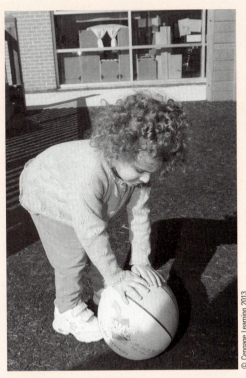

© Cengage Learning 2013.

Although foot-eye coordination is not fully developed until age 9 or 10, preschoolers enjoy practicing such manipulative skills as kicking a stationary ball.

Early-Elementary Children

Early-elementary children, also referred to as primary-grade children, are usually about 5 to 8 years old and in kindergarten to grades 2 and 3. In many ways, these children are developmentally similar to preschoolers. Yet their lives and learning experiences tend to change drastically upon entering public school—a situation NAEYC, the country's largest organization of early-childhood professionals, is greatly concerned about and has been attempting to change by educating teachers and parents as to what is developmentally appropriate for these young children.

Cognitively, for example, early-elementary children are more like preschoolers than upper-elementary children (Charlesworth, 2010). Yet in many public schools, all elementary children are treated similarly. Gone are the days of active learning; instead, early-elementary children are frequently expected to learn through lectures, textbooks, worksheets, and other seatwork. Subjects are studied in tightly scheduled time slots (Bredekamp & Copple, 2009), as opposed to being integrated. Student evaluations, rather than being determined by observation, often become grades based on the results of paperwork.

Opportunities for social development are also severely restricted, as children are expected to work individually rather than as part of a group. In addition, although primary-grade children are not yet physically mature and "are more fatigued by long periods of sitting than by running, jumping, or bicycling" (Bredekamp & Copple, 2009), their need for activity is usually ignored and suppressed during the elementary years.

In a developmentally appropriate early-elementary program, the emphasis will continue to be—as it should be during the preschool years—on active,

Kindergarten children may tire suddenly, but they recover quickly.

© Cengage Learning 2013.

integrated learning experiences that address the whole child. This means movement will continue to play a critical role in the primary grades.

Some general information about the characteristics and development of 5- to 8-year-olds can help you better plan movement activities appropriate for early-elementary children.

- Young children run into objects and each other because depth perception is a learned ability. By age 7, children should be able to travel freely throughout a room without collisions.
- Hand–eye and foot–eye coordination are not well established until age 9 or 10. Both are difficult for the youngest primary-age children due to slow reaction time.
- Kindergarten and first-grade children may tire suddenly, but they recover quickly.
- Physiologically, girls are about a year ahead of boys in development.
- Boys and girls share similar interests at the beginning of this age range, though these interests begin to diverge toward the end.
- Self-consciousness tends to become more of a factor toward the end of this age span.

Cognitive Development

As stated earlier, primary-grade children are cognitively more similar to preschoolers than to their upper-elementary counterparts. Thus, they still learn best by doing, and process should still receive more emphasis than product. These young children need experiences that allow them to explore and discover, to identify and solve problems, and to use and apply their burgeoning thinking skills. Traditional subjects will have greater meaning for them if they are integrated and relevant to children's lives.

naeyc
Standard 1a

One major difference occurs, however, between the preschooler's and the primary-grade student's cognitive level. During the early-elementary years, children begin to associate symbols with concrete experiences and, thus, to solve problems in their heads (Bredekamp & Copple, 2009; Charlesworth, 2010). They also begin to use logic in their attempts at understanding.

Another milestone is the realization that differences of opinion exist. Early-elementary children begin to accept this and to observe from other points of view—a significant development indeed.

Although still not able to think and solve problems as adults do, by the time they are 6 and 7 years old, primary-grade children have usually acquired the language skills of an adult. They talk almost nonstop. However, rather than seeing this as an annoyance, adults should do everything possible to encourage the newfound ability to communicate. In fact, whenever possible, adults should comment as necessary to prolong children's conversations. According to Charlesworth (2010), primary-level children "still respond to adult approval and to task success ... as criteria for their intellectual competence. Consequently, it is relatively easy to promote an atmosphere that enables them to feel good about themselves as learners."

Implications for the Movement Program.   Consider the following points:

- Primary-grade children continue to learn best by doing. (Movement is doing.)
- Task success promotes feelings of intellectual competence. (Movement education is success oriented.)
- Process is still more important throughout the primary grades than is product. (Movement exploration is a process that leads to discovery.)
- For content areas to have greater relevance to a young child, they should be integrated rather than studied in segments. (Movement, as discussed in Chapter 10, is a powerful tool in integrating traditional content areas.)

naeyc
Standard 1a

In short, movement is as important to primary-grade children as it is to younger children. Of course, because the learning situation tends to change in elementary school, the ways in which movement is experienced must also change. In the best of situations, primary-grade children receive daily movement instruction from a physical education specialist as well as curriculum-related daily movement experiences from their classroom teacher—and the specialist and classroom teacher work together to synthesize learning.

naeyc
Standard 4b

Of the cognitive developments taking place during this period, increased problem-solving and communication skills will probably have the greatest impact on the movement program. First, teachers can present a much wider range of problem-solving challenges to early-elementary children. By doing so, teachers will promote critical-thinking skills and help children learn how to learn. Teachers can test and stretch children's verbal skills by employing movement in the study of language arts and by soliciting ideas and feedback from children. Thus, by presenting children with challenges requiring interaction between partners or among group members, teachers can promote both problem-solving and communication skills.

Primary-grade teachers can expect their students' depictions of objects and animals to demonstrate much more realism at this stage. Because children's understandings and powers of concentration are greater, teachers can use a wider variety of music in the movement program and expect students to respond accurately to what they are hearing.

Sample Activities

The early-elementary child's level of cognitive development opens whole new possibilities for the movement program. For example, you can now explore laterality by using the terms *left* and *right*.

Body-Part Balances. Rather than assigning specific body parts for weight placement and balance activities, you can simply challenge children to place their weight or balance on a certain number of parts. You can also present more

(Continued)

challenges by stating, "Find [number] different ways to _____."

For instance, you might pose the following questions and challenges:

- Place your hands on the floor and show me how many ways you can move your feet without moving your hands.
- Find different ways to move with just one hand on the floor.
- Try putting just one foot but both hands on the floor. How many ways can you move the free foot?
- Put the top of your head on the floor and find at least four ways you can move the rest of your body.

Body-Part Relationships. Throughout this chapter, examples have been given of body-part activities appropriate for various development levels. During the early-elementary years, less emphasis will be placed on body awareness. However, exploring the possible relationships among body parts will require primary-grade children to think a bit more about the sum of their parts and the space they occupy. Toward this end, you can present challenges similar to the body parts challenges in Chapter 1.

10 Seconds. Primary-grade children are still attempting to grasp the concept of time, so an activity like "10 Seconds," adapted from Pica (2000b), can be helpful because it limits the time they have to perform a movement or movements. Explain that you are going to count 10 seconds in your head (count in your head so that your counting does not influence their movement) and that you will tell them when to begin and end moving. During that 10 seconds, you want them to show you how many different movements they can perform. After repeating this a few times, you can then ask them to prolong a single movement (like raising or lowering an arm or making a single turn) for 10 seconds, this time while you count out loud.

The Clock. In this activity, you act as the timepiece. You raise your right arm overhead to the 12 o'clock position, with your left arm down. You then sweep your right arm sideways in a smooth arc down to where it meets the left arm. When your palms touch, that is 6 o'clock. Both arms then separate and sweep out and up. When they meet overhead at 12, the activity is over. By watching the clock, the children should be able to determine the speed of their movements. They begin to move when the clock does. When the clock strikes 6, they know the activity is half over. Either ask the children to move any way they like while the clock hands are moving or assign them a specific movement with which they are familiar. Vary the speed of the clock as you repeat this activity.

One Step at a Time. _One Step at a Time_ is an album from Kimbo that is designed to help children understand the concept of time. Songs on the album include "Minute Hand/Hour Hand," "Yesterday-Today-Tomorrow," and "60 Seconds/60 Minutes."

A Different Approach. To enhance problem-solving skills and spatial awareness, choose a reference point, such as a table, a chair, or a column connecting floor to ceiling. Ask your students to find and remember their personal space and to approach the reference point in the following ways, always returning to their own personal space:

- in a straight path
- from one side and then from the other
- from the back
- in a curving (zigzagging) path
- walking forward to the reference point, but returning to personal space sideways
- walking sideways to the point, but returning backward
- walking forward partway to the point, making a half-turn, and continuing toward the point backward

Balancing on one body part only.

Affective Development

Perhaps the most significant social development during the early-elementary years is a growing interest in peers. Children easily establish—and abandon—friendships. Six- to eight-year-olds enjoy playing with one another in small groups. By first grade, children are beginning to compare themselves with others.

Standard 1a

Although these young children still respond to adult approval, peer acceptance becomes a stronger force than adult acceptance. The adult's role, therefore, shifts primarily to one of facilitator. Certainly, teachers and caregivers should strive to facilitate positive relationships among children.

Play, often seen as an activity for younger children, is still important in the cognitive and social development of primary-grade children. During the early-elementary years, however, growing gender awareness and differences tend to change the way children play. Children between the ages of 6 and 8 usually play with others of the same sex. Yet, although they may not choose partners of the opposite sex, if assigned to each other for an activity, they still seem to enjoy it (Haines & Gerber, 1999). Boys are usually more concerned with sex-role stereotypes than are girls (Miller, 2001).

Although the emphasis in learning through the primary grades should remain on process, early-elementary children do become increasingly interested in the final product. Task completion—and success—contribute to their feelings of self-esteem, with fears associated with achievement—or lack thereof—common between the ages of 6 and 11 (Charlesworth, 2010). A desire to excel begins in the second and third grades. Children in these grades like to be admired for doing things well.

Finally, although primary-age children show greater self-responsibility and are beginning to acquire a conscience, they still require adult assistance in achieving self-control and in monitoring their actions. Thus, teachers and caregivers must allow these children a certain amount of independence, encouraging them to take responsibility for themselves. However, teachers and caregivers must also remember that children of this age are sometimes too strict in their determination of what is right and wrong (Bredekamp & Copple, 2009).

Implications for the Movement Program. Perhaps because children of this age begin to compare themselves with one another, the natural conclusion has traditionally been that this is the age when competition should play a prominent role in movement activities. However, there are a great many reasons why cooperation, rather than competition, should continue to be stressed. For example, when students are given opportunities to work together toward a solution or common goal, they know they each contribute to the success of the venture. Every child plays a vital role in

naeyc
Standard 4c

the outcome, and each accepts the responsibility involved in fulfilling that role. Children also learn to become tolerant of others' ideas and to accept the similarities and differences of other children. In addition, cooperative activities are far less likely to cause inferiority feelings that so often result from comparisons made during

Cooperative group activities alleviate self-consciousness and help create feelings of belonging.

© Cengage Learning 2013.

competitive situations. Furthermore, according to Grineski (1993), self-esteem, motivation, and feelings of belonging are all enhanced through cooperative learning. Thus, physical educators and classroom teachers should make cooperative partner and group activities a major part of the curriculum. When competition is involved, it should be competition against oneself—that is, always striving to better an earlier performance. In addition, partner and group activities tend to alleviate the self-consciousness that begins to appear in older primary-grade children. When working with others, children are less focused on themselves than when they work individually.

naeyc
Standard 4b

To help break down sex-role barriers, teachers should avoid activities that involve any gender stereotyping. If, for instance, you ask children to run as though carrying a football in a big game, both boys and girls should be expected to respond. Similarly, activities that challenge children to take the roles of people in various occupations (from fire fighters to flamenco dancers, homemakers to hairstylists) warrant a response from all children, regardless of gender. To help get boys and girls together as partners, issue a challenge for children to get back to back with someone else as quickly as they can. They will be more concerned with how fast they can do it than with whom they are back to back.

Motor Development

Fundamental movement abilities are usually present by 5 years of age. By the age of 6, children are able to perform most locomotor skills in a mature pattern, with sliding and skipping commonly the last two locomotor skills acquired. In general, children can skip smoothly, alternating feet, by 5 1/2 years of age (Skinner, 1979).

naeyc
Standard 1a

Sample Activities

Many partner and group activities suggested for preschoolers are also appropriate for exploration with early-elementary children, as long as these activities are made somewhat more challenging. For example, if the children are forming letters, numbers, and geometric shapes in pairs, they should be assigned more difficult letters, numbers, and geometric shapes—and sometimes encouraged to choose their own.

Palm to Palm. In this partner activity, children consider the number of shapes they can assume with their arms and hands. Facing another child, who is standing close enough to touch, the first child forms a shape with her or his arms. (Any shape is acceptable as long as palms face the partner.) The partner then forms the identical shape, bringing hands palm to palm with those of the first child. As soon as contact is made, the first child chooses a new arm position, and the activity proceeds accordingly. After a while, the partners reverse roles.

Pass a Face. In this activity, children sit in a circle, and one child begins by making a face that is "passed" to the child to his right or left. The next child makes the same face and passes it along in the same direction. When the face has been passed all around the circle, the process is repeated, with a different child beginning.

Pass a Movement. Children stand in a circle and pass around an action. The first child might, for instance, bend at the waist and then straighten. Each child in succession must do the same.

Pass a Beat. Children stand in a circle. The first child claps out a rhythm (e.g., 1–2–3–4 at a moderate tempo, or quick-quick-slow). The object is for each child in the circle to repeat the rhythm exactly, keeping an even tempo all the way around. Even the interval between each child should be in keeping with the rhythm being passed.

Group Balance. Children stand in a circle, facing the center. Each child places his or her hands on the shoulders of the children on either side of them. Children must then maintain a steady balance through challenges to stand on only one foot, lean in various directions, rise on tiptoe, and such.

Let's Slither. Children begin by pairing off and stretching out on their stomachs, one in front of the other. The child in back takes hold of the ankles of the child in front, forming a two-person "snake" that starts to slither across the floor. This two-person snake then connects with another two-person snake. This process continues until the entire group has formed one big snake.

By the time most children are 6 years old, they are capable climbers. Between the ages of 5 and 7, children nearly reach the mature stage of throwing, being able to shift their weight to the foot on the same side as the throwing arm in preparation for the throw and then to transfer the weight to the opposite foot during the throw. By about 5.8 years of age, a child should be able to bounce a ball in place, catching each bounce (Skinner, 1979). Also between ages 5 and 6, children are usually able to kick a rolling ball and to accurately roll a ball to hit a target.

Early-elementary children are still physically active, with lots of energy and a desire to show off their newly acquired physical skills. During this time, development in all domains becomes integrated (Charlesworth, 2010). Gross motor skills are well developed—this, together with newly acquired cognitive and social skills, makes it possible for primary-grade children to take part in games involving rules and combinations of skills. They are also able to learn the steps and sequences of partner and simple folk dances (Haines & Gerber, 1999).

Implications for the Movement Program. Early-elementary children should be given as much opportunity as possible to practice and perfect their movement skills, with particular attention given to those skills that are newly acquired. Combinations of skills, whether assigned by the teacher or created by the children, should receive special emphasis. Not only will these combinations present greater challenges for the children, but they will also help prepare children for the games, dances, and movement activities that will likely be part of their later lives.

The primary grades present teachers with the perfect opportunity to incorporate dance (on a basic level) into the curriculum. Between the ages of 5 and 6, children are usually able to follow specific rhythm patterns (Mayesky, 2008), and the integration of the motor, cognitive, and affective domains enables children to work together, learning and performing dance steps and sequences. It is also significant that boys and girls at this level are usually still willing to cooperate.

Although primary-grade children are able to begin playing games involving rules and more complex skills, traditional games like kickball, basketball, and soccer are not developmentally appropriate at this level. Unless modified to meet the needs of young children, such competitive games are enjoyable only for those who have a chance for success. According to Grineski (1993), most participants fail due to the zero-sum (one winner and one loser) or negative-sum (one winner and many losers) results, characteristic of competitive situations. Furthermore, learning and practice opportunities are extremely limited during such games. In studies conducted by Grineski (1993), he discovered that 75 percent of ball contacts were made by 40 percent of the players during a third-grade soccer game; three students neither touched the ball nor ran the length of the gym during a fifth-grade sideline soccer game; and only 60 percent of the players touched the ball during a fifth-grade sideline basketball game.

Video

VIDEO: *ECE Health & Safety: School Age: Physical Development*

Sample Activities

A number of steps used in folk dance are simply combinations of locomotor skills. On their way to learning how to create and perform dances and master gymnastic and sports skills, children need to learn how to link the individual skills they have acquired to form movement "phrases," "sentences," and eventually "paragraphs."

Suggest combinations of skills that children must put together, in any order they choose, to form movement phrases. Possible combinations of locomotor skills include walk-leap-hop, run-jump-leap, or gallop-jump-hop, with possibilities for combinations of locomotor and nonlocomotor skills being walk-turn-jump, stretch-swing-jump, and hop-sit-roll. The children may perform as many repeats of each individual skill as they want, but they must link them without lengthy pauses or extraneous movements between the skills.

(*Continued*)

Step-Hop. A step-hop is a movement commonly performed in folk dances and in a basketball layup shot. Like the skip, it is a combination of a step and a hop. With the step-hop, however, the two movements have the same time value, and the accent is on the step (in skipping, the hop is accented). Provide an even 1–2 beat with your hands or a drum, and ask children to practice combining steps and hops to match that rhythm. Can they perform repeatedly one step followed by one hop?

"Mexican Hat Dance." Once the children are able to slide, the "Mexican Hat Dance" is a perfect introduction to a group folk dance. It should, of course, be divided into manageable components, with children learning the components individually before putting them all together. Music for this dance can be found in *All-Time Favorite Dances* and *Folk Dance Fun* (both offered by Kimbo).

In the primary grades, children should continue experimenting with locomotor movements performed with a partner. Once they are able to walk and run in synchronization, with one physical contact and in all possible directions, they should explore the possibilities for the remaining locomotor skills. Which are the easiest to perform together? Which are the hardest?

Obviously, teachers at the early- (and even upper-) elementary level must continue to plan movement experiences that offer all children opportunities for participation, practice, and success.

Children with Special Needs

Just as this textbook cannot do justice to the vast topic of child development, it also cannot fully address the subject of children with special needs or cover all the different special needs that teachers and caregivers may encounter. (For additional information, see "Resources for Children with Special Needs," the references at the end of this chapter, and the ever-increasing number of other resources now available on this topic.)

Although movement entails an additional challenge for children with special needs, movement education is well suited to these children. Its philosophy and practice lend themselves to inclusion of—and success for—all children. In addition, the benefits cited in Chapters 1 and 2 certainly apply to children with special needs. Coordination, listening skills, conceptual learning, and expressive ability are just a few of the areas enhanced through regular participation—at whatever level possible—in a movement program.

Standard 4b

Perhaps of greatest importance is the contribution that movement programs can make toward the special child's self-concept. Often children with disabilities fail to form a complete body image due to exclusion from physical activity. Similarly, because they do not necessarily perform the same way other children do, they develop a distorted body image (Gallahue & Cleland-Donnelly, 2007). Identifying and moving various body parts can "help the child discover how each body part fits into the whole schema of a human body. This enables the child to explore body boundaries and define his/her image" (Samuelson, 1981, p. 53). Achieving regular success in movement activities will contribute greatly to the child's confidence—perhaps offering for the first time an opportunity to feel good about him- or herself.

Another unique opportunity derived from the movement program is the chance to be part of a group. As the child's self-concept becomes more developed, he is better able to relate to others. As the child's movements and ideas are regularly accepted and valued, he receives greater acceptance from his peers. Becoming part of a group—making contributions, taking turns, following rules—has the additional benefit of enhancing social skills (Hibben & Scheer, 1982).

When incorporating children with special needs into movement experiences, you must be sure that your challenges can be met by all children. In general, every child will be able to respond in some manner. For example, Samuelson (1981) explained that the blink of an eye, the inhalation of a breath, and the twitching of fingers are all movements. Thus, they can be considered responses to challenges and can even be used for demonstration purposes, with the remaining children being asked to replicate these movements. Not only does this include the child with special needs, but it also places her in what is probably an unfamiliar role—that of leader.

Sometimes, of course, it will be necessary to adapt certain activities. For instance, some children with special needs have difficulty responding to an externally imposed rhythm (Krebs, 1990a). This does not mean rhythmic activities must be eliminated from the program; rather, it means that the teacher can simply allow certain children to move to self-imposed rhythms.

Music can be an especially helpful addition to movement programs involving children with special needs. These children often show high levels of response, motivation, and enjoyment when participating in music experiences (Edwards et al., 2008; Isenberg & Jalongo, 2000; Zinar, 1987). Thus, you may want to make music a greater part of your movement activities than you normally would.

Naturally, you should always consult parents and therapists regarding movement activities and possible modifications. Public laws require children who qualify for special services and who are under the age of 5 be given an individual family service plan (IFSP) and that school-aged children receive an individual education plan (IEP). Both plans are developed with input from parents, teachers, and service providers and outline short- and long-term goals in one or more developmental areas. Movement specialists who are in touch with parents, teachers, and therapists can help children meet their goals by determining appropriate objectives.

The following sections address the special conditions teachers and caregivers of young children are most likely to find physical impairments, hearing impairments, visual impairments, emotional disabilities, and limited understanding. Usually, a small number of children with these special conditions are included in the regular classroom—and their disabilities are not among the most severe. Because the presence of any of these conditions can have an impact on movement experiences, they are addressed here. Implications for the movement program, as well as suggested activities, are incorporated into the discussion of each condition.

Two final points should be kept in mind when working with children with special needs. First, we must recognize that just as no two children are alike, no two children with special needs are alike, even if their disabilities fall into the same category. All conditions have a range of severity and a uniqueness directly correlated to the uniqueness of the child with the condition. Most important, as Edwards et al. (2008) pointed out, we must recognize that "there are more similarities than differences between handicapped and nonhandicapped children."

Children with Physical Challenges

Children who are physically challenged are the fastest-growing population of children receiving special education services (Knight & Wadsworth, 1993). Physical disabilities may be caused by birth defects, accidents, or illness and include such neurological or musculoskeletal impairments as cerebral palsy, arthritis, poliomyelitis, spina bifida, and multiple sclerosis. Severe chronic illnesses like asthma, diabetes, leukemia, and hemophilia are also included in this category (Edwards et al., 2008; Knight & Wadsworth, 1993; Zinar, 1987).

Perhaps the one thing children with these conditions share in common is that their mobility is restricted in one way or another—and that, of course, will have an effect on their participation in movement activities. You, as teacher or caregiver, will have to understand the type and degree of the impairment and the physiological effects that movement may have on these children. Children with spina bifida, cerebral palsy, or arthritis, for example, will need periods of rest so that they do not experience pain or discomfort. Children with epilepsy are just like their peers except for occasional seizures, which are usually controlled through medication; however, climbing activities should probably be avoided (Gallahue & Cleland-Donnelly, 2007). Children with multiple handicaps often require extra assistance where the concepts of laterality and directionality are concerned (Edwards et al., 2008).

Zinar (1987) suggested a number of activities to help accomplish specific goals with children who have motor impairments. Among those goals are pretending to rock a baby to improve lateral movement of the upper arms and shoulders, tossing a balloon into the air and watching it descend to strengthen the back of the neck, and waving streamers while peers are marching to improve arm strength. According to Karnes (1992), though fingerplays offer good fine motor experience for children with muscle-control problems, those children might have to start with larger movements and gradually work toward smaller ones.

In general, the child with physical disabilities should be encouraged to participate at whatever level is possible. A child may have to substitute swaying or nodding the head for more difficult rhythmic responses. If the child cannot hold rhythm instruments, she can wear bells attached to elastics or Velcro placed around her wrists and simply become a musical instrument. Children in wheelchairs will have to experience locomotion on wheels rather than on foot—whether propelling themselves or being pushed by a peer. Krebs (1990a) suggested cane or crutch tapping as a substitute for hand clapping (or foot stomping) and replacing lower-body movements with upper-body movements.

The necessary modifications are often uncomplicated. Usually, it is simply a matter of focusing on what the children can do, as opposed to what they cannot.

Children with Hearing Impairments

Although of several types and degrees, all forms of hearing impairment involve some malfunctioning of the auditory mechanism. The majority of people with hearing impairments are not totally deaf; rather, they have varying degrees of hearing loss (Craft, 1990).

naeyc
Standard 1a

Often, when hearing losses are not immediately diagnosed, children with hearing impairments are thought to have cognitive disabilities or behavior problems, because their impairments make communication difficult and they may not have received messages concerning what is expected of them (Craft, 1990; Gallahue & Cleland-Donnelly, 2007; Zinar, 1987).

naeyc
Standard 4b

Movement, however, is usually not a problem for children with hearing impairments, unless there is damage to the semicircular canals. If so, the child will have balance problems, which can result in delays in motor ability. Children with damage to the semicircular canals should refrain from taking part in potentially dangerous balance activities—for example, climbing or tumbling actions requiring rotation—unless assistance is provided. Craft (1990) suggested that balancing skills taught in safe situations should be included in the program to help children with hearing impairments make maximum use of visual and kinesthetic cues in balancing.

For all children with hearing impairments, the major challenges involved in participating in movement experiences are related to the use of music and the presentation of instructions. Teachers and caregivers can take a number of steps to help lessen the latter problem. Children with difficulty hearing should be placed in the front of the room. Distractions like background music or others talking should be eliminated. Teachers, when speaking, should always face the child with a hearing impairment and avoid covering the mouth. Zinar (1987) also suggested that teachers speak in low tones (not low as opposed to loud but low as opposed to high pitched), because children with hearing impairments are better able to hear low-frequency sounds. Flicking the lights off and on is a signal that teachers can use to instantly get children's attention.

If the child uses sign language, the teacher should make every effort to learn simple signs that convey the day's objectives (e.g., walking, skipping, throwing). If sign language is not a possibility, teachers can communicate through facial expressions, gestures, and pantomime. For other communication ideas, the speech and language therapist (assigned by the school district) is a valuable resource.

During music activities, teachers must remember that although a child may not be able to hear the music, he will be able to feel it. Children with hearing impairments can place their hands on the CD player or the instrument being used to make music to feel the vibrations and establish a rhythm. Lying on a wooden floor often enables children to feel the vibrations with the whole body.

Imitation is another important tool in being able to experience rhythms with and without music. Children with hearing impairments should be encouraged to imitate their peers as they clap hands, stamp feet, play rhythm instruments, march, gallop, and skip. Teachers may need to repeat activities more often than usual to help children with hearing impairments gain a sense of rhythm.

Because movement education is one area that does not rely primarily on verbal communication, children with hearing losses can experience, as their peers do, all the benefits and joys of movement. For these special children, movement has the additional benefit of promoting social interaction that may be missing in other areas of their lives.

Children with Visual Impairments

The Education of All Handicapped Children Act (PL 94–142) defines children who are visually disabled as those whose visual impairments, even when corrected, adversely affect their learning. Included in the definition are blind and partially sighted children (Craft, 1990), more of whom are in public schools rather than in special schools for the blind (Zinar, 1987).

Standard 1a

Usually, a movement education program that meets the needs of children at all levels of ability only needs minor modifications to meet the needs of children who are **visually challenged**. Children with visual limitations tend to rely more heavily on adults than do sighted children and often display hesitation and caution when asked to move. However, they have to their advantage auditory and tactile skills that become increasingly stronger, and these senses can be used to enhance kinesthetic skills.

Standard 4b

When working with children with visual impairments, teachers have a number of methods they can use to help ensure greater success. Children with poor vision should be placed near the teacher so they can see more easily. Holding hands with the teacher or with a responsible partner—or having a partner place her hands on the hips or shoulders of the child with visual problems—are ways of using the tactile and kinesthetic senses to encourage movement and alleviate fear. The teacher can also use touch to help a child achieve an appropriate shape or position.

To make use of the auditory sense, the teacher should use verbal cues and clear, succinct descriptions when presenting challenges and when offering feedback. Statements like, "You are bending and straightening your knees to help you move up and down," have the additional benefit of increasing the child's body awareness. Such statements as, "Everyone swing their arms back and forth," help the visually impaired child realize that his body is like the other children's (Karnes, 1992).

Craft (1990) suggested enhancing visual cues through the use of such objects as brightly colored balls and mats that contrast with the background. Fluorescent tape placed on the edge of mats or on the floor can also help children who have some vision. When working with children who are blind, Craft recommended choosing activities that are not heavily dependent on visual input and feedback and thus require little or no modification.

Finally, if the child uses a cane, for safety, the entire class must learn how it is used.

Children with Emotional Disabilities

According to PL 94–142, a child with an emotional disability is "one who has an inability to learn that cannot be explained by sensory problems, health factors, or intellectual deficits; is unable to make and maintain satisfactory interpersonal relationships

with peers and adults; demonstrates inappropriate behavior; is generally unhappy or depressed; or develops physical symptoms in response to school or personal problems" (Gallahue & Cleland-Donnelly, 2007). According to Gallahue and Cleland-Donnelly (2007), estimates of the number of children with emotional disabilities range from 2 to more than 20 percent of the total population, meaning that even at the most conservative estimate, more than 1 million school-aged children have serious emotional disabilities.

Loovis (1990) reported that although the term emotionally handicapped is regularly used to describe all the children fitting this definition, these children exhibit quite varied behaviors, including hyperactivity, aggression "beyond what is considered normal or socially acceptable" (p. 195), withdrawal, impulsivity, and immaturity. These behaviors commonly result in a lack of self-control and a refusal to participate—the two most common problems encountered during the movement program. In addition, some evidence indicates that children with emotional disabilities also lag behind in physical and motor abilities, perhaps due to poor work habits, attention deficits, and other such common factors (Loovis, 1990). To effectively remedy the latter problem, Loovis recommended an emphasis on basic movement skills, including balance, execution of fundamental locomotor and nonlocomotor skills, and perceptual-motor activities.

To help alleviate discipline problems, a number of teaching tips can be employed. In general, the methods that are an inherent part of movement education lend themselves to greater success for children with emotional disabilities. For example, presenting activities that are challenging, yet not overwhelming, will encourage children to participate and will help guarantee success, which enhances self-esteem. Honest praise and positive reinforcement encourage desired behaviors. Dramatizing emotions and moving to action songs provide modes of self-expression and an outlet for feelings. Incorporating relaxation activities into the program promotes self-control.

Among the techniques specifically recommended for children with emotional challenges are the avoidance of physical contact during activities, shunning lyrics that could have disturbing associations for the children (e.g., "Rock-a-Bye Baby"), employing activities that require children to concentrate (e.g., "Bingo"), and, when appropriate, rewarding children by allowing them to assist in some way (Zinar, 1987).

Children with Limited Understanding

For the purposes of this text, children with limited understanding include children who are learning disabled and those who are mildly to moderately retarded. (Children with severe and

profound mental retardation are usually not included in the regular classroom unless one-on-one time with an aide is possible.)

Children with learning disabilities possess average or above-average intelligence but have difficulty using written or spoken language (Essa, 2008; Gallahue & Cleland-Donnelly, 2007). Because learning disabilities take many forms and are not as easily recognized as are physical disabilities, children who have them are often mislabeled as hyperactive, immature, or emotionally disturbed. Many of them have problems with motor control, including difficulties with body and spatial awareness, coordination, directionality, and stopping once they are in motion (Essa, 2008; Zinar, 1987).

ABOUT RESOURCES FOR CHILDREN WITH SPECIAL NEEDS

As the demand for information about, and materials for, children with special needs has increased, so has the supply. Human Kinetics (see Appendix 2) publishes several relevant books, including the following:

- *Moving with a Purpose: Developing Programs for Preschoolers of All Abilitie,* by Renee M. McCall and Diane H. Craft
- *Physical Activities for Improving Children's Learning and Behavior: A Guide to Sensory Motor Development* by Billye Ann Cheatum and Allison Hammond
- *Perceptual-Motor Behavior in Down Syndrome* by Daniel J. Weeks, Romeo Chua, and Digby Elliott
- *Strategies for Inclusion* by Lauren Lieberman and Cathy Houston-Wilson
- *Inclusion in Physical Education* by Pattie Rouse

Although many different definitions of mental retardation exist, two criteria must occur between conception and 18 years of age (Krebs, 1990b) to be considered retardation: below-average intellectual functioning and an inability to mature personally and socially with age. Children with mental retardation are usually also below average in motor development, possibly due to their cognitive difficulties and to a lack of opportunity for activity (Gallahue & Cleland-Donnelly, 2007).

In general, children with limited understanding—no matter what the cause—will have shorter attention spans and may become easily discouraged. Using a multisensory approach (providing children with chances to use body, voice, eyes, and ears—and often including music) and providing activities that incrementally become more challenging can help remedy these two problems. Children with mental challenges often require more repetition than do their chronological counterparts; therefore, they should not be asked to do two things at once (e.g., counting and clapping). Children with limited understanding may also rely more heavily on imitation. Teachers should accept this but should also be sure to offer praise and encouragement once the child begins responding in his or her own ways (Hirst & Michaelis, 1983).

Standard 4b

Movement, of course, can help improve problems with directionality, body and spatial awareness, and coordination. An activity like *Statues* (Chapter 2) can help children who have difficulty stopping to gain greater motor control. Simple, familiar songs and rhythmic activities can help strengthen memory and powers of concentration. And in all cases of children with limited understanding, movement should be used to reinforce academic concepts.

ASSIGNMENTS

1. Choose a movement theme (e.g., body awareness or an element of movement) and develop an activity that explores that theme at the infant level. Now make the necessary modifications to make the same activity appropriate for toddlers. Change it again to make it appropriate for preschoolers. Finally, change it to be appropriate for early-elementary children.

2. Observe the movement activities of a group that includes toddlers, preschoolers, and kindergarteners (or observe three separate groups). Note differences and similarities among the children in the cognitive, affective, and motor domains.

3. Create a "silly" movement activity that would have special appeal to 4-year-olds.

4. Write a justification of the need for physical education specialists and classroom teachers to collaborate on the movement experiences of their students during the primary years.

5. Create a movement activity and determine what adaptations could be made to accommodate children with physical, auditory, visual, learning, and emotional disabilities.

FIELD OBSERVATIONS

1. Talk to several early-childhood teachers or caregivers who conduct regular movement sessions in an effort to discover the length of time they are able to keep children of varying ages actively engaged in movement activities.

2. Observe a large group of children at play (preferably of varying ages) and note the different stages of social play you witness.

3. Observe a movement session that includes at least one child with special needs. To what degree is that child involved in the movement activities? If participation is minimal, what do you feel could be done to ensure greater participation?

REFERENCES

Albrecht, K., & Miller, L. G. (2001). *Innovations: Infant and toddler development.* Silver Spring, MD: Gryphon House.

Allen, K. E., & Marotz, L. (2000). *By the ages: Behavior and development of children pre-birth through 8.* Belmont, CA: Cengage Learning.

Bredekamp, S., & Copple, C. (Eds). (2009). *Developmentally appropriate practice in early childhood programs.* Washington, DC: National Association for the Education of Young Children.

Castle, K. (1991). *The infant and toddler handbook.* Atlanta: Humanics.

Charlesworth, R. (2008). *Understanding child development.* Belmont, CA: Cengage Learning.

Clements, R. L., & Schiemer, S. (1993). *Let's move, let's play: Developmentally appropriate movement and classroom activities for preschool children.* Montgomery, AL: Kinder-Care Learning Centers.

Craft, D. H. (1990). Sensory impairments. In J. P. Winnick (Ed.), *Adapted physical education and sport* (pp. 209–228). Champaign, IL: Human Kinetics.

Edwards, L., Bayless, K. M., & Ramsey, M. E. (2008). *Music and movement: A way of life for the young child.* Upper Saddle River, NJ: Prentice Hall.

Essa, E. (2010). *Introduction to early childhood education.* Belmont, CA: Cengage Learning.

Feldman, J. R. (1991). *A survival guide for the preschool teacher.* West Nyack, NY: Center for Applied Research in Education.

Frost, J. L. (1992). *Play and playscapes.* Clifton Park, NY: Delmar Learning.

Gabbard, C. (1998). Windows of opportunity for early brain and motor development. *Journal of Physical Education, Recreation, and Dance, 69,* 54–55, 61.

Gallahue, D. L., & Cleland-Donnelly, F. (2007). *Developmental physical education for all children.* Champaign, IL: Human Kinetics.

Garcia, C. (1994). Gender differences in young children's interactions when learning fundamental motor skills. *Research Quarterly for Exercise and Sports, 65,* 213–225.

Grineski, S. (1993). Children, cooperative learning, and physical education. *Teaching Elementary Physical Education, 4,* 10–11, 14.

Haines, B. J. E., & Gerber, L. L. (1999). *Leading young children to music.* Upper Saddle River, NJ: Prentice Hall.

Hammett, C. T. (1992). *Movement activities for early childhood.* Champaign, IL: Human Kinetics.

Harris, A. C. (1999). *Child development.* St. Paul, MN: West.

Hibben, J., & Scheer, R. (1982). Music and movement for special needs children. *Teaching Exceptional Children, 14,* 171–176.

Hirst, C. C., & Michaelis, E. (1983). *Retarded kids need to play.* New York: Leisure Press.

Isenberg, J. P., & Jalongo, M. R. (2000). *Creative expression and play in early childhood curriculum.* New York: Merrill.

Karnes, M. (1992). Music and movement with special needs children. In E. B. Church (Ed.), *Learning through play: Music and movement* (pp. 27–29). New York: Scholastic.

Knight, D., & Wadsworth, D. (1993). Physically challenged students. *Childhood Education, 69,* 211–215.

Kohn, A. (1992). *No contest: The case against competition.* New York: Houghton Mifflin.

Krebs, P. L. (1990a). Rhythms and dance. In J. P. Winnick (Ed.), *Adapted physical education and sport* (pp. 379–389). Champaign, IL: Human Kinetics.

Krebs, P. L. (1990b). Mental retardation. In J. P. Winnick (Ed.), *Adapted physical education and sport* (pp. 153–176). Champaign, IL: Human Kinetics.

Loovis, E. M. (1990). Behavioral disabilities. In J. P. Winnick (Ed.), *Adapted physical education and sport* (pp. 195–207). Champaign, IL: Human Kinetics.

Mayesky, M. (2008). *Creative activities for young children.* Belmont, CA: Cengage Learning.

Miller, K. (2001). *Ages and stages: Developmental descriptions and activities birth through 8 years.* Chelsea, MA: Telshare.

Parten, M. (1932). Social participation among preschool children. *Journal of Abnormal Psychology, 27,* 243–369.

Pica, R. (2000a). *Moving & learning series: Toddlers.* Belmont, CA: Cengage Learning.

Pica, R. (2000b). *Moving & learning series: Early elementary children.* Belmont, CA: Cengage Learning.

Pica, R. (2001). *Wiggle, giggle, & shake: 200 ways to move & learn.* Silver Spring, MD: Gryphon House.

Robert, D. L. (2001). Successful preschool movement programs. *Teaching Elementary Physical Education, 12,* 30–33.

Samuelson, E. (1981). Group development and socialization through movement. In L. H. Kearns (Ed.), *Readings: Developing arts programs for handicapped students* (pp. 53–54). Harrisburg: Arts in Special Education Project of Pennsylvania.

Sinclair, C. B. (1973). *Movement of the young child: Ages 2 to 6.* Columbus, OH: Merrill.

Skinner, L. (1979). *Motor development in the preschool years.* Springfield, IL: Thomas.

Sullivan, M. (1982). *Feeling strong, feeling free: Movement exploration for young children.* Washington, DC: National Association for the Education of Young Children.

Zinar, R. (1987). *Music activities for special children.* West Nyack, NY: Parker.

RELEVANT WEBSITES

For information regarding child development:

Child Development Institute:
www.childdevelopmentinfo.com

Centers for Disease Control and Prevention:
www.cdc.gov/ncbddd/child

Society for Research in Child Development:
www.srcd.org

Zero to Three:
www.zerotothree.org

For information regarding children with special needs:

Children with Special Needs:
http://www.childrenwithspecialneeds.com

Federation for Children with Special Needs:
http://fcsn.org/index.php

The Center for Children with Special Needs:
http://cshcn.org

For information regarding adapted physical education:

PE Central:
www.pecentral.org/adapted/adaptedmenu.html

KEY TERMS & DEFINITIONS

developmental appropriateness Consisting of age appropriateness, individual appropriateness, and social/cultural appropriateness. The former reminds us that there are universal, predictable sequences of development in all domains. The latter indicates that all children are individuals who develop according to their own timetables.

object permanence The realization that something that has been hidden still exists.

individual education plan (IEP) Plan developed for school-aged children who qualify for special services. Teachers, parents, and service providers work together to create short- and long-term goals in one or more developmental areas.

physically challenged The fastest-growing population of children receiving special education services. Includes those with disabilities caused by birth defects, accidents, or illness. In one way or another, the mobility of these children is restricted.

hearing impairment Malfunctioning of the auditory mechanism. Unless there is damage to the semicircular canals, which causes problems with balance, the major challenges for children with hearing impairments in movement programs are related to the use of music and the presentation of instructions.

visually challenged Describes a person who has visual impairments that, even when corrected, adversely affect their learning. With minor modifications, a movement education program can meet the needs of children who are visually impaired.

emotional disability A disability that affects a child's ability to learn and is not related to sensory, health, or intellectual problems. Such children are often depressed, have difficulties with social relationships, and demonstrate inappropriate behavior.

emotionally handicapped Children with emotional disabilities. Two of the most common behaviors ascribed to emotionally handicapped children are a lack of self-control and a refusal to participate.

limited understanding As used in this text, children with learning disabilities as well as those with mild or moderate retardation. Children with limited understanding usually have short attention spans and tend to become easily discouraged.

learning disabled Children who possess average or above-average intelligence but have difficulty in using written or spoken language.

social play Play that is divided into six categories: unoccupied behavior, onlooker behavior, solitary play, parallel play, associative play, and cooperative play.

mental retardation Most commonly refers to below-average intellectual functioning concurrent with an inability to mature personally and socially with age. Mentally retarded children usually are below average in motor development as well, possibly because of cognitive difficulties or a lack of opportunities for physical activity.

© Cengage Learning 2013.

CHAPTER

4

Content of the Movement Program

Learning Objectives

After completing this chapter, the student will be able to:

1 Define the elements of movement.

2 Create movement activities that promote understanding of the elements of movement.

3 Define locomotor, nonlocomotor, and manipulative skills.

4 Create movement experiences that promote development of locomotor, nonlocomotor, and manipulative skills.

5 Explain the differences between educational and Olympic gymnastics.

6 Create movement experiences falling under the category of educational gymnastics.

TERMS TO KNOW

elements of movement

personal space

general space

bound flow

free flow

locomotor skill

quality of movement

nonlocomotor skill

manipulative skill

creative dance

educational gymnastics

The decision as to what, specifically, will make up your movement program must ultimately be yours. Time, space, and availability or lack of equipment—and even regional weather—can all be determining factors. Of course, the developmental stages of your children will also influence your program planning.

The Elements of Movement

Critical to any program of movement education is the concept of movement variations, or extensions. This concept, discussed further in Chapter 8, allows for the discovery of unlimited movement possibilities for locomotor, nonlocomotor, and manipulative skills, as well as dance steps, gymnastic skills, and almost any other movement activity. Therefore, exploring the movement elements is an excellent starting point for any program.

For instance, if the locomotor skill of walking was being explored, there would be a number of choices regarding how to perform the walking: forward, backward, to the side, or in a circle (here the element of space is being used). In addition, the walk could be performed with arms or head held in various positions (shape), quickly or slowly (time), strongly or lightly (force), with interruptions (flow), or to altering rhythms (rhythm).

If we liken movement education to the study of grammar, the skills themselves can be considered verbs, while the elements of space, shape, time, force, flow, and rhythm are the adverbs modifying them. Each of these six elements of movement, listed in a general progression from least to most challenging, is described in more detail next.

Space

The element of space is divided into two components. The first, personal space, is the area immediately surrounding the body and includes whatever can be reached while a person remains in one spot. Personal space can be likened to a large bubble surrounding the body. The rest is referred to as shared or general space and is limited only by floors, walls, and ceilings.

Both general and personal space have three levels: low, middle, and high. When standing upright, one is at the middle level. Anything closer to the ground is considered the low level. Positions or movements performed on tiptoe or in the air occur at the high level.

Space also includes the bodily and spatial directions of forward and backward and right and left. Finally, movement performed through general space involves pathways, which will be straight, curving, or zigzag.

Sample Activities

To explore personal space, provide carpet squares or hoops for children or ask them to imagine they are each inside a giant bubble. Then present the following questions and challenges:

- Show me how low you can get in your personal space (in your "bubble" or on your "island" or "spot").
- Stay very low and move your arms all the ways you can all around your body.

- How high up can you get while staying in your own space? Find a way to get very high with your feet still on the floor. Now find a way with your feet coming off the floor.
- Explore the area in between very high and very low. Move your arms in as many ways as possible all around your body.
- How far apart can you place your feet? With your feet like that, move your arms all around your body.
- Do the same thing at a lower (higher) level.

(*Continued*)

To explore general space, give each child a hoop to pick up and hold around her or his waist. Or ask children to imagine they are each inside a giant bubble that stays all around them wherever they go. Now ask them to walk around the room without touching anyone else's hoop or bubble. Encourage them to make straight, curved, and zigzag paths (Figure 4.1). Once they have had ample time to experiment with a forward direction, ask them to try not touching one another while moving in a backward direction (with the back of the body going first). Can they do it with one (and then the other) side of the body leading?

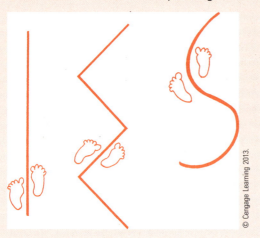

FIGURE **4.1** Pathways traveled through general space will be straight, zigzag, or curving.

If you have a large enough space, you can experiment with reducing the general space. First, allow children to explore all the available space. Then pretend you are a wall. A little bit at a time, move toward the children until they are moving in as little space as possible while still not touching one another.

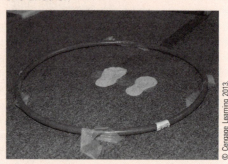

Hoops provide tangible evidence of personal space.

Shape

The study of shape relates to the various shapes the body is capable of assuming. This element is sometimes referred to as the relationship of body parts because whenever the relationship between or among body parts changes, so does the body's shape. For example, if an elbow is brought closer to a knee, the body bends and the spine curves. If that elbow is then taken as far from the knee as possible, the body must straighten.

Sample Activities

Making Shapes. Making Shapes (see Chapter 2) is a good introductory activity for exploring the element of shape. Children should also be challenged to experiment with the different shapes they can make with their bodies while performing locomotor skills.

The Mirror Game. In this activity, face the children and move slowly from one shape to another. The children pretend to be your mirror reflection and replicate each shape.

Numbers and Letters. A more advanced activity, appropriate for early-elementary children, is to challenge children to use their bodies to copy the shapes of numbers or the letters of the alphabet. Begin by reviewing numbers or letters with children, pointing them out on a chart or writing them on a chalkboard. Note that some have straight and zigzag lines; some, curved lines; and some, more than one kind of line.

Choose numbers or letters easily formed by the body and ask children to show them to you. You can also ask them to select partners and form the numbers and letters in pairs.

Sample Activities

Any movement can be performed at any speed. Spend a great deal of time exploring this with children. Which body parts can they move slowly? Which can they move quickly?

Exploring Time. To explore time with music, invite children to move appropriately to both slow and fast songs (see "Contrasting Elements," Chapter 7). To explore this concept with imagery, ask children to move like the following:

- a rabbit
- a bumblebee
- a turtle
- a snail or worm
- a race car
- a scurrying mouse
- an old car
- a stalking cat

Whenever children are executing any locomotor or nonlocomotor movements, be sure to challenge them to try the movements at different speeds. (Fast speeds will come most naturally to them, so you will most often be suggesting slower tempos!)

Time

The element of time relates to how slowly or quickly a movement is performed. Movement, however, is not only slow or fast; it also includes the range of speed in between. With young children, it is best to introduce this element by contrasting the extremes of slow and fast before exploring the continuum from one to the other.

Force

Force concerns how strongly or lightly a movement is performed and the amount of muscle tension involved. Tiptoeing, for instance, requires much less force and muscle tension than does stamping feet. Similarly, moving like a butterfly requires

Sample Activities

Statues and Rag Dolls. To introduce children to the concept of force, you can invite them to alternate between pretending to be a statue and a rag doll. Try this first while they are in a stationary position, and then ask them to try it while moving.

Robots and Astronauts. Have children alternate between moving like a robot and an astronaut floating weightlessly in outer space.

"Strong" and "Soft" Movements. This activity is excerpted from Pica (2000a). Ask children to do the following:

- Move very softly, like a feather floating. (Demonstrate with a feather if you have one.)
- Move very strongly, making lots of noise with their feet.
- Make strong movements with their arms, like propellers on a helicopter.
- Make light arm movements, like the wings of a bird sailing gently through the sky.
- Tighten all their muscles so they feel as stiff as robots. (If possible, use a Transformer or other robot toy for demonstration purposes.)
- Be floppy rag dolls with no muscles holding them up. (Show the children a rag doll as an example.)

As children perform any movement skills, encourage them to move both lightly and strongly.

© Cengage Learning 2013.

Sample Activities

Statues. Statues (see Chapter 2) is an example of an activity involving flow. To explore this element without music, ask children to move freely around the room until they hear your signal to freeze. As soon as they hear the signal, they must stop immediately and not move another muscle until they hear your signal to go again. Vary the time between signals, sometimes letting children experience free flow and sometimes interrupting frequently (bound flow).

Using Imagery. To explore flow with imagery, ask children to move like an eagle soaring, a tin soldier, a happy person with no cares, and a robot.

© Cengage Learning 2013.

Playing Statues offers children experience with bound flow.

much less force than moving like a dinosaur. With this element, it is best to contrast the extremes before exploring the continuum from light to strong.

Flow

The flow of movement is either bound (punctuated or halting) or free (uninterrupted). For example, **bound flow** would be motion resembling that of a robot or a series requiring children to hop-hop-stop, hop-hop-stop. **Free flow** is visible in the action of a skater gliding effortlessly across the ice or in the flight of an eagle. Free flow can also be likened to a sentence, which might have a breathing pause but not a complete pause until the period at the end.

Rhythm

Rhythm, although often associated with the element of time, is mentioned separately because of its many facets and benefits to students. This element not only relates to music but also encompasses the many rhythms of life. Words, for instance, have rhythm, as do the various locomotor activities (e.g., the rhythm of a run differs from that of a hop). People, in fact, possess their own personal rhythms for thinking and functioning (Gerhardt, 1973). The element of rhythm encompasses all of these aspects.

Sample Activities

Clapping. Clapping activities can demonstrate the rhythm of words. Sit in a circle with children. As you say your name aloud, clap one clap per syllable. Thus Rae Pica (pronounced Ray Pee-ka) would involve three claps, with a pause between the first and second claps. Then ask the children to do this activity with you. Go around the circle, saying and clapping the rhythm of each child's name (first name only or first and last, depending on the developmental level of your group).

Rhythms and Locomotor Skills. To explore the various rhythms of locomotor skills, ask children to perform a skill

(e.g., walking). After a moment, begin to beat a drum or clap your hands to the rhythm of their movement. Repeat with other locomotor skills. This allows children to concurrently hear, see, and feel the different rhythms.

Rhythms and Music. Clapping Rhythms and Exploring Common Meters (see Chapter 2 for both) offer other possibilities for exploring rhythm. In addition, any time you use music with a different "feel," you will be contributing to children's experiences with this movement element.

Locomotor Skills

Locomotor skills, sometimes called *traveling skills*, transport the body as a whole from one point to another. Although it is commonly believed that children acquire and develop locomotor skills automatically, they will be unable to reach a mature stage of development without practice, encouragement, and instruction. Failure to reach the mature level will hinder their ability to perform specialized movements in the future (Gallahue & Cleland-Donnelly, 2007).

Standard 1a

Children acquire the ability to execute locomotor skills according to their own internal timetables. The following represents a general developmental progression of locomotor skills. Each skill—crawl, creep, walk, run, jump, leap, gallop, hop, slide, skip, step-hop—is defined, and sample activities are provided for each.

Crawl

The crawl involves lying on the stomach, with head and shoulders raised off the floor and the weight of the upper torso supported by the elbows. Locomotion involves moving the elbows and hips.

Children should explore homolateral crawling, or simultaneously moving the arm and leg on the same side of the body. They should then explore crawling

Sample Activities

Talk to children about crawling, differentiating between it and creeping. Then ask them to pretend to be worms, snakes, or seals. Or perform The Eel group activity, which requires lots of cooperation (excerpted from Pica, 2001, p. 142).

The Eel. Talk to children about eels and show them a picture, if possible. Explain that eels are actually fish that look like snakes. One type of eel is the electric eel, which can grow up to six feet long and has the ability to shock in the way that electricity does.

Explain that the children will work together to form a very long eel, and then they are going to pretend the eel is

swimming in the ocean. The children begin by getting on the floor and moving individually, as they believe eels would. Then, at a signal from you, they start to join together, one by one, by taking hold of another child's ankles. When all the children are joined and moving like a giant eel, tell them that they have become an electric eel and you have just "turned on" their electricity. What would that look like?

If you find that the indiscriminate joining is too confusing for children, assign one child to take the ankles of another child by calling out their names.

ABOUT THE QUALITIES OF MOVEMENT

Not to be confused with the six elements of movement are the six **qualities of movement**, which you might also choose to explore with children. The following describes the six qualities of movement.

Sustained

Sustained movement continues through time and space without stopping and requires considerable control. Although movement at any speed can be sustained, this quality is usually associated with slow—even slow-motion—movement. Asking children to move as though in slow-motion instant replay will grant them experience with this movement quality.

Suspended

In suspended movement, the body often acts as a base of support above which one or more parts are temporarily interrupted in their flow of movement. In this case, the movement begins with an impulse, reaches its peak elevation, holds momentarily, and then continues once again. An example would be a swinging arm that stops momentarily overhead before swinging once again. Suspended movement involving the whole body requires control and balance. Playing Statues (Chapter 2) or Freeze qualifies as experience with suspended movement.

Swinging

Swinging takes the form of an arc or a circle around a stationary base. It usually requires impulse and momentum, except perhaps when the swinging part is merely released to the force of gravity. Swinging movement can be executed by the body as a whole, by the upper or lower torso alone, or by the head, arms, and legs. The easiest way to begin exploring this movement quality is to invite children to swing their arms in front-to-back and side-to-side directions.

Percussive

Percussive movement is punctuated and accented. A head moves percussively when it drops sharply forward and then returns to center. Feet move percussively when they run. Hands and arms move percussively when they rapidly strike the air. You can introduce this movement quality by asking children to pretend to run on hot sand that's burning their feet.

Vibratory

This quality relates to tremulous or quivering movement. Body parts that can depict vibratory movement might be a rapidly shaking head, an open hand trembling in the air, or shoulders moving in a rapid shimmy. Images that depict vibratory movement are a leaf quivering in the wind, a battery-powered toothbrush, and a baby's rattle being shaken. Rapidly shaking a maraca can inspire vibratory movement.

Collapsing

A collapse of the human body must always be executed with the necessary control to avoid injury. In addition to the body as a whole, other body parts can collapse, including the head (collapsing to chest, back, shoulder), an arm that has been suspended and then collapses through space, or the upper torso collapsing toward the lower torso. To introduce children to this movement quality, ask them to pretend to be puppets released from their strings.

with limbs in opposition, or cross-laterally, which means the left arm and right leg move together and then the opposite arm and leg move together.

Creep

This skill requires using the hands and knees or hands and feet to move the body through space. It is the child's first efficient form of locomotion. Children who have not achieved a mature level of cross-lateral creeping should be given many opportunities to practice, even at ages 4 and 5 or older (Sinclair, 1973).

Sample Activities

Creepers and Crawlers. Talk to children about the differences among creatures, such as a dog, a cat, a spider, a baby, a turtle, and a crab. Then ask them to show you how each of creature creeps. Ducks, Cows, Cats, and Dogs (see Chapter 10) is another great way to give children additional experience with creeping.

If you're working with infants, you can encourage them to creep or crawl by placing a desirable object or toy within their sight but just out of reach.

Tunnels set up as part of an obstacle course can give children opportunities to practice crawling and creeping.

© Cengage Learning 2013.

Walk

The walk moves the body through space by transferring weight from the ball and toes of one foot to the heel of the other. Continual contact is made with the floor. Limbs are used in opposition.

Infants begin to walk at about age 1; by the time children are 6, they have usually acquired a mature level of development. However, posture and foot alignment should be monitored. The body must be kept straight and toes pointed straight ahead, with the weight evenly distributed over all five toes. (Rolling in, with the small toes lifting off the ground, is a common problem.)

Sample Activities

As mentioned earlier, the elements of movement can be used to vary the way skills are performed. Following are examples of how you can use the elements of movement to modify walking. Note that these same examples can apply to all the locomotor skills.

Walking. Ask children to walk in the following ways:

- in place—slower, faster
- forward—slower; faster; in straight, curving, and zigzag pathways; as tall as possible; as small as possible; with tiny steps; with giant steps; in a funny shape; lightly; strongly; with pauses between steps
- backward—same as for forward walking
- sideways—same as for forward walking

Some examples for using imagery to explore walking are offered in Chapter 2. Other possibilities include walking as though sneaking up on someone, in deep snow, in a dense jungle, and in a haunted house.

Run

Running transfers the body's weight from the ball and toes of one foot to the ball and toes of the other. The body should be inclined slightly forward, and the arms should be slightly bent, swinging in opposition to the legs.

According to Sinclair (1973), running is one of the most demanding activities because it requires

> much of the heart, lungs, and muscles. For the young child it also makes demands on the nervous system for all parts of the body must be used alternately, symmetrically, and yet with synchronous timing; contraction and relaxation must alternate smoothly; an even rhythm must be maintained; balance makes new demands as strides lengthen and ground is covered rapidly. (p. 23)

Sample Activities

Running as Though ... To explore running with imagery, ask children to run as though on hot sand, finishing a long race, playing basketball, trying to catch a bus, and trying to score a touchdown. You can also encourage children to pretend they are in an imaginary track meet (perhaps at the Olympics). To provide additional motivation, accompany the activity with music that has an even beat and a tempo appropriate for running, such as the theme from the movie *Chariots of Fire*.

Jump

A jump propels the body upward from a takeoff on one or both feet. The toes, which are the last part of the foot to leave the ground (heel-ball-toe) are the first to reach it on landing, with landings occurring on both feet (toe-ball-heel). Knees should bend to absorb the shock of landing.

Leap

This skill is similar to a run, except the knee and ankle action is greater. The knee leads forward following the takeoff and is then extended as the foot reaches forward to land. The back leg extends to the rear while in the air. Once the front foot has landed, the back leg swings forward into the next lift. Leaps are often combined with running steps to achieve greater height and distance.

A jump propels the body upward from a takeoff on one or both feet. Landing occurs on both feet.

© Cengage Learning 2013.

Sample Activities

Jumping is explored in "Pop Goes the Weasel" and Rabbits and 'Roos (see Chapter 1 for both).

Exploring Jumps. Ask children to jump in the following ways:

- coming just a little way off the floor
- coming way off the floor
- with feet together
- with feet apart
- with feet alternately apart and together
- landing with one foot forward and the other back
- clicking heels together while in the air

To add imagery to the exercise, ask children to jump in these ways:

- as though they were bouncing balls, some bouncing high and some bouncing low
- pretending to reach for something above them
- as though startled by a loud noise
- as though angry (having a tantrum)
- with joy

Sample Activities

Preschoolers may be able to relate best to leaping through imagery or with a prop. Whichever way you prefer, be sure they practice leading with both left and right legs.

Using Imagery. Ask children to pretend to leap over a puddle, a hurdle, a tall building (like Superman would), or fallen trees in the forest (like a deer would).

Using a Prop. Hold a rope an inch or two off the floor and ask children to leap over it.

Gallop

The gallop is performed with an uneven rhythm. It is a combination of a walk and a run in which one foot leads and the other plays catch-up. Children will lead with the preferred foot long before they feel comfortable leading with the other foot.

Some young children learn this skill most easily when they can hear the gallop's rhythm. Teachers can provide rhythmic accompaniment with hands or a drum, or they can use the appropriate recorded music. "On Horseback" (Pica, 2000b) and "Giddy-Up" (Pica, 2000a) were written specifically for galloping, and Georgiana Stewart's album *Rhythms for Basic Motor Skills* (available from Kimbo and Educational Record Center) offers music for seven movement skills, including galloping.

Sample Activities

Fox and Hound. Hammett (1992, p. 15) offers a game called Fox and Hound in which children pretend that the lead foot is the fox and the back foot is the hound trying to catch the fox. The fox always gets away. Eventually, the feet reverse roles. Hammett suggests attaching pipe cleaners shaped like fox ears to shoes to help children remember which is the lead foot.

Cowboys, Cowgirls. Simply pretending to be horses—or cowboys or cowgirls riding horses—is a fun way for children to gain more experience with galloping. (If you have stick horses, be sure they are readily available to children.)

Hop

A hop propels the body upward from a takeoff on one foot (heel-ball-toe). The landing is made on the same foot (toe-ball-heel). The free leg does not touch the ground. Children are usually able to hop at about age 4. To help them maintain the balance necessary for successful hopping, encourage them to lean slightly in the direction of the support (hopping) leg to shift the center of gravity. If a child continues to have problems with balance, hold her hand on the side of the raised leg and hop with her. Children should practice hopping on the preferred and the nonpreferred foot.

Sample Activities

In and Out of the Hoop. Have children place their hoops on the floor in their personal space. Each child should hop in and out of the hoop all the way around it. Once they complete the circle, have them reverse direction and repeat on the other foot.

Over the Rope. Have children make a straight line with their jump ropes on the floor in their personal space. Instruct them to hop side-to-side over the rope, beginning at one end and hopping to the other. Then have them reverse direction and repeat on the other foot.

Slide

This movement skill is a gallop performed sideward. One foot leads and the other plays catch-up; the uneven rhythm remains the same as in the gallop. Because facing one direction and moving in another is difficult for young children, they will learn to slide much later than they learn to gallop. Once learned, the slide should be practiced in both directions.

Sample Activities

Sliding is best taught through demonstration and imitation. If you stand with your back to children, you can lead with the same foot they do. If you stand facing them, you will have to lead with the opposite foot.

"Ring Around the Rosie." Once all children can slide, a fun group activity is to practice sliding together. Have children form a circle and hold hands. Ask them to slide in one and then the other direction.

Skip

A combination of a step and a hop, the skip, like the gallop and the slide, has an uneven rhythm. With more emphasis placed on the hop than the step, the overall effect is of a light, skimming motion during which the feet only momentarily leave the ground. In the skip, the lead foot alternates. For many children, skipping initially on one side only is a normal developmental stage. Possibilities for teaching the skip include providing rhythmic accompaniment, holding the child's hand and skipping with him or her, breaking down the components of the movement, and demonstrating and imitating.

Sample Activities

"Ten Little Children." Cherry (1971, p. 45) offers a progression of skipping songs sung to the tune of "Ten Little Indians." For 2- to 3-year-olds, the lyrics prompt the children to lift one foot and then the other (e.g., "Lift one foot and then the other; repeat two times; all the little children …").

Three- to four-year-olds are encouraged to *hop* on one foot and then the other. The lyrics for 4- to 5-year-olds are, "Walk and hop and walk and hop now." At the teacher's discretion, the lyrics induce the "little children" to "skip and skip and skip and skip."

Step-Hop

Like the skip, the step-hop combines a step and a hop. With the step-hop, however, the step and the hop have the same time value—that is, it is performed with an even rhythm.

The step-hop is used often in folk dances. Like many other folk dance steps, it is a combination of basic locomotor movements. The step-hop is included here because (1) it has the same components as a skip, (2) it is a common movement

Sample Activities

Step-Hop. Introduce the step-hop to children by providing an even 1–2 beat with your hands or a drum and having children practice combining a step with a hop. They can begin by performing as many steps or hops in a row as they want, eventually reducing the number until they are alternating one

step with one hop. Can they match the steps and hops to your beats?

Later, use a piece of music in a 2/4 meter (at a moderate tempo) to continue exploring the step-hop. Use the elements of movement to vary the ways in which the children perform it.

(it can even be part of a layup shot in basketball), and (3) it is developmentally appropriate for primary-grade children.

Nonlocomotor Skills

Nonlocomotor skills are movements performed in place, usually while standing, kneeling, sitting, or lying down. Sometimes called axial movements, they involve the axis of the body rotating around a fixed point. Some textbook authors label them nonmanipulative skills, and others call them nontraveling skills.

Murray (1975) wrote that nonlocomotor movements should not be considered only as exercises or warm-ups. Rather, they serve as "points of departure for exploration and as instruments for creative expression" (p. 129). However, many nonlocomotor skills can certainly serve in both capacities.

It is perhaps even more difficult to list nonlocomotor skills progressively than locomotor skills. Many nonlocomotor skills are acquired at approximately the same point in a child's development, though some are more challenging than others. The order of the skills in this section represents a general developmental order of nonlocomotor skills: stretching, bending, sitting, shaking, turning, rocking and swaying, swinging, twisting, dodging, and falling. Each skill is defined, and sample activities provided.

ABOUT STAGES OF SKILL DEVELOPMENT

Until recently, it was assumed that children of the same age were at the same level of skill development. A physical education teacher planning lessons for second-grade classes, for example, asked all the children to perform identical tasks. Children who executed them well were given good grades; those who could not received lower or failing grades.

Today, it is understood that each child goes through a separate developmental process when learning every skill. Various stages of skill development are described by noted physical education textbook authors listed here.

Kirchner

Kirchner (2001) uses learning to ride a bicycle to explain the process everyone experiences in acquiring a new motor skill. If you think back, you will probably recall how unsteady your initial attempts were and how much concentration the effort required. Gradually, you became more proficient at keeping the bike upright, but stopping, turning, and other such tasks still required effort and concentration. Finally, with much practice, riding a two-wheeler became automatic.

Kirchner labeled these stages the initial phase, the intermediate phase, and the automatic phase. The first, as he described it, involves as much thinking about a skill as it does trying to perform it. The intermediate phase represents a gradual shift from the acquisition of the fundamentals of the skill to a more focused effort to refine it. In the final phase, the skill feels and looks automatic.

Gallahue

Gallahue (1993) described essentially the same three phases of motor learning that Kirchner used. However, Gallahue labeled them the initial stage, the elementary stage, and the mature stage.

The initial stage is "characterized by relatively crude, uncoordinated movements" (Gallahue, 1993, p. 23) and can be seen among 2- and 3-year-olds attempting to perform fundamental movement skills. The elementary stage, which seems to depend primarily on maturation, means greater control and coordination, though awkwardness and a lack of fluidity are still evident. Although Gallahue noted that this stage is typical of 3- to 5-year-olds performing fundamental movement

(Continued)

skills, he pointed out that many adults remain at the elementary stage in such skills as throwing, striking, and catching due to insufficient practice and instruction.

The mature stage can be attained in most fundamental movements by age 6 or 7, though children usually reach this stage at varying rates. This stage is characterized by "the integration of all the component parts of a pattern of movement into a well-coordinated, mechanically correct, and efficient act" (p. 25).

Graham, Holt-Hale, and Parker

Graham, Holt-Hale, and Parker (2009) chose four stages to describe what they called "generic levels of skill proficiency." The first, the precontrol level, represents the stage at which a child is unable to either "consciously control or intentionally replicate a movement." The authors used the example of a child's initial attempts to bounce a ball, during which the child spends more time chasing it than bouncing it. The ball, rather than the child, seems to be in control. Most preschool and kindergarten children are at the precontrol level.

At the control (advanced beginner) level, the movement is much closer to the child's actual intentions, although a good deal of concentration is still required. When children reach the utilization level in a particular skill, they do not have to think as much about how to execute the skill and are able to use it in different contexts. The proficiency level is the advanced stage and represents the stage at which a movement appears effortless and a child is able to use it in changing environments and repeat it with ever-increasing degrees of quality. Elementary-school children rarely reach the proficiency level in a skill.

Summary

Although each author chose to describe the various stages of skill development somewhat differently, they agree that there is a developmental progression in learning and acquiring a movement skill. What we, as educators, have to accept is that these levels cannot be unconditionally assigned to certain ages or grades. Rather, every child will move from the first to the last stage—however we choose to label them—as he or she learns each new skill and tries to master it.

Furthermore, it is not unusual to observe children in the same class who are at varying levels of skill proficiency. For example, primary-grade children who have been enrolled in gymnastics programs since they were preschoolers will often demonstrate utilization-level gymnastic skills, while those who have had no introduction to gymnastics will be at the precontrol level. Of course, those children who have had some experience with gymnastics will show control-level abilities.

How do you manage to teach all these children? This is where the indirect styles described in Chapter 8 come in handy. For instance, if you challenge children to balance on just two body parts, children at the precontrol level might respond by standing on two feet, control-level children might balance on two knees or on the buttocks in a V-sit, and someone at the utilization level just might perform a handstand. What is truly important is that all the children will have successfully answered your challenge.

Stretch

A stretch extends the body, its parts, and one or more joints vertically, horizontally, or any point in between. Perhaps more than any other, this nonlocomotor skill is commonly regarded as an exercise. Although frequently used as a warm-up, stretching better serves as a cooldown, preventing contraction of the exercised muscles. When using stretching for this purpose, children should be taught to hold a stretch for 8 to 10 seconds and not to bounce.

Sample Activities

Stretching. Stretching as a cat does or as though yawning are good introductions to this nonlocomotor skill. You can also have children experiment with gently stretching forward, backward, toward the ceiling, and toward the floor while standing, kneeling, and sitting. Then present the following challenges and questions:

- Lie on your back and show me how long you can be.
- Can you be just as long lying on your stomach?
- Can you stretch wide?

- Stretch one arm high and the other low (one toward the ceiling and the other toward the floor).
- Reach both arms to the right (one side). To the left (the other side).
- On your hands and knees, stretch one leg behind you and one arm forward.
- Show me that you can lie on your back and stretch one leg long and the other toward the ceiling.

Bend

A bend brings two adjacent parts of the body together, usually toward the body's center, using ball-and-socket or hinge joints. In addition to the body as a whole, many body parts can bend, including arms, fingers, legs, and the neck.

Bending and stretching are natural partners because once a body part has been bent, it must eventually straighten again.

Sample Activities

Bending. Have children stand and experiment with bending forward, backward, and to both sides. Then issue these challenges:

- Touch your knees and straighten.
- Touch your toes (with knees bent to avoid strain on the lower back) and straighten very slowly.
- Touch your toes and straighten halfway.

Then ask them to experiment with bending the waist, arms, and legs while kneeling, crouching, sitting, and lying on their backs, stomachs, and sides. Can they find any other parts of the body that bend?

Bending Versus Stretching. To explore and contrast bending and stretching, use imagery children can relate to. Possibilities include the following:

- Stretch to pick fruit from a tall tree.
- Flop like a rag doll.
- Stretch as though waking up and yawning.
- Bend over as though you were tying your shoes.
- Stretch to put something on a high shelf.
- Bend to pat a dog, an even smaller dog, or a cat.
- Stretch to shoot a basketball through a hoop.
- Bend to pick up a coin from the floor.
- Stretch as though climbing a ladder.
- Bend to pick vegetables or flowers.
- Stretch as though reaching for a star.

Sit

A sit moves the body from any level to a position in which the body's weight is placed on the buttocks or thighs. Although young children certainly know how to sit, exploring the ways in which it is possible to get into a sitting position can enhance body and spatial awareness.

Sample Activities

Exploring Sitting. Ask children to practice sitting from a standing, kneeling, and lying position, with and without the help of the hands. Have them sit at varying tempos onto both the buttocks and the thighs. Playing Cooperative Musical Chairs (played in a manner similar to Musical Hoops, Chapter 6) can provide additional practice with sitting from a standing position.

Shake

A shake is a vibratory movement involving tension and relaxation. It can be performed by the whole body or by individual parts. Children love to shake. They often view it as a somewhat silly movement. With very young children, you can introduce shaking by asking them to wiggle.

Sample Activities

Shake Like ... Use imagery to explore shaking. Ask children to shake like

- Jell-O when the bowl is moved
- a baby's rattle
- a leaf in the wind
- an electric toothbrush
- a very cold person
- a very scared person

Once children have explored shaking the body as a whole, ask them to discover how many individual body parts they can shake. Does the number of body parts that can shake change when the body goes from standing to kneeling to sitting to lying?

Musical accompaniment for shaking can be provided by "Shake It High/Shake It Low" (Pica, 2000a); "Wiggle, Wiggle, Shake, and Giggle" (Pica, 2000b); and Raffi's "Shake Your Sillies Out" from *Singable Songs for the Very Young.*

Turn

A turn is a partial or complete rotation of the body around an axis, causing a shift in weight placement. Turns can be executed dozens of ways, on a variety of body parts, at a variety of levels, clockwise and counterclockwise.

Graham, Holt-Hale, and Parker (2009) advise using the terms *clockwise* and *counterclockwise* with children, rather than *right* and *left,* to describe the direction of a turn. Until young children are familiar with any of these four terms, however, it may be best to simply ask them to turn first in one and then the other direction, perhaps using room markings to indicate the desired direction. For example, you

Sample Activities

Turning. Use the elements of movement to explore the skill of turning on the feet—for example, slowly, quickly, in both directions, and at high and low levels. Then ask children to discover other body parts on which they can turn. Possibilities include the knees, bottom, tummy, and back.

Ask, "What parts of the body can turn?" (Answer: The head and upper torso can turn, though neither can make a complete turn.)

might ask children to turn toward the chalkboard, the closet, or the windows. When children are developmentally ready, you can use the terms *right* and *left* and *clockwise* and *counterclockwise* to describe the direction in which they are turning (also including hand signals, if necessary).

Rock and Sway

Although the rock and the sway share the common trait of transferring weight from one part of the body to another, they are essentially different. A rock is the more forceful of the two, using greater muscle tension and suspension. A sway is an easy, relaxed motion that sustains rather than suspends.

Sample Activities

Swaying and Rocking. Demonstrate a gentle sway and ask children to imitate it. Or challenge them to sway like flowers or grass in the breeze. What else can they think of that sways? Then ask them to gradually increase the force of the sway until it becomes rocking. Does the rocking bring any images (perhaps a rocking chair or rocking horse) to mind?

Can rocking be performed in different directions (forward and backward, for example, in addition to side to side)? Reverse the process until gentle swaying is once again being demonstrated. It is also fun to practice swaying and rocking while holding hands in a circle or line.

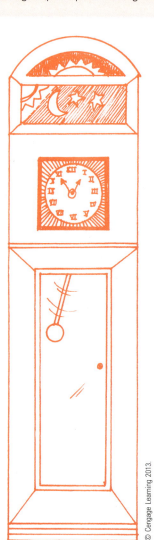

© Cengage Learning 2013.

Swing

A swing creates an arc or a circle around a stationary base. It usually requires impulse and momentum, except perhaps when the swinging part is merely released to the force of gravity. The swinging movement can be executed by the body as a whole, by the upper or lower torso alone, or by the head, arms, or legs (one at a time, unless the body is suspended off the ground).

© Cengage Learning 2013.

Twist

Unlike a turn, which rotates the whole body, a twist rotates a part of the body around an axis. The neck, trunk, arms, and legs are the body parts most easily twisted. Wrists, ankles, shoulders, and hips can be twisted to a lesser extent.

Sample Activities

Swing Like ... Use a jump rope or another appropriate object to demonstrate swinging. Then challenge children to discover how many parts of the body can swing. Encourage them to explore swinging back and forth and side to side. Prompt specific responses by presenting the following challenges:

- Swing your head like a windshield wiper.
- Swing your head like the clapper in a bell.

- Swing your arms like an elephant's trunk (or the pendulum of a clock).
- Swing your body as though you were on a flying trapeze.
- Find at least two more ways you can swing your body.

Sample Activities

Twisting is fun to do in conjunction with pretending.

Twist Like ... Ask children to twist in these ways (excerpted from Pica, 2000a):

- like the inside of a washing machine
- like a screwdriver when someone is using it
- like a wet dishrag being wrung (if you have one, show children how this looks)
- as though wiping their bottoms with towels

- as though digging a little hole in the sand with a foot
- as though wiping with a towel and digging a little hole in the sand with a foot at the same time

Challenge children to discover other ways they can twist their bodies and body parts, perhaps to the accompaniment of such tunes as "Peppermint Twist" or Dire Straits's "Twisting Around the Pool."

Dodge

A dodge usually uses the whole body as it shifts quickly and forcefully to avoid an object (or person) moving toward it. When combined with the run, the dodge becomes a locomotor skill. However, it is often performed from a stationary position, where it may involve such other nonlocomotor movements as bending, stretching, twisting, or falling.

Sample Activities

Pretend to Dodge ... Use imagery to introduce the dodge to children. Ask them to pretend to dodge a flying ball, a limb falling from a tree, a snowball, and a crowd of people in a busy department store.

Fall

A fall moves the body from a higher position to a prone, supine, or on-the-side lying position. Falls are often sudden, forceful movements, but they may also be executed slowly and limply. Either way, the body should be relaxed to avoid injury.

Introduce children to the fall by concentrating first on collapsing. Sullivan (1982) suggested an activity in which each child stands in his or her own personal space and makes the body stiff and tight. For each activity below, start the children in Sullivan's recommended position.

Wet Noodle. At a signal from you, tell children to "let go immediately of the stiffness and collapse to the floor like a wet noodle" (Sullivan, 1982, p. 119). Then ask them to rise in slow motion, make their bodies stiff again, and repeat the process several times. (This would make an excellent relaxation exercise. If used in this way, children should always end as "noodles.")

Fall Like ... You can also use imagery to explore falling. Ask children to fall like a limp rag doll, a puppet released from its strings, bowling pins being struck by a bowling ball, raindrops, snowflakes, Humpty Dumpty from a wall, and a melting candle.

Manipulative Skills

To most early-childhood professionals, the word *manipulatives* conjures up images of puzzles, blocks, and other such materials that develop fine motor skills in young children. In the physical education field, manipulative skills involve gross motor skills and an entirely different object. In some physical education texts, manipulative skills are described as gross motor movements involving force imparted to or received from objects. Others characterize manipulative skills as activities using some implement, usually with the hands but sometimes with the feet or other body parts. For the purposes of this text, manipulative skills will be described as any gross motor skill in which an object is involved, or manipulated.

For clarity, the manipulative skills are divided into two categories. The first group consists of pushing, pulling, lifting, and striking—skills that can initially be explored with imaginary objects, allowing children to become familiar with the body movement itself. (Some very young children may experience greater success with a tangible object. You will have to use your judgment.)

Pull

A pull entails resistance and is used to move something from one place to another toward the base of support. With this movement, the arms are first extended and then usually bent. Pulling may be prolonged by combining it with a locomotor movement, usually a walk.

Pull ... Challenge children to pull something imaginary in each manner listed below:

- with both hands
- with one (and then the other) hand
- alternating hands
- forward, downward, upward, and then sideward
- strong and hard
- lightly (against less resistance)
- slowly and then quickly
- with short (and then long) movements

Push

A push moves something, also against resistance, from one place to another away from the base of support. A push starts with the arms drawn in and continues into an extension of the arms. The push may also be extended by combining it with a locomotor movement. For young children, pushing seems to be more difficult than pulling (Sinclair, 1973).

Infants who are walking often enjoy pushing or pulling objects as they walk. By providing them with pull-push toys, you can give them not only additional practice with pushing and pulling but also greater incentive to practice walking.

Sample Activities

Push ... Pull ... Push ... Repeat the "Pull" activity but substitute pushing. To contrast pulling and pushing, ask children to move as if they were pushing a swing, pulling a rope, pushing heavy furniture, pulling a kite, pushing a balloon into the air, pulling a wagon or sled, pushing a car stuck in mud or snow, pulling a balloon from the sky, and pushing a shovel.

ABOUT CREATIVE DANCE

Not to be overlooked is the possibility of making **creative dance** part of the content of your movement program. Although the terms *creative movement* and *creative dance* are often interchanged, they are not technically the same.

Although it is true that discovering the ways it is possible to move an arm or perform everyday movements falls under both categories, one factor distinguishes creative dance from creative movement. Preschool children themselves have told Stinson (1988) that the difference between dance and other movement is that dance is "magic." In other words (words that perhaps we adults can better understand), creative dance is an art form. Although it is based on natural movement and not the stylized movements used in ballet and other theatrical dancing, it is indeed art, and it is the form of dance most appropriate for young children.

According to the National Dance Association (1990), movement must first be expressive (i.e., the body is used as an instrument to express ideas and feelings) if it is to be considered dance and therefore art. Other factors of dance are intent, form, and awareness. The National Dance Association further states,

> Intent means that the movement is chosen by the dancer—not necessarily pre-planned, but under the dancer's own control … The artistic form that a dancer or choreographer creates may be very complex. On the most basic level—that which is appropriate for young children—dance form involves a beginning, middle, and an end. Thus "dancing" is separate from "not-dancing" and each dance has a sense of wholeness. Awareness means sensing oneself moving. For example, walking may be used as dance movement, but the dancer senses the feet as they contact the floor, with lightness or strength, lingering or with quickness. This kind of awareness is the magic that transforms any particular movement into dance movement. (p. 3)

Creative dance, like other art forms, is important in early-childhood education. Through creative dance, young children are given opportunities to express ideas and personal feelings, to learn more about themselves and others, and to make connections with different art forms and the rest of the world. To learn more about making creative dance part of your movement program, refer to Gilbert (1992), Joyce (1993), and Cone (2004).

© Cengage Learning 2013.

The "magic" of creative dance gives children an opportunity to express their ideas and personal feelings.

Lift

A lift transports an object from one place to another, often from a lower to a higher level. Because this skill may require carrying the object, it can also be a locomotor movement. When lifting from a low to a high level, the knees must be bent and then straightened as the lift is made.

In lifting, pulling, and pushing, the arms, legs, and trunk work together.

Sample Activities

Pretend to Lift. Ask children to pretend to lift something that is very light. Have them first pretend to use both hands, then one hand, and finally the other hand. Can they show you how it would look to lift this object from low to high and from high to low? Challenge them to repeat the process, but this time pretending that the object is very heavy. How does that make lifting different? What would it look like to lift something very hot? What about something filled to the very brim with liquid that must not be spilled?

Strike

A strike is a strong movement of the arm (or arms) propelled in any direction for the purpose of hitting an object. The arm must bend to initiate the strike, extending with both force and speed. When performed without an implement (e.g., a bat or golf club), the movement abruptly stops, with no follow-through in the motion of the arm.

Sample Activities

See Chapter 2 for the "Make-Believe Striking" activity.

Hit the Air! Challenge children to hit the air with both arms; with one (and then the other) arm; alternating arms; upward, downward, sideward, forward; and with long, short, and medium extension of the arms. Have them do this while standing, kneeling, and sitting.

The second group—throwing, kicking, ball rolling, volleying, bouncing, catching, striking, and dribbling—are considered the more traditional manipulative skills. Because of the visual–motor coordination required by manipulative skills, these are usually more difficult for young children than are the locomotor and nonlocomotor movements. Adapting the equipment to the child, rather than expecting the child to adapt to the equipment, can make a significant difference in success levels.

Throw

Throwing consists of using the hands to move an object away from the body through the air. Following the infant–toddler phase of throwing small objects (food, bottles, etc.) in a downward direction (overhand), most children progress from a two-hand underhand throw to a one-hand underhand throw to a one-hand overhand throw (Kirchner, 2001). Often, the size and weight of the ball dictate the type of throw.

Sample Activities

Throwing "Soft." Infants love to throw things and should be given plenty of soft items to practice with. You will also need plenty of patience on hand, as you will be expected to retrieve the thrown objects. Although it may seem that an infant is getting some perverse pleasure from seeing you "fetch," she is not only practicing her throwing skills but also learning a valuable lesson in cause and effect.

Target Practice. Accuracy is not the first objective in teaching young children to throw. Rather, they must initially become familiar with the throwing action itself. Begin simply by providing foam or yarn balls and asking children to practice throwing them against a wall. When children are ready for a greater challenge, ask them to throw at a large target, such as a hoop hung on the wall, the inside of a large box, or a rubber trash barrel. As they become more proficient, you can decrease the size of the targets.

© Cengage Learning 2013.

A two-handed throw.

Kick

Kicking imparts force to an object (usually a ball) with the leg and foot (most often the side or top of the instep). This skill requires eye–foot coordination, body control and coordination, and accuracy of force and direction. Kicking for distance should be practiced frequently to develop a mature kicking pattern, whereas kicking for accuracy should not be a concern until after the mature pattern has been mastered (Gallahue & Cleland-Donnelly, 2007).

Sample Activities

Kicking Practice. Hammett (1992) advised beginning with beach balls because they are difficult to miss. Ask children to kick the beach ball in any way they can, both with the preferred and the nonpreferred foot. If space is limited, balloons can be substituted. Hammett then suggests that children be asked to kick a beach ball over and under a jump rope held by two classmates. With more skilled children, a large foam ball can replace the beach ball.

Ball Roll

Like throwing, ball rolling involves moving a ball away from the body with the hands, but rather than through the air, the ball travels along the ground.

Sample Activities

As with throwing, accuracy is not the initial objective in teaching children to roll a ball. Begin simply by asking them to roll balls of various sizes toward the wall.

Using Targets. When children feel comfortable with ball rolling, substitute smaller targets such as plastic bowling pins and empty soda bottles. Begin with large balls and gradually decrease their size.

Downhill/Uphill. If you have access to inclines, children will enjoy rolling balls down them (this is a great way to ensure success for very young children) and discovering that the balls do not go as easily uphill.

Ball-rolling skills are most often associated with games like bowling and kickball but are also used in such activities as boccie, shuffleboard, and curling. Gallahue and Cleland-Donnelly (2007) wrote that the basic pattern is also seen in underhand throwing (including softball pitching) and lifesaving rope-tossing activities.

Volley

For the purposes of this text, volleying is defined as striking (imparting force to) an object in an upward direction with the hands or other body parts (excluding the feet). Typical body parts used for volleying include the head, arms, and knees, as witnessed during a soccer game. Accurate visual tracking is necessary for this skill.

When working with young children on volleying, lightweight, colorful objects, such as balloons and beach balls, should be used to help ensure success.

Sample Activities

Two-Hand/One-Hand Volley. Provide a medium to large balloon for every child. Challenge children to try hitting the balloons upward and forward with both hands. The next step is to volley the balloon with just one (the preferred) hand, later trying it with the nonpreferred hand. Finally, challenge children to volley the balloon with different body parts. How many different body parts can they use to volley?

Bounce

Bouncing, sometimes referred to as dribbling, signifies striking an object (most often a ball) in a downward direction with one or both hands. According to Gallahue & Cleland-Donnelly (2007), the developmental progression seems to be "(1) bouncing and catching, (2) bouncing and ineffective slapping at the ball,

Sample Activities

Bounce and Catch. Begin this activity with large playground balls or small beach balls. Have children start by bouncing and catching the balls using two hands. Vary the number of bounces between catches.

Bounce, Bounce, Bounce. Once children become proficient with bouncing and catching, challenge them to bounce continuously with two hands. The final challenge is to bounce with one (the preferred) hand and eventually with the nonpreferred hand.

(3) basic dribbling with the ball in control of the child, (4) basic dribbling with the child in control of the ball, and (5) controlled dribbling with advanced abilities." Although bouncing a ball does not have much application later in life, it is an excellent tool for developing eye–hand coordination.

Catch

The catching skill of receiving and controlling an object with the hands requires children to focus on the approaching object and make the adjustments necessary to receive it. Catching can be difficult for some children, who experience fear as the object approaches. Using soft, colorful objects (scarves, beanbags, balloons, yarn balls, and even teddy bears) and large, soft balls (beach and foam balls) can alleviate the fear and make visual tracking easier.

Sample Activities

Catch It! Children begin by catching their own bounced ball. The next challenge is to catch an object thrown by someone who is able to throw accurately. Once children achieve a certain measure of success, they can try catching an object (ball, beanbag, balloon, etc.) that they have tossed into the air.

Strike

Striking, as it is used here, refers to imparting force to an object by using an implement, such as a racket, paddle, or bat. Graham, Holt-Hale, and Parker (2009) contended that this is one of the last skills children develop because visual tracking is not refined until the upper-elementary years and eye–hand coordination is more challenging at greater distances from the body. They also stated that the difficulty of striking increases with the length of the implement. However, with the proper modifications to the equipment (lightweight, short-handled implements and lightweight objects to be struck), young children can experience success with this skill.

Sample Activities

Batting Challenges. A good rule for exploring this skill is that at first, the object and the child should be stationary. For example, have the child use a bat to strike a ball off a cone or tee. Next, the object moves but the child remains still (e.g., the child hits a pitched beach ball with a paddle or a large, lightweight bat). The final challenge occurs when the object and the child move (e.g., keeping a ball in the air with a paddle).

Dribble

In the context of this book, dribbling refers to the manipulation of a ball with the feet. Force is imparted to the ball horizontally along the ground. However, unlike kicking (in which the ball can also travel in a vertical direction), the goal is not to impart force for distance. Rather, the ball is controlled by keeping it close to the feet. Dribbling requires eye–foot coordination, which is not fully established until age 9 or 10, and a great deal of body control.

Stages of Dribbling. Children should first practice dribbling with a beanbag, which is less dynamic than a ball. Later, children can progress to a small beach ball or playground ball (8 to 12 inches in diameter), attempting to control the ball with the insides and outsides of their feet. Next, provide a pathway (and later an obstacle course) for them to dribble through. Encourage them to alternate feet while dribbling.

Educational Gymnastic Skills

Gymnastics teaches children body-management skills on the floor and with small and large apparatuses. It also develops strength, stamina, and flexibility, which links it to the health-related components of physical fitness. Although this applies to both educational gymnastics and the more traditional, Olympic-style gymnastics, a vast difference in approaches exists between the two.

Olympic gymnastics is stunt-oriented, and the ability to execute the required stunts determines success or failure. Performances "are compared against a set standard, such as the Olympic '10,' and typically against others' performances" (Belka, 1993, p. 1).

Educational gymnastics, on the other hand, is child oriented and a natural progression of the exploration of fundamental movement skills. Its use of exploration and discovery allows children to progress at their own pace—and, thus, to experience much success in body management.

Five skills—rolling, transferring weight, balancing, climbing, and hanging and swinging—are developmentally appropriate for preschool and primary-grade children. These skills can introduce children to the experiences characteristic of gymnastics. Mats or carpeting should be used for rolling and transferring weight.

Roll

Rolling is a horizontal transfer of weight that can take many forms and that can move in forward, backward, or sideward directions. It is one of the most basic movement activities and is excellent for developing balance (Skinner, 1979), as well as body and spatial awareness. Unlike Olympic gymnastics, which often begins with the forward roll, educational gymnastics considers the forward roll an advanced skill.

Log Rolls. Log rolls involve long, stretched bodies with arms overhead, rolling in both directions. Once children are able to keep their bodies (and direction) straight while performing log rolls, ask them to try initiating the rolls with first the upper and then the lower torso.

Footsie Rolls. A more advanced activity is footsie rolls, in which pairs of children lie on their backs with the soles of their feet together and then attempt to roll without their feet breaking contact.

Egg Rolls. Egg rolls require getting into an egg shape—kneeling, with arms crossed and resting on the mat, knees pulled into the chest, and head tucked. The child then rolls sideways in both directions.

An activity for initiating the forward roll through convergent problem solving is included in Chapter 1.

Transfer Weight

Transferring weight, in its simplest definition, is the smooth shift of the body's weight from body part(s) to body part(s). Locomotion, such as walking, is considered weight

Sample Activities

Weight Transfer. In this activity, children experiment with placing weight on various body parts and then transferring that weight to other parts. Explain the placement of weight by telling children that only the body parts you assign will be touching the floor. They will then move their weight from those body parts to the next one(s) you mention. (Move somewhat quickly from one position to another so that children are not required to balance on any one body part for too long.) Make it their goal to transfer the weight as smoothly as possible.

Body parts can include hands and knees, knees and elbows, knees alone, the tummy (nothing else should be touching the floor), the back, one (and then the other) side of the body, the bottom only, hands and feet, and just the feet.

transfer because it moves the body's weight from foot to foot. However, transferring weight can also take place without locomotion, as when an individual moves from a lying to a sitting position (simple weight transfer) or shifts the body's weight from the feet to the hands (advanced).

Balance

When a person is balanced, his or her center of gravity is over the base of support, whether that base is a foot, two feet, two hands, or the head and hands. Balance over a wide base is, of course, easier than over a narrow one. Like transferring weight, balancing is possible both when moving and while remaining stationary; it is, in fact, necessary to both moving and remaining stationary.

© Cengage Learning 2013.

Maintaining balance while moving is known as dynamic balance.

MORE ABOUT OLYMPIC AND EDUCATIONAL GYMNASTICS

Olympic

- Stunt oriented
- Children's performances compared with performances of others
- Children traditionally compete against one another
- Mastery of specific skills required
- Traditional demonstration/imitation method of instruction (command style) used
- Children often scored on their performances
- Often consists of skills too advanced for most preschoolers
- Customarily requires use of large apparatuses beyond the capability of most preschoolers
- Often developmentally inappropriate

Educational

- Child oriented
- Children's performances compared only with their own previous performances
- Children compete against selves to improve skills
- Children progress at own developmental rates
- Exploratory approach (problem solving) used
- Children rewarded intrinsically through success achieved
- Natural outgrowth of exploration of fundamental movement skills
- Children explore possible uses of large apparatuses according to their level of ability
- Developmentally appropriate

Sample Activities

Walking a Tightrope. A basic introduction to balance is walking a tightrope, whether imaginary or created with masking tape, string, or rope. (Note that younger children will benefit from having a visible "tightrope.") Begin by asking children to walk forward along the tightrope, placing one foot in front of the other. When they are ready, challenge them to try moving sideward and then backward. (These activities can later be transferred to a low balance beam, if available, giving children a chance to actually move above the ground.)

Low and High Balancing. Young children should practice balancing on various body parts at low and high levels. Challenge children to do the following balances at a low level: on two hands and one knee, on one hand and one knee, on bottom only, on knees only, on tummy only, and on one knee.

Challenges for a high level include on tiptoe, on one foot (flat), on the other foot (flat), on tiptoe with knees bent, on tiptoe with eyes closed (briefly), and on tiptoe on one foot only (briefly).

Balances that occur in a stationary position, like standing on one foot, are known as static balances. Maintaining balance while moving (for example, walking along a balance beam) is called dynamic balance.

Climb

Children love to climb and are often fearless in their attempts to do so. This skill involves "pushing and pulling and supporting one's weight while moving the body up or down" (Belka, 1993, p. 6). Climbing contributes to leg, arm, upper trunk, and shoulder strength.

Climbing requires apparatus. However, if the necessary equipment is not available indoors, most playground structures will suffice.

Hanging and swinging help develop arm, upper trunk, and shoulder strength.

© Cengage Learning 2013.

Sample Activities

Monkeys! No one hangs and swings better than a monkey, and children love to pretend to be monkeys. Challenge them to hang and swing with two arms, one arm (trying it on both sides), and eventually in an inverted position (with supervision only).

MORE ABOUT CATEGORIES OF MOVEMENT SKILLS

Locomotor Skills

- Crawl
- Creep
- Walk
- Run
- Jump
- Leap
- Gallop
- Hop
- Slide
- Skip
- Step-hop

Manipulative Skills

- Pull
- Push
- Lift
- Strike
- Throw
- Kick
- Ball rolling
- Volley
- Bounce

- Catch
- Strike
- Dribble

Nonlocomotor Skills

- Stretch
- Bend
- Sit
- Shake
- Turn
- Rock and sway
- Swing
- Twist
- Dodge
- Fall

Gymnastic Skills

- Roll
- Transfer weight
- Balance
- Climb
- Hang and swing

Hang and Swing

Hanging and swinging, like climbing, require apparatus. These activities help develop arm, upper trunk, and shoulder strength. Most children will use an over-grasp and can hang for four or more seconds (Sinclair, 1973). Arms should remain fairly straight (the elbow should be slightly bent) while hanging and swinging.

Without supervision, children should hang from apparatus no higher than their heads. Even with supervision, the apparatus should not be more than twice the child's height. Children should also be taught to dismount (i.e., let go) on a backward rather than a forward swing, as a forward swing usually propels them higher into the air.

ASSIGNMENTS

1. Not all the skills described in this chapter are explored in every movement program. Choose those skills you consider most critical for preschool children and provide justification for your choices.
2. Create one activity for each movement element and skill.
3. Explain, in your own words, how the movement elements and skills are used in conjunction with one another.
4. Using early-childhood or physical education supply catalogs, compile a wish list of equipment you consider necessary for exploring manipulative and educational gymnastic skills.

FIELD OBSERVATION

1. Observe a preschool class at a gymnastics center. Is the class content educational or Olympic gymnastics? Explain the reasons for your determination.

REFERENCES

Belka, D. (1993). Educational gymnastics: Recommendations for elementary physical education. *Teaching Elementary Physical Education, 4,* 1–6.

Cherry, C. (1971). *Creative movement for the developing child.* Carthage, IL: Fearon.

Cone, T. P., & Cone, S. L. *Teaching children dance.* (2004). Champaign, IL: Human Kinetics.

Gallahue, D. L., & Cleland-Donnelly, F. (2007). *Developmental physical education for all children.* Champaign, IL: Human Kinetics.

Gallahue, D. L. (1993). *Developmental physical education for today's children.* Dubuque, IA: Brown & Benchmark.

Gerhardt, L. (1973). *Moving and knowing: The young child orients himself in space.* Englewood Cliffs, NJ: Prentice Hall.

Gilbert, A. G. (1992). *Creative dance for all ages.* Reston, VA: AAHPERD.

Graham, G., Holt-Hale, S., & Parker, M. (2009). *Children moving: A reflective approach to teaching physical education.* New York: McGraw-Hill.

Hammett, C. T. (1992). *Movement activities for early childhood.* Champaign, IL: Human Kinetics.

Kirchner G. (2001). *Physical education for elementary school-children.* Blacklick, OH: McGraw-Hill.

Joyce, M. (1993). *First steps in teaching creative dance to children.* Columbus, OH: McGraw-Hill.

Murray, R. L. (1975). *Dance in elementary education.* New York: Harper & Row.

National Dance Association. (1990). *Guide to creative dance for the young child.* Reston, VA: National Dance Association.

Pica, R. (2000a). *Moving & learning series: Preschoolers & kindergartners.* Belmont, CA: Cengage Learning.

Pica, R. (2000b). *Moving & learning series: Toddlers.* Belmont, CA: Cengage Learning.

Pica, R. (2001). *Wiggle, giggle, & shake: 200 ways to move & learn.* Silver Spring, MD: Gryphon House.

Sinclair, C. B. (1973). *Movement of the young child: Ages two to six.* Columbus, OH: Merrill.

Skinner, L. (1979). *Motor development in the preschool years.* Springfield, IL: Thomas.

Sullivan, M. (1982). *Feeling strong, feeling free: Movement exploration for young children.* Washington, DC: National Association for the Education of Young Children.

RELEVANT WEBSITES

For activities, resources, and more:

PE Central:
 www.pecentral.org

Moving & Learning:
 www.movingandlearning.com

The Perpetual Preschool:
 www.perpetualpreschool.com

KEY TERMS & DEFINITIONS

elements of movement How a movement is performed. If we liken movement education to the study of grammar, the skills themselves can be considered verbs, while the six movement elements—space, shape, time, force, flow, and rhythm—are the adverbs modifying them.

personal space The area immediately surrounding the body, including whatever can be reached while remaining in one spot. It can be likened to a large bubble surrounding the body.

general space Space that is normally limited only by floors, walls, and ceilings. It may also be referred to as *shared space.*

bound flow Describes movement that is punctuated or halting, such as the movements of a robot.

free flow Uninterrupted movement, such as is visible in ice skating.

locomotor skill Transports the body as a whole from one point to another. Although it is commonly believed that children acquire and develop locomotor skills automatically, in fact, children are unable to reach a mature stage of development without practice, encouragement, and instruction.

nonlocomotor skill Movement performed in place, usually while standing, kneeling, sitting, or lying. Involves the axis of the body rotating around a fixed point. Some textbooks describe these skills as nonmanipulative skills.

manipulative skill In this text, any gross motor skill that involves an object being manipulated.

creative dance An art form based on natural movement rather than the stylized movements used in ballet or other forms of theatrical dancing.

educational gymnastics A child-oriented, natural progression of the exploration of fundamental movement skills that teaches body management—on the floor and with small and large apparatus—and develops strength, stamina, and flexibility through exploration and discovery. Educational gymnastics is not similar to Olympic gymnastics, where the student's ability to execute stunts determines success or failure.

quality of movement Divided into six categories: sustained, suspended, swinging, percussive, vibratory, and collapsing.

PART TWO

Planning for Movement and Music

5   Lesson Planning

6   The When, Where, and What of Movement Sessions

7   Choosing and Using Music

© Cengage Learning 2013.

CHAPTER

5

Lesson Planning

Learning Objectives

After completing this chapter, the student will be able to:

1 Describe a lesson plan.

2 Explain the rationale for developmental progression in lesson plans.

3 Create a lesson plan using a variety of themes.

4 Create a lesson plan using a single theme.

5 Create a lesson plan using a single unit theme.

TERMS TO KNOW

lesson plan
objectives
primary theme
observation cues
developmental progression
movement theme
unit theme

Much of lesson planning is a matter of personal choice. You can choose a lesson plan format from the numerous possibilities in physical education texts, or you can create one of your own. You may choose to build your lesson plans around movement themes, in which case you will have to decide whether a lesson will consist of a single theme or a variety of themes. Or you may choose to build your lesson plans around content areas or classroom themes. There are, however, some general suggestions for lesson planning.

Gallahue and Cleland-Donnelly (2007) wrote, "Experience has shown that teachers who fail to plan are really in essence planning to fail." As often mentioned, movement education is success oriented. Thus far, we have considered the term *success* only as it applies to children participating in movement experiences. Yet success should also be the result for those who are facilitating the movement experiences. Well-prepared lesson plans can help ensure that this will be the case.

Creating Lesson Plans

A **lesson plan**, as defined by Weiler, Maas, and Nirschl (1988), "specifies procedures for teaching one class period of a planned learning unit" (p. 43). However, there may be as many ways to create lesson plans as there are teachers. Here are some suggestions to get you started on devising your own.

naeyc
Standard 4b

1. The lesson plan should be considered a flexible guideline (Kirchner, 2001), because no two classes are ever alike. Even children of the same age will be at different levels of motor ability, experience, and emotional maturity. Thus, you will have to adapt your lessons accordingly. You should also be aware of—and open to—the idea that changes can occur as you go along, either over time or during an individual lesson. For example, you may decide, based on your observations during one lesson, that you would like to further develop a particular activity or skill, thus causing you to change your next lesson plan. Or the children may make a suggestion you had not considered or ask to repeat something they especially enjoyed. (For more on flexibility, see Chapter 9.)

2. Although you do not want to be rigid in your preparation and use of lesson plans, you want to have clear—and realistic—**objectives**. Although it may seem overwhelming to do all at once, the best plan of attack is to know what objectives you would like the children to meet during the entire school year. You can then break these into goals for weekly or daily lesson plans.

If, for instance, your prime objective is for your kindergarten children to experience some success with all the basic locomotor and nonlocomotor skills, you must first define what you mean by success. You can then begin to prepare your schedule accordingly. What activities will you include in each lesson to help children reach this goal by the end of the year? What exactly do you want them to accomplish in each meeting? Of course, you may decide you also want to include objectives for the cognitive and affective domains as well as the physical. For example, do the children demonstrate understanding of the three levels in space (cognitive)? Are they able to cooperate effectively during a partner activity (affective)?

Graham (2008) advises being realistic and specific. He wrote that expecting children to learn to volley a ball in a 30-minute class is an example of an unrealistic and overly general goal. Rather, you should set a narrower focus that provides

One of your primary—and constant—objectives should be the children's enjoyment.

© Cengage Learning 2013.

a guideline for observation and evaluation—for example, "The children will learn to bend their knees as they receive and volley a ball." Thus, the yearly objectives are rather like a sumptuous banquet, and the daily or weekly objectives are the many, many ingredients that go into making the banquet possible.

3. The more experienced you become at teaching, the less time and detail will be necessary in your planning. (This is certainly good news in light of the previous discussion.) It only makes sense—the more familiar and comfortable we become with anything, the less concentration it requires.

Take the lesson plans themselves. When you first begin teaching movement, you will likely find that the more detailed the lesson plans are, the easier the actual teaching will be. Figure 5.1 provides an example of a lesson plan outline that allows you to record most of the specifics in teaching a movement class.

The first four items—class, skill level, length of lesson, and number of meetings per week—are helpful for teachers with several classes each week, especially if the classes are not identical. The space allotted for equipment allows the teacher to list the materials required for a specific lesson and to make a quick and easy inventory before the class.

Primary theme refers to the lesson's main focus—for example, a movement element or skill, or a classroom theme—with the secondary theme(s) being the subfocus. If the primary theme is jumping, the secondary theme might be the movement element of force. The lesson would then involve jumping lightly and heavily. The objectives (also written on the lesson plan) might then be that children learn to land toe-ball-heel, with knees bent, and demonstrate an understanding of the difference between light and heavy jumps.

The next part of the lesson plan format has space to list the activities, organization/equipment needs, and observation cues for each activity. (An actual lesson plan would require more space for the activities than shown.) Organization simply means the formation in which an activity will be performed—for example, circle, single-file lines, scattered, and so on. Small Xs representing students' bodies can be used to demonstrate the formation of choice. Any equipment required for the activity can also be noted here. (You can later review this

FIGURE **5.1** Sample lesson plan outline.

Class _____ Skill Level _____

Length of Lesson _____ Lessons per Week _____

Equipment Needed _____

_____

Primary Theme _____

Secondary Theme(s) 1. _____

2. _____

Objectives (physical, cognitive, and/or affective) _____

_____

Activities	Organization/Equipment	Observation Cues

Notes

_____

_____

_____

section to prepare your overall list of equipment and note that information at the top of the lesson plan.)

naeyc
Standard 3b

Until you become adept at observation and evaluation, you will certainly want to write observation cues on the lesson plan itself. Observation cues are questions you will ask yourself as you analyze the children's movement based on your lesson's themes and objectives. You will also use these cues to help children refine their movements. (For more on this topic, see Chapter 8.) For instance, using the jumping theme and objectives as an example, the observation cues appearing on the lesson plan might be: "Are the children landing with knees bent? Are their heels coming all the way to the floor, or are they landing on the balls of their feet only? Are they demonstrating a clear difference between light and heavy jumps? Is there a discernible difference in the amount of muscle tension being used for each?"

The last section should be used immediately following a class (or as soon after as possible) to make notes regarding your evaluation of the activities, the children's performance, and your own teaching. These notes can help you make the necessary adjustments in future lessons.

naeyc
Standard 4b

4. The number of activities you plan for a single lesson will vary according to the ages of the children and the time allotted for movement. Regardless of the number of activities, a lesson plan should have a beginning, a middle, and an end.

The beginning should be an activity that focuses children on you and on the reason you have come together: to move! If you want to add an element of predictability to your movement sessions, begin each one with the same activity (e.g., touching head, shoulders, knees, and toes). On the other hand, you might choose an opening activity that specifically focuses children on the theme of that day's lesson. Whichever you decide, you will get the session off to the best possible start by making the first activity fun.

You will get your movement session off to the best possible start by making the first activity fun.

The middle of the plan is the body of the lesson, or the activities you have designed to meet the outlined objective(s). The activities should build on one another and flow easily from one to the next. Writing them down will keep you focused on the tasks at hand and avoid lulls in the lesson (Graham, 2008; Sullivan, 1982).

The end of the lesson, which, like the beginning, could be the same activity each time, should bring closure to the session and wind the children down. (For more on this, refer to "The Role of Relaxation" in Chapter 9.)

5. To maintain interest and order, the activities you plan should alternate between lively and not so lively. This may mean following a locomotor activity with a nonlocomotor activity or an activity that moves through general space with one performed in personal space, perhaps sitting or even lying down. Another possibility is to follow an activity involving the whole body with one requiring the use of only the hands or arms. (For more on pacing sessions, see Chapter 9.)

Activities that involve the whole body and move the child through general space should alternate with less-lively activities.

Developmental Progressions

Although much choice is available with regard to the design of lesson plans and the movement program itself, one factor must be present in all instances if a program is to be truly successful. That factor is developmental progression. In other words, you must begin at the beginning and proceed in a logical, developmental order from there.

What should be "the beginning"? There is no one right answer to this question. You must determine this for yourself, depending on the developmental level of the children with whom you are working. There are, however, some guidelines you can follow in making this determination.

With young children, the initial focus of the lessons should be on the elements of movement, rather than on the movements themselves. This can be somewhat confusing—naturally, you cannot have one without the other. For example, if the focus of a lesson is pathways and you ask the children to gallop in zigzag paths, they will be concentrating on the zigzags (the movement element), but they will also be practicing the gallop (a movement skill). Thus, the two are interrelated. Initially, however, your objectives should be concerned with their understanding of the movement elements and not necessarily with the quality of their execution of the movement skills.

Chapter 4 outlined a general developmental progression for the movement skills (locomotor, nonlocomotor, manipulative, and educational gymnastics). Based on these progressions, therefore, you would not explore skipping before working on the locomotor skills leading up to the skip. Likewise, you would not focus on dodging before exploring simpler nonlocomotor skills. The same applies for the exploration of the movement elements. In general, the developmental progression for the movement elements—from least to most challenging—is space, shape, time, force, flow, and rhythm.

Space—in particular, personal space—is the logical starting point for a movement program with young children. To further narrow the focus, however, we should consider two underlying principles: (1) The young child is concerned primarily with self, and (2) before children can focus on moving their bodies and the various body parts, they should be able to identify body parts. Thus, identifying body parts while in personal space is the most logical answer to the question regarding where to begin.

In working with children ages 2 to 8, you could choose to begin at the same point with all of them, regardless of age. However, in keeping with the premise that you should begin where the child is, you would adapt the particular activities according to each child's developmental stage. For example, you might begin all of your lessons—for toddlers, preschoolers, and early-elementary children—with a focus on body-part identification. You might then challenge toddlers simply to point to the various body parts whose names you call out. With preschoolers, you might play a game of Simon Says (without the elimination process). You could also play Simon Says with the early-elementary children but with a substantially increased pace.

naeyc
Standard 1a

Three general progressions should be remembered when planning your lessons:

1. Children should work individually before exploring movement with a partner and then in cooperation with a group.
2. For the most part, children will first use the body as a whole. They can be asked later to move both arms and/or both legs together, separate from the rest of the body. Laterality (using either the left or right side of the body) is then introduced, followed by the opposition of body halves. Here students discover, for example, that the lower half of the body can bend while the top half stretches. Finally, body parts are isolated and used individually. Use of parts such as hands and the face can be introduced early, but much experience is required before a child can isolate and move only the head, hips, or shoulders.

Most children ages 3 to 5 prefer pretending to be an airplane over pretending to fly the airplane.

3. In general, children between the ages of 3 and 5 would rather pretend to be something than pretend to do something. In other words, they would rather pretend to be an airplane than pretend to fly that plane. Only much later can they demonstrate how such experiences might feel. Thus, the natural progression is being, doing, and then feeling (Pica, 2000a).

You, of course, are the only one who can judge when it is time to move from one step to another. You may have to rely on some experimentation to make your judgment. For instance, if children have been working individually for quite a while, you can try a partner activity. If it is successful, you know they are ready to add more partner activities to their repertoire. If, on the other hand, the initial attempt results in chaos or lack of understanding, children should continue to work individually a little longer.

As mentioned, there are no fixed formulas for the developmental design of lesson plans. However, if you keep the preceding points in mind and plan your activities and lessons so they build on one another—and give yourself permission to make changes based on trial and error—you will create a successful movement program.

Using a Variety of Movement Themes

Some teachers, perhaps abiding by the adage "variety is the spice of life," prefer to create lesson plans with multiple themes, rather than a single theme throughout. Because there are no hard-and-fast rules concerning the "best" way to plan lessons, this is a perfectly acceptable option. It does not, however, lend itself to classroom or unit themes, as classes sometimes explore only one unit theme per week or month. But it is possible to create lesson plans using a variety of movement themes.

Standard 4c

A movement theme, as opposed to a classroom or unit theme, is based on a movement element or skill. Thus, a lesson plan with multiple movement themes might focus on body-part identification, one element of movement, one locomotor skill, and one nonlocomotor skill. Figures 5.2 and 5.3 present examples of lesson plans, adapted from Pica (2000a), that use multiple movement themes. The lessons are appropriate for preschoolers. However, depending on the children involved, each lesson might include too many activities for a group of young preschoolers to complete in one session.

In Figure 5.2, the first activity—Simon Says—focuses on body-part identification and is a great opening activity because children enjoy it and it immediately

FIGURE **5.2** First sample lesson plan using multiple movement themes.

Simon Says

This game is an excellent body-parts activity and a good way to begin because it is familiar to most children. In the traditional game, those who need to participate the most are usually the first to be eliminated! You can enhance all the children's enjoyment if you play Simon Says without the elimination process. Instead, play the game with the children arranged in two circles. If a child moves without Simon's "permission," she or he simply transitions from one circle to the other.

"Simon" might make the following requests:

- Raise your arms.
- Touch your head.
- Stand up tall.
- Touch your toes.
- Touch your shoulders.
- Pucker up your mouth.
- Stand on one foot.
- Place hands on hips.
- Bend and touch your knees.
- Close (open) your eyes.
- Reach for the sky.
- Give yourself a hug.

Let's Walk

This activity provides an excellent opportunity for you to observe the children's strengths and weaknesses regarding posture and alignment, weight distribution, and use of body parts—while the children simply have fun walking. Observing closely, have the children walk freely (with good posture and alignment), in place, forward and backward, on tiptoe, on heels, and with tiny (giant) steps.

Any of these challenges can be modified by using the elements of movement. For example, you might challenge the children to walk in place as lightly as possible (the movement element of force), or to walk as slowly as possible (the movement element of time).

The Tightrope

For this very basic introduction to balance, you need tightropes, whether imaginary or created with masking tape, yarn, or string on the floor. Most young children find a visible tightrope much easier to walk on. Be sure to make enough available so children do not have to wait long for a turn.

After presenting the tightropes, ask the children to pretend they are tightrope walkers in the circus, balancing high above the crowd. You might want to remind them there is a net below, and real tightrope walkers extend their arms to the sides for better balance.

If you use visible tightropes as opposed to imaginary ones and the children have to wait for their turns, you might have those waiting pretend to be other circus characters (clowns, lion tamers, trapeze artists, etc.).

Exploring Up and Down

Pose the following questions and movement challenges:

- Do you know what up and down mean? Show me with your body.
- Can you make your body go all the way down? All the way up?
- How high up can you get?
- Can you go down halfway?
- Make yourself so tiny I can hardly see you.
- Show me you can become as huge as a giant.
- Pretend your feet are glued to the floor. Can you move your body up and down without those feet moving?

(Continued)

FIGURE **5.5** Second sample lesson plan using single movement theme.

Let's Stretch

Stretching is always a good exercise, whether it's the arms, legs, or trunks doing the stretching. Lead the children through a little of each, remembering to stretch forward, backward, toward the ceiling, and toward the floor. (*Note:* Knees should always be slightly bent when stretching toward the floor.)

Let's Bend

Explain that bending is another fun way to move the body. Then ask them to do these movements, demonstrating if necessary:

- bend forward, then backward, then to the side
- touch their knees and straighten
- touch their toes and straighten very slowly
- touch their toes and straighten halfway

Exploring Up and Down

Ask children whether they know what *up* and *down* mean. Have them show you with their bodies. Then pose the following questions and movement challenges:

- Show me you can make your body go all the way down. Can you go all the way up?
- How high up can you get?
- Go down halfway. What does that mean to you?
- Make yourself so tiny I can hardly see you.
- Make yourself as huge as a giant.

Exploring Straight and Round

Talk about *straight* and *round*, showing children examples or pictures of these shapes and discussing how they differ from each other. What other things can they think of that are either straight or round? Then ask them if they can show you these things with their bodies.

Straight

- ruler
- wall
- pencil

Round

- pancake
- ball
- Frisbee

from Pica (2000b), the lesson plan in Figure 5.4 uses the theme of body-part identification. Though not technically a movement element or skill, body-part identification is an important starting point and can be considered part of the exploration of personal space. This lesson plan could easily be the first movement session conducted with children ages 18 to 36 months.

The lesson plan in Figure 5.5 focuses on the nonlocomotor skills of bending and stretching, which also incorporate exploration of up and down (the levels in space) and the concepts of straight and round (the element of shape).

In considering a developmental progression of lessons using a single movement theme, it is important to realize that each movement element and skill has its own progression. If you choose to design your program this way, you will not want to plan your first lesson around one element of movement, your second around the next element of movement, and so forth. It also would not be practical to plan to cover every aspect of one movement element before exploring the next.

Rather, you could plan to initially acquaint your students with the least-challenging aspects of the least-challenging movement element (i.e., space). Once the children have mastered the introductory concepts, you can move to the least-challenging aspects of the next movement element. Remember, however, that repetition is important to young children; thus, it will benefit them to periodically review concepts they have previously experienced.

Using a Single Unit Theme

Many schools and child care centers design their yearly curriculums around weekly or monthly themes. A quick flip through any thematically organized curriculum resource will display the most popular of these themes: self-concept, the senses, hygiene, nutrition, families and friends, seasons, weather, animals, occupations, transportation, and holidays and celebrations. All these relate in some way to the children's lives—which, of course, is why they have become the most popular units. All of these, with a little imagination, not only lend themselves to field trips, art activities, story time, and such but also to movement activities.

Teachers who organize the rest of their curriculum around a single unit theme usually choose a similar plan for their movement programs. Their focus, rather than being on the development of motor skills or the mastery of movement elements, is on providing a kinesthetic alternative to the exploration of these themes. For example, if the weekly unit were occupations, some of the activities planned might include field trips to such places as the firehouse, a bakery, and a hospital. The class might receive visits from parents or community members representing various careers. The children's artwork would then revolve around what they had seen and heard. During circle time, you might read such stories as Dee Ready's *Mail Carriers, Dentists,* and *Farmers,* or you might play a song from Ronno's *People in Our Neighborhood.* Math and science projects could include baking, taking temperatures, counting teeth, and planting seeds.

These activities offer children a multimodal approach to learning about occupations. The children are receiving opportunities to hear, see, feel, and do. However, to truly address a kinesthetic learning style, movement activities should also be planned. And this is easy enough to do. For instance, do the children also want to dance to one of the songs from Ronno's album? Depicting the actions described in Dee Ready's books will ensure greater comprehension and retention. Similarly, during group time—or any time the children need to better grasp a concept—they can be invited to show you. For example, what does it look like when bread rises? What shape is an envelope? A stamp? A mailbox? Can the children demonstrate seeds growing? Do seeds grow quickly or slowly?

In keeping with the occupation theme, the following excerpt from *Moving & Learning Across the Curriculum* (Pica, 2007) demonstrates other bodily/kinesthetic ways of teaching awareness of and respect for various occupations and career choices.

- Talk to the children about the different jobs it takes to run a community. Ask each child, in turn, what they want to be when they grow up.
- As each child answers your questions, ask her or him to demonstrate an action performed by a person holding that job. The rest of the children then imitate the action.
- Repeat the process until every child has a turn.

Or, alternatively, you can call out an occupation and challenge children to call out a corresponding action. Choose one at a time for children to perform while singing

"This is the way we..." to the tune of "The Mulberry Bush." (For example, "This is the way we paint the house" or "This is the way we slide down the pole.") (p. 252)

The lessons in Figures 5.6 and 5.7 are adapted from Pica (2001) and show complete movement lessons devoted to the exploration of a single theme. The theme in the first lesson (Figure 5.6), which is appropriate for preschoolers, is pets and falls under the broader heading of animals and the content area of science.

The lesson theme in Figure 5.7 is the sky, which falls under the broader heading of nature and the content area of science. This lesson plan is appropriate for early-elementary children and demonstrates how various aspects of a single theme can be physically explored.

Developmental progression is a bit more abstract in lessons organized around unit themes. In studying the lesson plan in Figure 5.7, for instance, you might wonder how you will know if your students are ready to be "clouds" or the "solar system." More appropriate questions might be: At what stage of cognitive development are the children? Will they grasp the concepts involved? Are they ready to work cooperatively as a group? Does the lesson require them to

FIGURE **5.6** Sample lesson plan using a single unit theme: Pets.

Content Area: Science

It's a Dog's Life
Discuss various canine traits with children and the way dogs move when they perform the following activities. Then, stressing realism, ask children to show you how a dog moves when it does the following:

- Wags its tail
- Fetches a newspaper
- Shakes your hand with its paw
- Buries a bone
- Begs
- Plays catch
- Rolls over

Cats
Although there are a number of characteristics considered typical of felines; cats, like people, all have personalities distinctly their own. Do any of the children have cats at home? What kind of personalities do they have? How do those cats move when they behave in the ways listed below?

Stressing realism, ask children to show you how a cat moves when it is behaving in the following ways:

- Playing with a toy
- Being affectionate
- Stalking a mouse or bird
- Cleaning itself
- Rubbing against furniture
- Being afraid of something
- Curling up to go to sleep

Turtles
Show children a picture of a turtle. Then discuss turtles and their characteristics. Have the children ever seen or had a turtle? How did it move?

Ask children to assume the shape of a turtle and show you how a turtle hides inside its shell. Then ask them to come out of their "shells" and show you how slowly a turtle moves.

FIGURE **5.7** Sample lesson plan using a single unit theme: The sky.

Content Area: Science

Clouds

Ask children for their impressions of clouds. How many different kinds of clouds have they seen? What do they think clouds are made of? Have they ever sat looking up at the sky, watching the clouds form the shapes of objects or animals? (If possible, take the children outside or to the window to do just that before this activity.)

Ask children to move like big fluffy clouds, wispy clouds, dark storm clouds, and clouds drifting and slowly changing shape.

If time allows, ask children to cooperate as a group, with each child beginning as a single cloud but gradually drifting together and apart, forming larger and then smaller clouds. Sometimes two clouds will drift together to form a floating shape; sometimes larger groups of clouds will join and separate.

The Solar System

Talk to the children about the solar system, which includes nine planets that revolve around the sun. The planets are, in the order of their distance from the sun (from nearest to farthest), Mercury, Venus, Earth, Mars, Jupiter, Saturn, Uranus, Neptune, and Pluto. The solar system also consists of moons (Earth has only one) and stars.

If you like, you can show children pictures of the planets, discussing the characteristics of each. You should also discuss solar and lunar eclipses, which are described in the activity.

For the activity itself, you will need as many scraps of paper as there are children. On each piece of paper, write the name of a planet or sun, moon, or star. Have each child pick a piece of paper from a container. They then form a "solar system."

The sun, of course, will be in the center, "radiating light." The planets should each revolve around the sun at an appropriate distance (Mercury, for instance, will be the closest and Pluto the farthest away). The stars should "twinkle," and the moon revolves around the earth (from west to east, if you can work that into the exercise). When the moon blocks the sun, a solar eclipse occurs; when the moon is in the earth's shadow, that's a lunar eclipse. How do the children want to depict solar and lunar eclipses?

(This is a difficult activity, and it may take many repetitions before it is performed smoothly.)

Sunrise/Sunset

Talk to your group about the rising and setting of the sun. Have they ever watched a sunrise or sunset? Explain that the sun rises in the east and sets in the west, and it takes from early morning to early evening (and sometimes longer) for the sun to move from east to west. (Remind them, of course, that the sun does not actually move; Earth revolves around it.)

Ask the children to each get into a very small shape on one side of the room (the eastern side, if possible). Then they pretend to be the sun slowly rising over the horizon. Once fully risen, the sun moves in very slow motion—shining all the while—across the "sky" (to the other side of the room) and begins setting, until it is no longer in sight.

If you like, you can accompany this activity with a piece of slow, soft music, helping to set the mood and tempo.

understand movement elements or perform movement skills for which they are not yet ready?

Whether the classroom teacher is planning movement activities to accompany a weekly or monthly theme or a movement specialist is working in conjunction with the classroom teacher to enrich the academic experience, exploring content areas through physical activity is valuable for young children in numerous ways, as detailed in Chapters 3 and 11.

ASSIGNMENTS

1. Determine how you want to design your lesson plans—built around a variety of movement themes, a single movement theme, or a single classroom theme. Justify your choice in writing.
2. Choose an age group and make a list of movement objectives you would want them to meet in a school year. (You can use the information in Chapter 3 to determine what objectives are realistic for children of a particular age.)
3. Using the sample lesson plans in Figure 5.1, create three lessons that are appropriate for the age group you selected in assignment 2. These lessons should include objectives that will help children meet the yearly goals you have outlined. They should also demonstrate a developmental progression (both within the lessons themselves and from one to the next).

FIELD OBSERVATION

1. Test one or more of the lessons you created in assignment 3 with a group of children. Did it work as planned? What, if anything, would you do differently when next planning a lesson?

REFERENCES

Gallahue, D. L., & Cleland-Donnelly, F. (2007). *Developmental physical education for all children*. Champaign, IL: Human Kinetics.

Graham, G. (2008). *Teaching children physical education*. Champaign, IL: Human Kinetics.

Kirchner, G. (2001). *Physical education for elementary school-children*. New York: McGraw-Hill.

Pica, R. (2000a). *Moving & learning series: Preschoolers & kindergartners*. Belmont, CA: Cengage Learning.

Pica, R. (2000b). *Moving & learning series: Toddlers*. Belmont, CA: Cengage Learning.

Pica, R. (2001). *Wiggle, giggle, & shake: 200 ways to move & learn*. Silver Spring, MD: Gryphon House.

Pica, R. (2007). *Moving & learning across the curriculum*. Belmont, CA: Cengage Learning.

Sullivan, M. (1982). *Feeling strong, feeling free: Movement exploration for young children*. Washington, DC: National Association for the Education of Young Children.

Weiler, V. B., Maas, J. M., & Nirschl, E. (1988). *A guide to curriculum planning in dance*. Madison: Wisconsin Department of Public Instruction.

RELEVANT WEBSITES

For physical and movement education resources:

National Association for Sport and Physical Education:
www.naspeinfo.org

PE Central:
www.pecentral.org

PE4Life:
www.PE4LIFE.org

PE Links 4U:
www.pelinks4u.org

Moving & Learning:
www.movingandlearning.com

KEY TERMS & DEFINITIONS

lesson plan Usually a detailed procedure for teaching one class period of a learning unit.

objective Intended goal to be accomplished over a period of time (e.g., by the end of a lesson or by the end of the school year).

primary theme The main focus of a lesson.

observation cue Question asked to help analyze and refine children's movements.

developmental progression Beginning at the beginning and proceeding from there in a logical, developmental order.

movement theme A theme based on a movement element or skill; differs from a classroom or unit theme.

unit theme A classroom topic explored over a period of time (e.g., a week or a month).

© Cengage Learning 2013.

The When, Where, and What of Movement Sessions

Learning Objectives

After completing this chapter, the student will be able to:

1 Determine how to fit movement into the schedule.

2 Describe the best ways in which to use the available space for movement experiences.

3 Determine appropriate group sizes for movement activities.

4 Determine the best attire for children participating in movement activities.

5 Describe the role of props and equipment for children participating in movement activities.

6 Create movement activities using a variety of props typically available in early-childhood settings.

TERMS TO KNOW

group time
group size
unrestrictive clothing

How do you fit movement into an already busy schedule? How much and what kind of space is required? What size groups should you work with? What should children wear? Will you need equipment and props? Of course, many factors will influence the answers to these questions. Among them are the ages of the children (group movement sessions are not appropriate for infants), the number of children and assistants you have, the space you have to work in, the equipment available to you, the funds that may or may not be available for purchasing new equipment, and the human resources for constructing equipment you may or may not have at your disposal.

Experience and personal preference can also play roles in the decisions you make. For instance, if you are a fledgling instructor, you may make some initial choices for scheduling and group size that continue to change as you gain experience. Or you might feel strongly that children should explore movement with minimal—or no—props or equipment. Although every situation is different and you will ultimately make—and continue to make—decisions based on the logistics of each situation, the following information can help establish a framework from which to begin.

Scheduling

With the many physical, social, emotional, cognitive, and creative benefits to be garnered from movement education, young children deserve the opportunity to experience planned movement activities daily. Yet daily movement sessions are seldom offered in early-childhood programs or the primary grades. The reasons for this are many and varied, ranging from lack of time to lack of space to lack of money for hiring specialists.

In elementary schools, movement is typically planned only if the school employs a physical education specialist. Due to budget cuts, however, physical education teachers are seeing children less often and for shorter periods or are being removed completely from staff rosters. The responsibility for movement education then falls to the classroom teacher, who commonly feels inadequately trained for such a task or is already pushed to the limit trying to meet all the curriculum objectives demanded by the recent clamor for accountability. Similar situations exist in early-childhood programs, as evidenced by the comment of the director of a privately owned kindergarten, who stated, "We don't have time for movement; we're too busy preparing the children for first-grade academics." However, an increased understanding of how children learn, the need to address the whole child, and the importance of physical fitness have led classroom teachers and early-childhood professionals to make greater efforts to overcome the problems of incorporating movement education into their programs.

naeyc
Standard 4b

What, then, is the best way to go about arranging **group time** for movement? Because children are comforted by predictability, the best plan is to schedule movement sessions for the same time each day or each week (see Figures 6.1 and 6.2). Most early-childhood programs, whether half or full day, already schedule one or more periods for large-group activities. Because these periods typically alternate with quieter activities, such as time to explore learning centers or nap time, they can easily be used for movement. One note of caution: These activities should also

Video

VIDEO: *ECE/Play: Daily Schedules - Program Planning (Child Care in Action)*

FIGURE **6.1** Group activities are scheduled three times in this example of a full-day program for 4- and 5-year-olds.
Excerpted from E. Essa. (2007). **Introduction to Early Childhood Education,** *5th ed. Copyright 2007 by Delmar Learning.*

7:30–9:00	**Staggered arrival:** Teachers greet children and talk to parents; self-selected activities such as books, manipulatives, play dough, and blocks
7:30–8:30	**Breakfast available**
9:00–9:20	**Group time:** Introduction of day's activities; story or discussion related to day's topic
9:20–10:30	**Activity time:** Self-selected activities from learning centers, or teacher-planned projects
10:30–10:40	**Cleanup time**
10:40–11:00	**Snack**
11:00–11:15	**Small-group activity:** Teacher-initiated, small-group activity to reinforce specific concepts
11:15–12:00	**Outdoor time:** Self-selected activities
12:00–12:20	**Group time:** Recap of morning; story; music
12:20–12:30	**Wash for lunch**
12:30–1:00	**Lunch**
1:00–3:00	**Nap:** Transition to nap and sleep for those requiring a nap
1:00–1:30	**Rest:** Quiet individual activity for nonsleepers
1:30–3:00	**Activity time:** Self-selected activities, both inside and outside; as sleeping children wake, they gradually join others
3:00–3:20	**Snack**
3:20–4:00	**Activity time:** Continued self-selected activities both inside and outside
4:00–4:10	**Cleanup**
4:10–4:30	**Group time:** Closing of day; story; movement activity
4:30–5:30	**Staggered departure:** Self-selected activities until all children leave

alternate with periods in which children have a chance to work or be alone. Otherwise, children may temporarily tire of being together as a group, and your movement experiences may end up more frustrating than fulfilling.

If lack of time is a concern but you feel strongly about offering children movement every day (or as many days as possible), particularly in light of young children's need for repetition, one option is to set aside a 30- to 45-minute period at the beginning of the week during which you complete one whole lesson plan. Then, during the remainder of your movement sessions, which could each be as brief as 15 to 20 minutes, you would use the same lesson plan, repeating those activities that required extra work or ones your children especially enjoyed (Pica, 2000).

naeyc
Standard 1a

FIGURE **6.2** Essa's sample half-day program for 3- and 4-year-olds includes two group times.
Excerpted from E. Essa. (2007). **Introduction to Early Childhood Education,** *5th ed. Copyright 2007 by Delmar Learning.*

8:50–9:00	**Arrival**
9:00–9:20	**Group time:** Introduce day's activities; story, music
9:20–9:40	**Snack**
9:40–10:30	**Activity time:** Self-selected activities
10:30–10:40	**Cleanup time**
10:40–11:00	**Small-group activity**
11:00–11:40	**Outdoor time**
11:40–11:55	**Group time:** Closing and recap of day
11:55–12:00	**Departure:** Gather belongings; teachers talk to parents briefly

The age of children is the most significant factor in determining the length of your sessions. Even so, great disparity is found among the suggestions offered by some experts. For example, Sinclair (1973) suggested,

> For two-year-olds and younger three-year-olds, one or two simple motor tasks might be sufficient; for children in the older four- and five-age bracket, group activity might be successful for a period of 20 minutes—seldom longer unless there is a sharp change of pace or focus. For full-day programs indoors, vigorous activity should be offered at least four times during the day; for shorter programs indoors, two or three times may be sufficient. (pp. 85–86)

On the other hand, Fowler (1981) contended that children "can be involved happily in movement activities for as long as 45 minutes or more, providing that the teacher is prepared to offer a wide variety of activities that range from vigorous and challenging tasks to those which are quieter and less demanding" (p. 108). Fowler also recommended "at least two opportunities during the day for movement if children are in school all day" (p. 109). Sullivan (1982) suggested that 7- and 8-year-olds can easily manage a 1-hour session, while classes for 3-year-olds are best kept at 15 minutes per day. And Stinson (1988) simply said that children themselves should determine the length of each session. Once they are "finished," she asserted, the most you can expect from them is "going through the motions" (p. 42).

Standard 4c

As mentioned, every situation is different. A small group will require less time to complete a lesson than will a large group. A mixed-age group may or may not take more time to complete a lesson. A very young group will certainly need more time to get through fewer activities. With a young group, it also usually takes longer for transition into and out of group activities. Due to the natures of children and movement exploration, lessons with the same number of activities can last 45 minutes one day, the next day only 30 minutes, and the following day just 20. Probably as the year progresses and the children (and you) gain more experience, the sessions can be extended.

When planning, one thing is certain: you must remain flexible. Children's moods vary from day to day. The weather can force you to explore indoors what you had planned for outdoors. Carefully planned lessons can take much less—or more—time than expected. Simply put, where movement and young children are concerned, you should be prepared to occasionally (and perhaps frequently) play it by ear.

Standard 4b

It is better to overplan than underplan so that you do not find yourself finished with a lesson long before the session is scheduled to end. Keep a list of activities from previous lessons that could use some additional work or were particular favorites of the children. Or compile a list of extra activities to choose from—locomotor and nonlocomotor, vigorous and quiet—just for those occasions when class runs short. You can also ask children for ideas.

Space

Is there such a thing as the perfect space in which to conduct movement sessions? To some teachers, it must seem a rare commodity indeed. But as the saying goes, "Where there's a will, there's a way." In a field test conducted by Gilliom (1970), teachers held movement sessions in a gym, half of a gym (with another class in the other half), a multipurpose room, a blacktopped school yard, a grassy school yard, a wide hall, a classroom with desks pushed to the edges, a stage, a cafeteria, and a lobby.

Of these, a gym is certainly the ideal. It usually offers a large, open space (although if too large, boundaries should be established, as described in Chapter 9) and a smooth, resilient wooden floor. It typically does not contain objects like pieces of furniture with pointed corners that would be hazardous to moving children. The gym also has the advantage of being a place that children associate with movement. As such, it can help set the proper mood. If a gym is not

A gymnasium or motor skills room offers open space and is a place children associate with movement.

available, you will have to choose an appropriate area. Here are some points to bear in mind:

- Find or create the most open space you can. (Space set aside for circle time is often large enough for movement.) Each child should have a personal space to call his or her own. Participants should be able to move freely through general space without colliding. If you must use a classroom, push the furniture to the walls or, if possible, set up a permanent movement center in the room.
- Sometimes what seems like too little space can actually be adequate for movement. For instance, ask children to gallop in a circle, rather than back and forth across the area, to ensure that they have a chance to gallop "full out." You can also divide a large group in two, asking half the group to act as the audience while the other half performs an activity. In this case, keep activities brief to avoid too much time spent waiting. Also, ask the audience to watch for something in particular so that they are participating visually. If you cannot perform locomotor skills indoors, consider planning nonlocomotor activities for the classroom and locomotor activities for outdoors.
- Whenever possible, avoid cement or concrete flooring; it does not yield. Wooden surfaces are the best for movement; a carpeted floor is second best (unless the carpet is laid over cement). If using a cement floor is unavoidable, decrease or eliminate high jumps, leaps, falls, and other such movements from your program.
- Find an area with as few distractions as possible. Distractions can be caused by people coming and going, excessive noise, or equipment and objects that provide either a safety hazard or overwhelming temptation (like tables "begging" to be climbed on or wheel toys just "asking" to be ridden). If the material distractions cannot be removed, consider covering them before your movement sessions to help eliminate the temptation.
- Take all possible safety precautions. Place obstacles along a concrete wall to prevent children from running into them or put foam rubber on sharp corners of furniture that must remain in the area.

Although problems are bound to exist with any location, most issues can be overcome. With a little creativity and a lot of desire, just about any space can become a movement space.

MORE ABOUT WORKING CONDITIONS

When I first started my company, Moving & Learning, I hired and trained instructors and sent them to local child care centers and preschools to teach my movement program. Once a month, we would get together to share stories about what was or was not working. Often, what was not working turned out to be the space in which the instructors and I were trying to teach.

Floor-to-ceiling columns throughout the movement area were a problem for one instructor. These columns posed a definite hazard to children, who did not always look where they were going. The only solution was to wrap the columns in padded material, similar to how pipes are wrapped for insulation in a cold basement.

Another instructor informed us that in one center, the only room in which to conduct movement sessions had a wood stove in the middle. During warm weather, the heavy cast iron object could be extremely dangerous if a child were to trip and fall against it. In cold weather, when lit, it posed two dangers. Although detracting from the space available for movement, the only alternative in this situation was to surround the object with a barricade, such as a series of gates, like those used to keep children from falling down stairs.

The most problematic situation I ever encountered had several factors working against it. The center's director had determined that the larger basement area would be more appropriate than the classrooms for movement. The floor, of course, was cement; and although covered with indoor/outdoor carpeting, it limited the movements we could explore. A large fan was going at all times, which circulated the air nicely but was impossibly noisy, so I was unable to use a range of vocal expressions to elicit what I wanted from the children. The space was also long and narrow, which sometimes kept the children and me from being able to see one another and also allowed children to remove themselves quite a distance from the group. But the biggest problems were the many distractions. Play equipment lined one side of the area, offering irresistible temptation to some children. The kitchen was on the other side. Because this was a large child care center, there were three or four kitchen employees constantly bustling about and lots of clanking of pots and pans. The program director's office was at one end of the basement and the restrooms at the other, resulting in an endless stream of people coming and going. If I had previously imagined the worst possible scenario for teaching movement, this situation would have made an almost perfect match.

I taught in that space twice before asking the director if we could use the classrooms instead. She agreed, and everyone was happier. Although space was limited and furniture had to be moved before my arrival, the cozier, more familiar area was less stimulating and thus more appropriate for these particular children. With fewer distractions, less noise, and greater visibility, we were able to get down to the business of having fun with movement.

Unfortunately, the situations described here are far more common than are "ideal" working conditions. When I started my business, I had been unprepared for them. After reading this chapter, you will not have to be.

Group Size

Many factors come into play in terms of the size of the group. The first consideration in determining group size must be the space available to you. If the space is only large enough to accommodate half of your class at a time, you may have to make arrangements for the other half. If aides or other teachers are available, they can attend to the nonparticipating children as they circulate through the learning centers, or they could take children to the playground or library. Perhaps half of your class could go to another classroom during movement sessions. If so, you might want to reciprocate by allowing your colleague's groups into your room while he or she is conducting movement sessions.

If your space does accommodate all the children, you must ascertain how many students you feel comfortable working with. Will you be working alone, or will you have assistance? If you are a beginning teacher, you probably would do best with small groups. If circumstances allow, you can increase the size of the group as you gain experience.

Sullivan (1982) suggested one adult for every five 3- and 4-year-olds and one adult for every 10 to 15 older children. She also recommended groups with anywhere from 8 to 15 children so that there are enough children to "generate energy from members" but not too many children for individual attention.

Naturally, the situation itself will be the ultimate determinant. Seasoned teachers realize that a vast discrepancy frequently exists between the ideal group size and the group size they must actually work with. (Many teachers find themselves working alone with as many as 25 preschoolers.) One bit of advice you should make every effort to follow is Stinson's (1988) recommendation to keep children in groups to which they are accustomed, because they are already used to being together and to interacting as a group.

Attire

Most young children dress casually enough, so clothing is not usually a problem. The two most important considerations are that children wear **unrestrictive clothing**, allowing for freedom of movement, and that their clothing not increase the possibility of injury. Overly long pant legs, for example, could cause a child to trip, and tights are slippery on most surfaces.

If you find that you often have children dressed inappropriately for your movement sessions, consider asking for parents' assistance. Tell them why you make movement part of your curriculum. Explain movement's many benefits and how essential it is for children to experience movement in unrestrictive attire. Ask parents to send an extra T-shirt and pair of shorts so their children will have the appropriate clothing for movement sessions.

If health regulations do not forbid it and the floor's surface is clean and smooth, you should absolutely encourage children to move in bare feet. Children have been moving in sneakers for physical activity for so long we seem to have forgotten that feet do have sentient qualities. They can be used to grip the floor for strength and balance, and their different parts (toes, ball, sole, heel) can be more easily felt and used when bare. Furthermore, there is evidence indicating that going barefoot strengthens feet and improves body alignment. Young children also feel a natural affinity for the ground that can be enhanced by removing all the barriers between it and the feet. In addition, toes accidentally stepped on and body parts accidentally kicked are much less likely to be hurt by bare feet than by those wearing sneakers or shoes.

Children who are reluctant to remove shoes and socks can be encouraged by concepts like "barefoot time" or, for toddlers, "tippy-toe time." They will also become more enthusiastic about bare feet if you remove your shoes and socks. (To save time and eliminate potential chaos, establish and practice routines for removing and retrieving footwear. Socks should be put inside shoes and shoes lined up against a wall or placed in each child's cubbyhole before the movement session.)

Of course, sometimes children cannot perform barefooted (for instance, when a child is wearing tights). If the choice comes down to sneakers or stocking feet, choose the sneakers. Even on a carpet, it is much too dangerous to

Whenever possible, children should be encouraged to move in bare feet.

© Cengage Learning 2013.

move in socks or tights. In addition, if children sense that it is easy to slip, their freedom of movement will be greatly restricted.

Equipment and Props

The most important—and only absolutely necessary—prop in children's movement experiences is the human body. Some consider music to be the second most important. Using additional props and equipment, however, can enhance movement experiences and certainly merits consideration, especially in light of a study determining that children play harder and longer when their child care centers provide such portable pieces of equipment as balls, hoops, and jump ropes (Bower et al., 2008).

Equipment like mats, inclines, balance beams, crawl-through shapes, and climbing structures offer many movement possibilities that children might not otherwise encounter. Manipulating objects provides opportunities to move in new ways that require different levels of coordination. It also lets them become comfortable with objects (Weikart, 2007). In addition, focusing on the movement of a prop can help alleviate self-consciousness and encourage children who might not otherwise want to participate.

The decision to incorporate props and/or equipment into the movement program is often more a practical, rather than a personal, choice. Are the materials available? If not, is there funding to purchase some or all of what is desired? Are parents willing to donate their time and expertise to help make some equipment? Is there space for storing equipment?

Sanders (1992) suggested that schools with limited budgets could start by purchasing small items—and only those not easily homemade—then gradually acquire other items. His book outlines activities that require equipment and offers instructions for making such items as ribbon sticks, rhythm sticks, target boards, beanbags, balance beams, and balance boards.

When purchasing equipment, you will find many possibilities listed in early-childhood catalogs, such as Childcraft, J. L. Hammett, Kaplan, and Lakeshore Learning (see Appendix 2). Because equipment is their business, physical education suppliers like Flaghouse and Play with a Purpose (Appendix 2) offer a greater selection of materials and, sometimes, better quality (see "Selecting Equipment: Practical Considerations" later in this chapter).

In the following pages, some of the relatively small, inexpensive props commonly found in early-childhood and early-elementary programs are discussed and activities are suggested for each.

FIGURE **6.3** Provide children with access to balls of different sizes and textures.

© Cengage Learning 2013.

Balls

Because the majority of manipulative skills described in Chapter 4 consist of ball-handling skills, balls are necessary for any program in which these skills are taught.

A wide variety of balls should be available to children (Figure 6.3). Beach balls and balls made of foam or yarn are easier for young children to catch, and eliminate the fear of being hit that often occurs with harder balls. Because small balls are easier to throw and large ones easier to catch and bounce, many sizes should be offered. Children will usually select equipment with which they can have the greatest success and will vary their choices according to need and developmental progression.

Hoops

In the past, there was little choice in hoops that could be purchased; a hoop was a hoop. Today, hoops are available in a variety of colors and in different sizes and styles (Figure 6.4). According to Hammett (1992), the 24-inch flat hoop is the most versatile, offering the best possibilities for manipulation and other activities. Flat hoops also tend to be sturdy and outlast the less-expensive tubular ones.

Sample Activities

One-Ball Activity. An introductory-level activity requiring one ball per child is to simply ask children to move the ball all around the body, using both hands, the preferred hand alone, and then the nonpreferred hand. How many ways can they accomplish this task? Challenge them to try it with balls of different sizes and textures.

Partner Activity. Curtis (1982) suggested a partner activity in which pairs of children attempt to move while holding a ball between them without using hands. The ball can be balanced between the children's backs, tummies, hips, foreheads, or shoulders. Can they sit down and stand up without losing the ball?

Passing Overhead. Passing a ball overhead is appropriate for small groups of children. In this activity, children stand in a single-file line. The first child passes a ball overhead to the next child without looking back, and so on down the line. The last child then comes to the front. This is repeated until all the children have had a chance to be first. To make this activity more challenging, have the children pass the ball by alternating passing it overhead and then through their legs (Pica, 2000).

Activity Suggestions. For activity suggestions exploring specific ball-handling skills, refer to "Manipulative Skills" in Chapter 4.

FIGURE **6.4** Hoops held upright can be crawled through or used as targets.

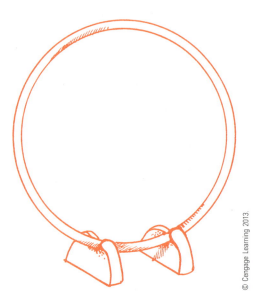

© Cengage Learning 2013.

Sample Activities

Possibilities abound for using hoops. They can be spun, rolled, swung, jumped (like a rope), twirled around the body or various body parts, tossed and caught, and crawled through (when held upright by a person or by hoop holders). They can also be used as targets. When lying flat or held around the waist, they offer an example of personal space.

The Concept of Around. To explore the concept of around, provide each child with a hoop. Challenge children to discover how many body parts the hoop can be twirled around (clockwise and counterclockwise). Direct them to try twirling it around the waist, the neck, an arm, a wrist, a leg, or an ankle. Can they do it both quickly and slowly? While remaining in place and while moving through general space? With the body at different levels?

Exploring In and Out. To explore in and out, ask children to place their hoops flat on the floor and find how many ways they can move into and out of them. (Possibilities include stepping, jumping, leaping, and hopping.) Ask them to walk around the hoop with one foot in and one foot out, trying it in both directions. What other locomotor skills can they perform this way? Challenge them to discover how many other ways they can be inside and outside the hoop at the same time. Possibilities include having feet on the outside and hands on the inside, sitting or kneeling inside with hands and feet on the outside, lying on back or tummy inside the hoop with arms and/or legs extending over and outside the hoop, or balancing on different body parts inside the hoop with arms and/or one leg extended over and outside.

Musical Hoops. Hammett (1992) suggested a game of Musical Hoops as a fun alternative to Musical Chairs. In this game, hoops are scattered throughout the room, with one child inside each hoop. When the music starts, children walk around the room. When the music stops, they step inside

the closest hoop. Each time the music starts, a different locomotor skill is substituted. To make this a cooperative game, remove one or two hoops as the music plays. When the music stops, children have to share the remaining hoops. When there is only a single hoop left, children must decide how to share it. (One possibility is for each child to place one foot inside the hoop.)

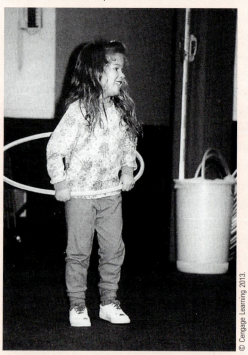

© Cengage Learning 2013.

To explore the concept of around, challenge children to discover how many body parts the hoop can be twirled around.

FIGURE **6.5** Beanbags are more fun and educational today than ever before!

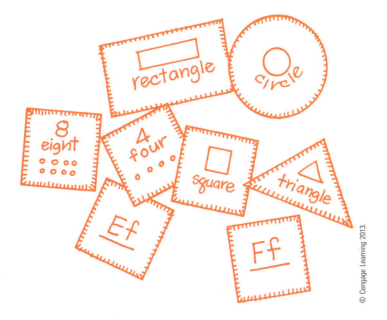

© Cengage Learning 2013.

Beanbags

Beanbags are more fun today than ever before and offer a great variety of learning experiences (Figure 6.5). They come in different geometric shapes, in numerous colors (with the name of the color sometimes printed on the bag), and with letters (upper- and lowercase) and numbers (numeral and written word) printed on them—in English, Spanish, and French. There are even beanbags with sign language.

Streamers

Streamers, sometimes called ribbons (or ribbon sticks, if they are attached to sticks), can be made from lightweight cloth, satin ribbon, plastic surveyor's tape, plastic

Sample Activities

Children enjoy (and have much success) throwing and catching beanbags, which are lightweight, flexible, and colorful. When used with target boards, boxes, hoops, or tires, beanbags provide practice with throwing for accuracy. Beanbags can also be manipulated with the feet, offering some introductory experience with dribbling. These activities are invaluable for developing eye–hand and eye–foot coordination.

Exploring Positions. To explore concepts like up and down, near and far, high and low, and front and back, ask children to move a beanbag around the body at all possible levels. How far away from the body can they get the beanbag? How near to the body without touching it? Ask them to explore all the possibilities while standing, kneeling, sitting, and lying.

Balancing Beanbags. Perhaps the most popular beanbag activity is balancing a beanbag on various body parts. From the simplest challenge (balancing the bag on the palm of the hand) to the more difficult (balancing it on an elbow, a knee, or the nose), children love to test their skills this way. At first, challenge them to see on how many parts they can balance the beanbag while remaining in their personal space. How many ways can they find to move the body part balancing the beanbag? Later, you can suggest that they try balancing the beanbag on different body parts while executing various locomotor skills.

Beanbags and Music. To combine beanbag activities with music, choose "Me and My Bean Bag," "Bean Bag Activities," or "Bean Bag Fun" (available from Kimbo Educational Records).

FIGURE **6.6** Streamers and ribbon sticks can be homemade or purchased from catalogs.

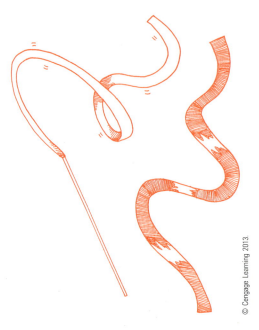

© Cengage Learning 2013.

ribbon, crepe paper, or even strips of newspaper (Figure 6.6). Commercial ribbon sticks can be purchased from early-childhood and physical education supply catalogs.

Because streamers extend beyond the body and can cause injury if they catch someone across the face or in the eye, children will need a lot of room to move. Keep in mind that injuries can occur even with shorter ribbons made especially for young children.

Scarves

You can purchase inexpensive chiffon scarves (8 to 16 inches square) in department stores or through early-childhood or physical education supply catalogs. (In catalogs, these scarves are sometimes listed as juggling scarves.) Or you can purchase sheer fabric in a variety of colors by the yard. This fabric can be

Sample Activities

Pathways Around the Body. Streamers are ideal for exploring the concepts of over, under, around, in front of, and behind—the pathways around the body. With very young children, you may have to make specific suggestions for moving the streamer (e.g., in small and large circles, or swinging). When children are developmentally ready, simply ask them to discover how many ways they can find to move the streamer over, under, around, in front of, and behind various body parts.

Pathways Through the Air. Pathways through the air, like the arcing pathway made by a home run ball on its way out of the park, are more abstract than those made by the feet on the ground. Streamers can help make these aboveground pathways "visible." Children enjoy pretending the air is a

giant chalkboard and their streamers pieces of chalk. Ask them to "write" various letters in the air or draw favorite shapes. Then introduce them to typical streamer patterns—circles, spirals (small circles), swings, figure eights, and zig-zags (snake-like movements).

Ball, Hoop, and Ribbon Activities. If you wish to explore moving to music with balls, hoops, or ribbons, you may want to check out *Ball, Hoop and Ribbon Activities for Young Children* by Carol Hammett and Elaine Bueffel (from Kimbo). Or you could simply play pieces of music in different styles, asking children to move their props in whatever way the music makes them feel. Hap Palmer's "Movin'" is a good choice.

Scarves are easier to manipulate and therefore more appropriate than streamers for toddlers.

© Cengage Learning 2013.

ripped and does not require sewing seams. Because you can get many scarves from a single yard, purchasing the sheer fabric is a relatively inexpensive option. If you need a truly inexpensive alternative, paper towels will suffice.

Although scarves can serve many of the same purposes as streamers, some children find scarves easier to manipulate because they are smaller and do not extend as far from the body.

Rhythm Sticks

Rhythm sticks, also known as lummi sticks, are common and popular items in early-childhood and elementary settings. They can be homemade or purchased from catalogs. Either way, they should be lightweight, no longer than 18 inches (although a maximum of 12 inches is best for young children), and one-half to one inch in diameter. If homemade, an alternative to wooden doweling is PVC pipe, available at hardware and plumbing supply stores.

Because they are short and manageable, rhythm sticks are excellent for familiarizing young children with the feel of a held object. This will prepare them for manipulating short- and long-handled implements, such as rackets, paddles, and hockey sticks.

Sample Activities

If the scarves are large enough, children can explore the same aerial pathways and designs suggested for streamers.

Tossing and Catching. Scarves are also excellent for developing tossing and catching skills. They float slowly enough to give children ample time to adjust. If you use brightly colored scarves, they are also easy to focus on. In addition, for children who are developmentally ready, scarves are fun and practical for juggling.

Arm and Leg Movements. Tying large scarves around children's wrists and ankles can motivate them to see what effect various arm and leg movements have on the scarves. Play music of different tempos and moods so children can alter their movements each time you repeat this activity.

Peekaboo. With infants, add scarves to games of peekaboo. You can also use scarves to increase awareness of object permanence by hiding and then revealing small toys placed under the scarves.

Whether purchased from catalogs or homemade, rhythm sticks should be lightweight and no longer than 12 inches (for young children) to 18 inches.

Sample Activities

Stick Sounds. For a beginning stick activity, give children time to experiment with striking two rhythm sticks together and determine the different sounds that they can create. Suggest that they try both loud and soft sounds and that they use different parts of the sticks.

Rhythm Stick Positions. Suggest that children try some of these movements (see Figure 6.7), which are commonly associated with rhythm sticks:

- drumming: use the floor as a drum and the rhythm sticks as drumsticks
- rapping: both sticks are held vertically, one above the other, and the two ends are struck together; this is more challenging because the ends are so small
- hammering: one stick is held vertically, like a nail, and the other stick is used as a hammer
- scraping: also known as "Peel the Carrot," because one stick is held horizontally, like a carrot to be peeled, as the other is moved along it like a vegetable scraper

Quiet Moves. Movements that make little or no sound include rolling the sticks around one another, shaking them, flipping and catching one or both, and lightly tapping various body parts with them (e.g., heads, shoulders, knees, and toes).

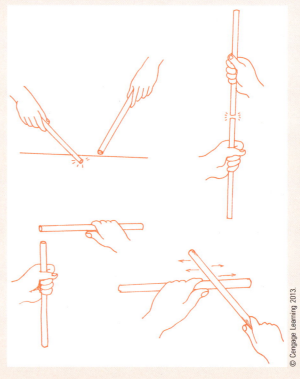

FIGURE **6.7** Drumming, rapping, hammering, and scraping.

Tapping to a Beat. The most common use for rhythm sticks, of course, is tapping them together in time with a musical beat. Musical selections for this activity should have a strong, even beat. Marches, with their even 1–2 rhythm, are most appropriate. You will want to begin with children using the rhythm sticks while sitting, gradually advancing toward the more developed skill of simultaneously marching and playing the sticks. Weikart (2007) referred to this complex combination of locomotor action—what the feet are doing— and nonlocomotor action—what the hands are doing—as integrated movement.

Rhythm Sticks and Music. Kimbo Educational offers several albums for rhythm stick activities: *Multicultural Rhythm Stick Fun, Lively Music for Rhythm Stick Fun,* and the popular *Simplified Rhythm Stick Activities.*

Parachutes

Whereas the previously mentioned props are primarily intended for individual use, parachutes are designed to be used by groups of children. Thus, they are excellent for promoting cooperation.

Before beginning parachute activities, you should introduce the children to the three ways to grip the chute: (1) palms down, (2) palms up, and (3) one

Making a giant wave with a parachute.

Children enjoy the challenge of bouncing balloons on the parachute and trying to keep them inside the circle.

Sample Activities

The two main possibilities for exploration with a parachute are moving it up and down and rotating it.

Passing the Parachute. To rotate the chute while remaining in place, children simply pass it to the right or left. This excellent introductory activity familiarizes children with gripping the parachute.

Making Waves. Challenge the group to create waves by using large arm movements to raise and lower the chute. They can experiment with this while sitting, kneeling, and standing. Ask, "Does a change in level have any effect on the waves?" Experiment with unison movement (all the children raising and lowering their arms at the same time) and with alternating movement (one child raises her arms as the next lowers his, and so on around the circle).

Making Ripples. Challenge the group to make small ripples by moving their arms up and down in opposition (one hand going up and the other coming down).

Keep It Bouncing! Once children are adept at making waves and ripples, place a lightweight ball or other object in the center of the chute. Challenge children to keep the ball bouncing.

The Igloo. Another in-place movement children enjoy is creating an "igloo." They start by holding the parachute close to the floor. They raise it, reaching as high into the air as possible, and then pull it quickly back down, trapping air under the chute. Once the children have the knack of this, they can lie down as the parachute is lowered, hands on the inside and bodies on the outside. Older children can hold the parachute with crossed hands, turning to face the outside as the parachute is lowered. This places them inside the igloo when the chute is brought to the floor.

Circling with the Chute. Challenge children to hold the parachute at waist height and discover how many locomotor movements they can use to move the parachute in a circle. Can they find a way to rotate the parachute while facing it (i.e., sliding)? Be sure children practice moving in both directions.

Kimbo offers several recordings to stimulate parachute play, including *Playtime Parachute Fun for Early Childhood*, by Jill Gallina.

palm up and the other down. With all three grips, the thumb should be held in opposition to the fingers. Unless a certain grip is required for a particular activity, children should simply use the most comfortable grip.

Parachutes can be purchased from catalogs or government supply stores or be made from sheets (brightly dyed if possible).

ABOUT SELECTING EQUIPMENT: PRACTICAL CONSIDERATIONS BY KEITH GOLD, PRODUCT MANAGER, FLAGHOUSE, INC.

Being an early childhood professional carries the great responsibility of caring for the "future of our society." Part of that responsibility involves keeping the children safe.

When selecting equipment for the children's use, all items must first pass the "difficult to swallow" test. Additionally, any item a child could mouth or lick should be tested for toxicity and proven safe if accidentally ingested. All materials, including the inks and dyes, should be nontoxic. A typical problem area is the ink used on products like foam dice and beanbags.

Another area of concern with beanbags is what is inside them. Some manufacturers use peas or other bean products. This filler is not recommended as it can attract vermin into your classroom. You should look instead for beanbags filled with plastic pellets. Reinforced stitching will inhibit ripping. Also available are beanbags covered with gym-mat material, which is washable and generally antifungal and antibacterial. These may cost a bit more than fabric-covered bags, but are well worth the investment when considering their longer life and greater hygienic value.

This gym-mat material is also important when purchasing shapes, wedges, and tumbling or safety mats. Many of the early childhood suppliers sell lightweight vinyl shapes in cute designs, using yellow foam as filler. These are generally inexpensive pieces that have a one- to two-year life. At the opposite end are professional-quality mats constructed of nylon-backed vinyl, weighing at least 13 to 15 ounces, and with nylon stitching. They are antifungal, antibacterial, flameproof, and tear-proof. These items, while not necessarily cute and certainly more expensive than low-end shapes, are functional and have an 8- to 10-year life, thus costing your program much less in the long term.

Safety and practicality also come into play when purchasing other common items, like hoops, parachutes, and balance beams. Traditionally, hoops were bendable, hollow plastic, with the pieces stapled together. Today hoops come staple-free, with plastic inserts, or in one-piece molded forms that are virtually unbreakable. Parachutes can now be bought with handles all around the outside edges so small hands can grip them more easily. And regardless of the balance beam you choose—and the variety includes padded beams very close to the ground, variable-height beams, foam beams, wooden beams, and beams made of plastic links that bend and curve—a safety mat should be placed underneath it because a falling child can be injured from any height.

As a rule of thumb, common sense and some experience should tell you whether a product seems safe and of good value. Your biggest problem may be lack of knowledge as to what is available. With this in mind, when you are ready to purchase new items, do not hesitate to ask questions, including questions about the materials used to construct the products. And remember, no matter what equipment you use, no product is completely safe without proper supervision.

ASSIGNMENTS

1. Design a weekly schedule for a full-day and a half-day program, incorporating movement into it daily.
2. Write a sample letter addressed to parents, justifying the necessity of children moving in bare feet.
3. Write a statement regarding your philosophy concerning the use of (or the decision not to use) props.
4. Using early-childhood and/or physical education supply catalogs, prepare three five-year plans for purchasing equipment, based on annual allotments of $50, $100, and $200.

FIELD OBSERVATION

1. Observe movement sessions held with toddlers, preschoolers, and early-elementary children. Note the length of the sessions and your observations regarding the children's staying power. How long did the sessions last? Did the children lose or maintain interest?
2. While observing the previously mentioned sessions, also note the spaces in which they are held. Are any ideal? If any have drawbacks, how does the teacher compensate? Could you do anything differently to minimize the drawbacks?

REFERENCES

Bower, J. K., Hales, D. P., Tate, D. F., Rubin, D. A., Benjamin, S. E., & Ward, D. S. (2008). The childcare environment and children's physical activity. *American Journal of Preventive Medicine*, *34*(1), 23–29.

Curtis, S. R. (1982). *The joy of movement in early childhood.* New York: Teachers College.

Essa, E. (2010). *Introduction to early childhood education.* Belmont, CA: Cengage Learning.

Fowler, J. S. (1981). *Movement education.* Philadelphia: Saunders College.

Gilliom, B. C. (1970). *Basic movement education for children: Rationale and teaching units.* Reading, MA: Addison-Wesley.

Hammett, C. T. (1992). *Movement activities for early childhood.* Champaign, IL: Human Kinetics.

Pica, R. (2000). *Moving & learning series: Preschoolers & kindergartners.* Belmont, CA: Cengage Learning.

Sanders, S. W. (1992). *Designing preschool movement programs.* Champaign, IL: Human Kinetics.

Sinclair, C. B. (1973). *Movement of the young child.* Columbus, OH: Merrill.

Stinson, S. (1988). *Dance for young children: Finding the magic in movement.* Reston, VA: AAHPERD.

Sullivan, M. (1982). *Feeling strong, feeling free: Movement exploration for young children.* Washington, DC: National Association for the Education of Young Children.

Weikart, P. S. (2007). *Round the circle.* Ypsilanti, MI: High/Scope.

RELEVANT WEBSITES

For equipment:

Flying Start:
www.flaghouse.com/Flying-Start

Play with a Purpose:
www.pwaponline.com

Sportime:
www.sportime.com

(For more websites, refer to Appendix 2.)

For rhythm stick activities:

Kimbo Educational:
www.kimboed.com

Educational Activities:
www.edact.com/files/lyrics/cd55.pdf

KEY TERMS & DEFINITIONS

group time Period set aside for large-group activity that can be used as movement sessions.

group size The ratio of adults to children. Experts suggest one adult for every five 3- to 4-year-olds and one adult for every 10 to 15 older children.

unrestrictive clothing Attire that allows for freedom of movement and lessens the possibility of injury.

© Cengage Learning 2013.

Choosing and Using Music

Learning Objectives

After completing this chapter, the student will be able to:

1 Determine how to choose music to enhance children's movement and music education.

2 Cite and describe different aspects of musical variety.

3 Use the five aspects of musical experiences to enhance children's music and movement education.

4 Create activities using a variety of musical elements appropriate to early childhood.

TERMS TO KNOW

styles of music

texture

tempo

accelerando

ritardando

volume

crescendo

decrescendo/diminuendo

staccato

legato

pitch

phrase

form

rhythm

141

Although it is important for children to experience movement without music (so they can get a sense of their own personal rhythms), it is not surprising that accompanying movement activities with music is often the more popular way of exploring movement. Music, after all, is enjoyable and provides an additional source of inspiration. It can be energizing or relaxing. It can make abstract concepts like slow and fast, light and strong, or free and bound more concrete. It can help a child hear and feel the difference between the rhythm of a skip and that of a step-hop or between sustained and suspended movement. Music is also a source of new ideas for activities. Finally, movement is an important instructional tool in the music education of children (Andress, 1991).

Choosing Music

Teachers and caregivers often say they have a difficult time finding music for movement—they do not know where to look or what to look for. But "movement" music is all around us, if only we remain open to the possibilities.

Standard 4b

Two critical factors should be recognized when making musical selections. The first is the quality of the music you provide. Quality listening experiences have been linked to the ability of children to concentrate and to their later language development (Jarnow, 1991). Therefore, the recordings you choose to accompany movement activities must be clear and uncluttered. If you expect students to move to the music's rhythm, that rhythm must be easily heard. If instrumentation is the focus of the listening/movement activity, then the instrumentation must be distinctive. If you are asking children to respond to the lyrics of a song, the words must be audible.

Throughout their lives, children will have far too many opportunities for less-than-perfect exposure to music. They will hear it played in the background in doctors' offices, elevators, and supermarkets. They will hear it played indiscriminately at home, at school, and in the car. And they will learn to tune it out.

Haines and Gerber (1999) contended that the child "must be exposed to good musical sound, for anything less will inhibit or damage her awakening sensitivity." When selecting music for movement activities (or for any other purpose in your classroom), you should remember that there is a major difference between hearing and listening. Listening involves perception; hearing does not. If you want students to really listen to the music as they move, it must be music that invites them to listen.

Second, variety is also critical—from both the student's and the teacher's point of view. Variety not only helps maintain interest but also familiarizes students with musical elements and movements they might not otherwise experience. Following are several aspects of musical variety—styles, periods, nationalities, and textures—to consider when selecting music.

Styles

Style is difficult to define. Styles of music technically differ from one another in how they treat form, melody, harmony, sound, and rhythm. For the most part, however, people can simply judge one style from another. We know, for instance, that rock and roll certainly differs from opera, but most of us would have trouble saying why. Other examples of musical styles include jazz, folk, country, bluegrass, blues, rhythm and blues, disco, gospel, new age, swing, and

Dixieland. Some of today's styles include hip-hop, techno, and rap. Chances are, your students are exposed primarily to the music they hear on radio and television, which can offer only limited movement possibilities and does little to broaden music education.

Periods

It would take an extensive course in music history to cover all that past ages have produced. The periods of classical music alone offer an almost unlimited number of possibilities for use with children.

From the Renaissance, for example, came pieces such as "Greensleeves," which is played during Christmastime under the title "What Child Is This?" Bach's many works were products of the Baroque era, as was Pachelbel's lovely Canon in D Major. From the Classical period are Haydn's "Surprise Symphony" (Symphony No. 94 in G Major) and Mozart's "Eine Kleine Nacht Musik" ("A Little Night Music"). The Romantic period gave us Prokofiev's *Peter and the Wolf,* the waltzes, and Tchaikovsky's *Swan Lake, Nutcracker Suite,* and the forceful and expressive "1812 Overture."

All of these selections easily lend themselves to movement, as do those belonging to the decades of American music. The 1920s, for example, were the years for the Black Bottom, the Charleston, and other flappers' dances. The 1930s ushered in an era of Latin rhythms. The 1940s produced the big bands and their particular brand of swing. Elvis Presley was a product of the 1950s, which introduced rock and roll. During the 1960s, young people were performing such solo dances as the Swim, the Pony, and the Mashed Potato to the accompaniment of Top 40 hits. With disco in the 1970s, partner dancing returned and opened the way for a revival of ballroom dancing in the next decade. The 1980s saw an eclectic variety of musical styles, including everything from punk rock to new age, as well as a fusion of styles from various parts of the world. In the 1990s, country music and line dancing were especially popular, with swing making a comeback at the end of the decade. At the beginning of the 21st century, hip-hop has replaced country as the most popular music in America. Few of us can imagine what the upcoming decades might bring.

ABOUT THE MUSIC AND MOVEMENT CENTER

Standard 4b

Learning centers offer children opportunities to further explore their interests, both individually and in small groups (Figure 7.1). When you provide a music and movement center in your classroom, children can listen to music, play instruments, and experiment with sound or movement at their own developmental levels and without adult supervision. To achieve maximum success with your center, keep the following points in mind.

Location is critical. Choose an area where children making noise will not disturb those involved in quieter activities. Church (1998) suggested a spot near the dramatic-play space or next to the circle time area. Teachers can designate certain times of the day when the music/movement center is open or closed. The area should be large enough so children can actually move.

Make your center inviting. If you have space, a table and chairs and additional comfortable seating (beanbag or beach chairs, throw pillows, and/or scatter rugs) let children know that they are welcome to take their time in the center. Movement and music pictures hung on the walls will inspire children and identify this as a special place.

Make your center accessible to young children. Tape or CD players should be easy for children to reach and operate. Remove the tabs from the tops of cassettes so that it will be impossible to record over them. Materials should be stored in easy-to-open containers and on easily reached shelves. Instruments should be readily available.

© Cengage Learning 2013.

FIGURE **7.1** An example of the "ideal" music and movement center.

Periodically change the materials (e.g., recordings, props, instruments, and other sound-making devices) for maximum interest and experimentation.

Though space and funding often keep us from achieving the ultimate, imagining it can help. The following wish list includes items found in the ultimate music and movement center:

- A CD player designed for children, with a wide variety of CDs—some with recordings of the children's own voices, others labeled with pictures that represent the songs
- A listening center for the CD player, with several headphones and a jack box so several children can listen at once (this material is listed as "Music or Audiovisual Equipment" in early-childhood supply catalogs, such as those from Kaplan, Lakeshore, and J. L. Hammett; see Appendix 2)
- Percussion instruments—maracas, tambourines, castanets, finger cymbals, and rhythm sticks
- Melodic instruments—bells, small keyboards, tone bars, xylophones, and a piano (to really achieve the ultimate)
- Miscellaneous, constantly changing sound sources: coffee cans, paper bags, or oatmeal containers filled with beads or sand; coffee-can or oatmeal-box drums (i.e., with lids); different-sized stainless steel mixing bowls; blocks of wood; kitchen tools; and a variety of rocks
- A prop box, possibly including scarves, streamers, elastic bracelets or anklets with bells sewn on them, and rag dolls or stuffed animals to serve as dance partners
- Acrylic mirrors so children can observe and vary their movements
- An ever-changing selection of books to read or look at while listening
- A small selection of art materials to encourage children to combine drawing with music and to offer a rich creative experience (Church, 1998)

Of course, if your music and movement center is going to be welcoming, accessible, efficient, and successful, it has to be maintained. Everything in the center should have a special place, and children should learn to return each item to its appropriate spot. Andress (1973) suggested plastic bleach bottles with cutout sections, ice cream cartons, shoe boxes, silverware trays, and coffee cans with plastic lids for storage containers. Cup hooks under a shelf are appropriate for hanging small items like castanets and triangles; many other instruments can be hung on a pegboard. Most important, children must be taught to handle every item in the music and movement center with care and respect.

Nationalities

The world is peopled with hundreds of nationalities, each of which has its own musical heritage: Polish and Mexican polkas, German and Austrian waltzes, Italian tarantellas, Irish jigs, Scottish Highland flings, and English folk songs. African chant and drum music, calypso, reggae, the hora, Latin rhythms, Greek dances, Native American songs, Spanish flamencos, and many, many others are further examples. All inspire different movements and contribute to children's multicultural education.

Textures

Although it may surprise many Top 40 devotees, songs do not always consist of vocals backed by guitar, bass, and drum. In addition, every instrumental number does not have to be orchestral. Exposure to varying texture means students will become accustomed to hearing and moving to sounds produced by different instruments. For example, a piece consisting only of percussion instruments (an African number, perhaps) may produce percussive and staccato movement (punctuated, like bound flow). In contrast, a violin sonata by Johannes Brahms would generally tend to result in balletic or legato (smooth, like free flow) motion. Other musical textures are created by solo piano, full orchestra, brass, woodwinds, voice alone (a cappella), electronic instruments, acoustic guitar, or harp, to name a few.

Although children may not enjoy everything you play for them, your enthusiasm, coupled with continued exposure, can make a difference in how they perceive music (see "More About the Magic of Exposure"). Even if they never learn to fully appreciate all the music they hear, they will at least make future choices based on knowledge rather than on ignorance.

Of course, most of us do not have music collections encompassing everything suggested here, nor do we have the funds to buy everything we need. But most of us do have local libraries with librarians whose expertise we can rely on. You can also call on music teachers and/or invite parents to bring in music important to their families. Take advantage of these resources, keeping variety and quality in mind.

Using Music

There are certainly more ways to incorporate music into the curriculum than can be covered within the scope of this book. For our purposes, we will consider how music, together with movement, can provide the well-rounded introduction to music discussed in Chapter 2. We will look specifically at the musical experiences children should have and the musical elements children should encounter. All these elements can be explored through movement.

Two points must be made in regard to music and the teacher of young children. First, you need not be an expert in the field of music—or have an experienced singing voice—to offer children valuable musical experiences. Children are not critics, and they will not be judging you on the quality of your singing, instrument playing, or musical creations. Second, you must possess only two qualifications to make music part of your program: a desire to do so and a willingness to participate. Remember, children learn much from your example.

naeyc
Standard 4c

It is not necessary to be an expert in the field of music—or have an experienced singing voice—to offer children valuable musical experiences.

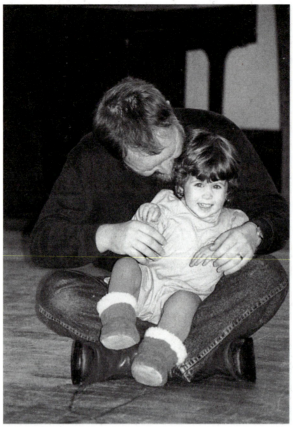

© Cengage Learning 2013.

You must also understand the value of repetition. There will be lots of it, whether you plan it or not, and understanding its importance to children will make it easier to accept! Jarnow (1991) wrote,

> A song or album may sound the same to you every time you hear it, but to [a] child, each listening period is another opportunity to gain mastery of it. By hearing the same music over and over again, she absorbs combinations of tones, rhythms, words, phrases, concepts, and emotions … [It] takes on an importance akin to that of an old friend who offers reassurance and comfort at each meeting. (p. 25)

Sometimes children do not like a song the first time they hear it. Only after repeated exposure does it become familiar and "safe" to them, rendering it

MORE ABOUT THE MAGIC OF EXPOSURE

Your children are not going to enjoy all the music you play for them. Like adults, they have musical preferences. In fact, some evidence indicates that the musical preferences of young children are fairly set and not easily changed (Achilles, 1992). But exposure is a powerful factor in bringing about change, especially if the exposure is coupled with enjoyment.

Several years ago, a teacher at one of my workshops shared a story about her husband. His profession was installing siding on homes. For a while, he was working on a home owned by people who loved polkas. Day in and day out, the sound of polkas floated through the windows, exposing him to a style of music he had never paid much attention to. At the end of one day, he went home to his wife and announced, "You know? I like polkas!"

Exposure can make a difference. So expose your students to a wide variety of music. Show them how much you enjoy it all, and you will open whole new worlds for them.

suitable for their approval. Other children—toddlers especially—may not sing a song until they have had many chances to just listen. Finally, there will be times when you instigate the repetition—for example, when a single tune provides examples of two or more musical elements. With each repetition, you can focus children's attention on yet another aspect of the composition, changing not only the way they listen but also the way they respond in movement.

Musical Experiences

Five aspects of musical experiences should be part of every child's life: moving, listening, singing, playing, and creating (Edwards et al., 2008; Haines & Gerber, 1999). Of course, there is considerable overlap and interrelatedness among the five aspects. Listening is a part of all musical experiences, but movement can be, too. In Chapter 2, we examined the role of movement in a child's general music education. Now, we will look briefly at the role of the other four aspects of musical experiences and how movement can enhance each of them.

Standard 4b

Listening. As mentioned earlier, there is a difference between listening and hearing. The latter requires no concentration; the former does. To really listen, one must pay attention and focus the mind on what is being heard. According to Haines and Gerber (1999), the ability to pay attention is a learned skill, and "active listening" is required if children are to make sense of their environment and communicate with it.

The examples in Chapter 2 of children tiptoeing to soft music and stamping feet to loud music, swaying to a 3/4 meter and skipping to a piece in 6/8 require active—or focused—listening. Children must be able to perceive the different dynamics between soft and loud music and must feel the difference in rhythm between the 3/4 and the 6/8 meter. Having heard and perceived, their bodies respond accordingly.

Standard 1a

Singing. The stages of vocal expression, beginning in infancy, move from cooing and babbling to chanting to singing (although a child's early attempts are rarely on pitch). Because most children love to sing and often break into

Children need focused listening experiences.

© Cengage Learning 2013.

spontaneous song, music becomes part of every program that involves children, even when it is not consciously planned.

Adding hand motions and other actions to songs can contribute to singing activities, enhance listening, and add greater meaning to lyrics. Some children are reluctant to sing but are willing to perform such actions and are thus involved in the activity. You should not be concerned, however, if children are unable to sing and move at the same time. Learning to do both simultaneously is a normal developmental process; teaching the words before adding the actions can encourage this process (Edwards et al., 2008).

naeyc
Standard 1a

Playing. Playing instruments and exploring environmental sound should occur early and often in a child's life. Both contribute to the child's overall music education and provide an awareness of sound that can enrich daily living.

Like singing and moving simultaneously, playing and moving at the same time is more challenging than doing either alone. However, when children reach the stage where they are able to do both, one activity will enhance the other—for example, marching while playing a rhythm instrument contributes to children's enjoyment and sense of rhythm.

Creating. Although others limit this category strictly to the creation of music, Haines and Gerber (1999) take a broader view of the creative process in relation to music as a whole:

> We believe that every child has the capacity to take the ingredients of music and to make from them a recipe, however simple, that is peculiarly his own, that delights and satisfies him, and that can often be shared with others. To create, the child needs a basic vocabulary of musical experiences and skills … As these are acquired, … so the creative acts of music making will appear.

The authors go on to describe creating through active listening, moving, singing, and playing, lending further evidence to the interrelatedness not only among the five aspects of musical experiences but also between the benefits of movement and music education.

Moving and playing an instrument at the same time is more challenging than doing either alone, but children will eventually be able to do both simultaneously.

© Cengage Learning 2013.

Adding hand motions and other actions to songs contributes much to singing activities.

© Cengage Learning 2013.

Musical Elements

Some musical concepts are too advanced for young children to grasp. Others are important only to those who go on to study music seriously. But there are many musical elements young children can and should experience, including tempo, volume, legato and staccato, pitch, phrases, form, mood, and rhythm. These can all be explored through movement, offering children a multisensory approach that gives the concepts greater meaning and makes a longer-lasting impression.

Tempo. Tempo is the speed at which music is performed, which means this musical element is related to the movement element of time. The best way to introduce tempo is by contrasting the extremes—very slow and very fast. Once children can recognize and move to fast and slow music, you can begin introducing the more challenging concept of the continuum from very slow to very fast and the reverse. Accelerando is the term for music that begins slowly and then gradually increases in tempo. Ritardando indicates a gradually decreasing tempo. The following are examples of pieces demonstrating various tempos.

Slow. Possibilities include Pachelbel's *Canon*, the first movement of Beethoven's "Moonlight" Sonata, the second movement of Antonín Dvořák's "New World Symphony" ("Largo"), and Chopin's nocturnes. In addition, many new age recordings consist primarily of slow pieces, as do several of George Winston's solo piano albums (including *Autumn, Winter into Spring, December,* and *Summer*). Another choice is "Slow-Motion Moving," found in Pica's *Moving & Learning Series*.

Fast. As you know, there is no shortage of fast music. However, if you want to use something other than pop selections, classical pieces include Rimsky-Korsakov's "Flight of the Bumblebee," Mozart's *The Marriage of Figaro,* and Rossini's *William Tell Overture*. In addition, Hap Palmer's *The Feel of Music* includes a song called "Quickly and Quietly."

Slow and Fast. Several children's recordings offer songs contrasting these two tempos.

- "Song About Slow, Song About Fast" from Hap Palmer's *Walter the Waltzing Worm*

- "Fast and Slow March" from Hap Palmer's Creative Movement and Rhythmic Exploration
- "Slow and Fast" from Hap Palmer's *The Feel of Music* (an album that specifically relates the characteristics of music to movement)
- "The Slow Fast, Soft Loud Clap Song" from *Songs about Me* from Kimbo Records
- "Moving Slow/Moving Fast" from Rae Pica's *Moving & Learning Series: Toddlers, Moving & Learning Series: Preschoolers & Kindergartners,* and *Moving & Learning Series: Early Elementary Children*
- "Marching Slow/Marching Fast," also from the *Moving & Learning Series*

Accelerando. Strauss's "Acceleration Waltz" is an excellent example of the concept of accelerando. Other excellent examples include "Beep Beep" (often referred to as "Little Nash Rambler"), a song made popular by The Playmates in the 1950s, and "Getting Fast/Getting Slow" from the *Moving & Learning Series*. Brahms's "Hungarian Dances" also uses accelerando, ritardando, and abrupt changes in tempo.

Volume. Part of the broader category of dynamics, which also involves the accenting of certain tones, volume refers specifically to the loudness or softness of sounds. According to Haines and Gerber (1999), many people incorrectly associate big or high movements with loud music and small, low movements with soft music. However, because volume is better equated with movement's "relative strength or weakness, its firmness or gentleness," this musical element truly goes hand in hand with the movement element of force. When music is soft, moving with a great deal of muscle tension would be an unlikely response. On the other hand, when music is loud, it is not likely to conjure up, for example, images of butterflies floating.

Again, the best way to introduce volume is by contrasting extremes. Once children can move well to loud and soft music, you can begin introducing the continuum from one to the other. Crescendo is the term for music that begins softly and gradually gets louder. Decrescendo (sometimes called diminuendo) refers to a gradually decreasing volume.

Soft. The previous suggestions for slow music are also appropriate for soft music. "Soft Sounds" can be found on *Adventures in Sound*, available from Melody House (Appendix 2). Lullabies are also excellent examples of soft music. Many recordings available to early-childhood professionals are made specifically for "quiet times."

- Hap Palmer's *Quiet Places* and *Sea Gulls*
- Joanie Bartels's *Lullaby Magic I* and *Lullaby Magic II*
- Derrie Frost's *Quiet Time* and *Daydreams*
- *Quiet Moments with Greg and Steve*
- *Lullaby Time for Little People, Let's Visit Lullaby Land,* and *Daydreams,* all available from Kimbo Records

In addition to these, an entire page of offerings from well- and lesser-known artists is available in the Educational Record Center catalog.

Loud. Again, loud music can easily be found. One piece that children especially enjoy is Tchaikovsky's "1812 Overture." Another option is from the album *Adventures in Sound*, which includes the song "Loud Sounds."

Loud and Soft. Children's songs that offer contrast between these two dynamics include "Soft and Loud," from Hap Palmer's *The Feel of Music;* "Play Soft, Play Loud," from Jill Gallina's *Rockin' Rhythm Band;* "Moving Softly/Moving Loudly," from the *Moving & Learning Series;* and "The Slow Fast, Soft Loud Clap Song," from *Songs About Me,* available from Kimbo.

Crescendo and Decrescendo. Ravel's *Bolero* is a classic example of crescendo. From Edvard Grieg's *Lyric Suite* is "Norwegian Rustic March," which includes both crescendos and decrescendos, as does "Getting Louder/Getting Softer" from the *Moving & Learning Series*.

Staccato and Legato. Staccato and legato relate to the movement element of flow and are part of the broader category of articulation, which also includes correct breathing, phrasing, and attack. Legato, which corresponds to free flow, indicates that music is to be played without any noticeable interruptions between the notes. In other words, the music flows smoothly. Staccato, on the other hand, is more punctuated and, therefore, corresponds with bound flow.

Any song you sing with children can be performed in either manner. You might try a piece like "Twinkle, Twinkle, Little Star" to get a feeling for these musical elements. First, sing the song in an easy, flowing manner, demonstrating legato. Then try it in a choppy style, adding brief pauses between syllables, to experience staccato.

Portions of Haydn's "Surprise" Symphony are staccato, while "Aquarium" from Camille Saint-Saens's *Carnival of the Animals* is an example of legato. Pica and Gardzina's "Robots and Astronauts" and "Staccato/Legato," from *Moving & Learning Series: Preschoolers & Kindergartners* and *Moving & Learning Series: Early Elementary Children* are examples of both elements in one song.

Pitch. Pitch is the highness or lowness of a musical tone. With this concept, the use of high and low movements is most appropriate. In Haines and Gerber (1999), Haines has written two songs, "High Is Where the Birds Go" and "Low Is Like a Tunnel," to demonstrate the contrast between high and low pitches. The song "High and Low," found on cassettes and CDs accompanying both *Moving & Learning Series: Preschoolers & Kindergartners* and *Moving & Learning Series: Early Elementary Children,* moves from low to high pitches and the reverse. It also asks children to begin in a crouch, raising and lowering their bodies with the rising or descending pitch.

Phrases. A phrase is a division of a composition, commonly a four- or eight-measure passage, that represents a musical thought or idea. A musical phrase is similar to a sentence.

Phrases are best introduced to children through listening experiences. By singing a familiar song and pausing between phrases, you can make them aware of this musical concept. Once they grasp it, you can ask them to accompany the song with movement, pausing where you pause. A later, more challenging request would be to have children change movements or direction at the beginning of each new phrase.

The use of high and low movements is most appropriate for exploring the concept of pitch. Children should first be challenged to raise and lower their arms in response to a rising or descending pitch.

© Cengage Learning 2013.

ABOUT MUSICAL INSTRUMENTS

Musical instruments typically are divided into three categories: string, wind, and percussion. Looking at the instruments that fall into each classification, you can see that the varying sounds produced will similarly result in varying movements. Children are unlikely to respond to sounds produced on a bongo in the same way that they would respond to sounds produced by a flute.

String instruments produce sound by means of vibrating strings. Among the most common instruments in this classification are guitar, violin, viola, cello, double bass, banjo, mandolin, ukulele, and harp.

Sound is created with a wind instrument when the player blows into or over a mouthpiece. This classification is grouped into two families: brass and woodwind. Belonging to the former are, among others, the trumpet, trombone, French horn, and tuba. The flute, oboe, clarinet, and saxophone are among those falling into the woodwind family.

An object that produces sound when hit with an implement, or is shaken, scraped, or rubbed, is considered a percussion instrument. This category includes such instruments as the cowbell, cymbals, lummi sticks, xylophone, triangle, rainstick, and, of course, drums.

A simple Google search shows there is no shortage of information on making musical instruments with and for children. For a book on the topic, try *Making Musical Instruments with Kids: 67 Easy Projects for Adults Working with Children* by Bart Hopkin (See Sharp Press, 2009).

For online instructions, the following are among the many options available:

- http://www.makingfriends.com/musical_instruments.htm
- http://familycrafts.about.com/od/toppicks/tp/makemusic.htm
- http://www.artistshelpingchildren.org/musicalinstrumentsartscraftstideashandmadekids.html
- http://familyfun.go.com/crafts/crafts-by-type/music-instruments/musical-instruments/

You can also find online video instructions at http://www.ehow.com/videos-on_5019_make-musical-instruments-kids.html.

A source for purchasing adaptive musical instruments for children with special needs is A Day's Work: http://www.adaysworkmusiceducation.com/.

"Row, Row, Row Your Boat" is an appropriate and fairly simple song to begin with, as the first two lines constitute one phrase and the second two lines another. Start by singing it at a slow to moderate tempo. Gradually increase the tempo as children begin to grasp the concept. When children are ready, play various recordings of the song, finding new ways to challenge them to match their movements to the phrasing. (Raffi sings this song on *Rise and Shine.*)

Form. Form is the overall design of the phrases that constitute a song's organization. It is often designated by letters (e.g., "Row, Row, Row Your Boat," "Pop Goes the Weasel," and "Ring Around the Rosie" are in an AB form; because of its repeating final phrase, "Twinkle, Twinkle, Little Star" is in an ABA form). Once young children have become familiar with musical phrases, they will eventually begin to notice repeated or contrasting phrases and to respond accordingly with movement. Repeated phrases call for repeated movements, while contrasting phrases call for contrasting movements (e.g., strong and light, small and large, or forward and backward).

Mood. Feelings are often conveyed by music, and very often young children are the first to pick up on the mood of a song and to respond to it. This ability seems to be due to the as-yet-undiminished sensitivity of the young child's ear and to his or her as-yet-undiminished willingness to show a physical response.

Children frequently react to happy music by skipping, dancing, running, twirling, bouncing up and down, or performing similar movements. Lively pieces like Bach's "Musette in D Major" from his *Anna Magdalena Notebook* or Bobby McFerrin's "Don't Worry, Be Happy" can evoke such actions. By contrast, Samuel Barber's 20th-century classical piece "Adagio for Strings," which has a sad feeling to it, usually quiets the children and slows their movements. Brahms's "Lullaby" is a perfect example of a song that conveys a particular mood; it makes its listeners want to sleep!

Your role as teacher is to make children aware of how different music affects them. Talk to them about how certain songs make them feel, the musical elements involved, and why they think the songs evoke the responses they do.

Rhythm. Rhythm, according to McDonald and Simons (1989), is the "organization of sounds, silences, and patterns into different groupings" (p. 290). Within the context of this book, rhythm will consist of the concepts of beat and meter.

The beat in music is the recurring rhythmic pulse that is heard (and felt) throughout a piece. Very young children are not developmentally ready to match their movements to a beat. Rather, when you first introduce this concept to children, you should synchronize instrumental accompaniment to their rhythm. Watch them walk, run, gallop, and execute other locomotor skills, and then, on a hand drum, beat out a rhythmic pattern that matches their movements. When they change their movements, change the beat. They will soon realize that they are responsible for creating rhythm. Eventually, they will be able to move "at one" with the beat of a musical accompaniment.

Meter indicates a basic group of beats. When a meter is stated, the top number refers to the number of beats in a measure; the bottom number indicates the kind of note that equals one beat. For example, 2/4 means there are two quarter notes per measure, with 6/8 indicating six eighth notes to the measure.

The four most frequently used meters in Western music—2/4, 3/4, 4/4, and 6/8—were defined in Chapter 2. The 4/4 meter is certainly the most common in Western music, particularly in Top 40 songs. You will find 2/4 used in polkas and many marches, with 3/4 most often found in waltzes but also in ragtime. Many folk songs and some marches are written in 6/8.

Because some interesting qualities can result from exposure to less common meters, it is worth the effort to track down pieces in 5/8, 7/8, 5/4, and others. Hap Palmer's "Five Beats to Each Measure," from *The Feel of Music*, as well as "A Not-So-Common Meter" (in 7/8), from *Moving & Learning Series: Preschoolers & Kindergartners*, are examples of less commonly used meters.

How can you manage to expose your students to all these musical elements? The answer is simple: When you choose varying styles, periods, nationalities, and textures to play, you will automatically be exposing children to different tempos, volumes, articulations, pitches, phrases, forms, moods, and rhythms. Think variety, and plan to provide your students with a well-rounded music (and movement) education. As pointed out at the beginning of this chapter, you do not have to worry if you have never had any music education yourself. As you can see, "There is a great deal that the 'ordinary,' nonmusical caregiver or teacher can do" (Wolf, 1992, p. 56).

Video

VIDEO: *ECE/Child Development: "Infants & Toddlers: Communication Development" (Child Care in Action)*

ABOUT THE COPYRIGHT LAW AND YOU

The reproduction of sound recordings is so simple—and is so often done—that teachers may not realize that by copying recordings (or parts of them), they are sometimes violating the copyright protection granted to the authors of original works of authorship. In most cases, it is illegal to duplicate sound recordings. There are exceptions, however, and some of them deal specifically with educators.

Section 107 of the Copyright Act covers "fair use." Although the courts have considered and ruled on the doctrine many times, there is still no real definition of fair use. However, four factors should be considered in determining whether a particular use is fair:

- the purpose and character of the use, including whether such use is of commercial nature or is for nonprofit educational purposes
- the nature of the copyrighted work
- the amount and substantiality of the portion used in relation to the copyrighted work as a whole
- the effect of the use on the potential market for or value of the copyrighted work

Although it may seem, based on the first point, that duplicating recordings can be justified if "for nonprofit educational purposes," it is actually the fourth point that teachers must seriously consider. In guidelines established regarding the educational uses of music, copying "for the purpose of substituting for the purchase of music" is specifically prohibited.

In other words, if you are recording musical selections from a previously purchased CD for teaching purposes, you are not violating the law. If, on the other hand, you are duplicating music to share it with a friend or colleague so he will not have to buy the CD, then that is "substituting for the purchase of music." (Artists like Hap Palmer and Ella Jenkins do not earn salaries for the time they spend creating music. Instead, they earn royalties based on the number of their recordings sold. So substituting for the purchase of music does have an effect on the potential market, as stated above.)

Does copying a musical selection or two from a library-owned recording constitute "fair use?" If you have tried and failed to locate a particular recording owned by a library or colleague, is there no possibility of purchase? These questions—and others like them—are questions only you can answer, based on your understanding of the copyright law and fair use.

For more information, visit http://www.copyright.gov. You can speak to an information specialist by calling 202-707-3000 from 8:30 a.m. to 5 p.m. Eastern Standard Time, Monday to Friday. Or you can call the Forms Hotline (202-707-9100) 24 hours a day to request circulars. Circular No. 1 has information pertaining to copyright basics, and Circular No. 21 is entitled "Reproduction of Copyrighted Works by Educators and Librarians."

Sample Activities

Chapter 2 provided suggestions for exploring rhythmic groupings and common meters. Statues was described as an activity that develops listening skills and helps children differentiate between sound and silence. Because the music stops and starts, Statues also provides children with experience in the movement element of flow. You can also use the activity to explore musical phrases by always pausing at the end of a phrase. Finally, you can explore the concept of mood by choosing a piece with a different feeling every time you play.

As a movement resource, this text cannot fully develop the subject of music in early childhood. To make music a larger part of your curriculum, refer to the many fine music resources listed throughout the book and in Appendix 2. The following activities, however, can offer you a starting place, provide you with examples of the benefits of using movement and music to enhance one another, and spark ideas of your own.

Contrasting Elements. To provide children with an understanding of the musical element of tempo and the movement element of time, choose one of the songs suggested that contrasts slow and fast music (or choose two separate pieces—one slow and one fast). Challenge children to move in the following ways to each tempo:

You can use a similar activity to enhance understanding of the musical element of volume and the movement element of force. Select a single song that contrasts volumes, or choose two separate pieces. Ask children to move in the following ways to each volume:

- Soft:
  Tiptoeing
  Patting the floor or body with hands
  Pretending to float
  Swaying gently
  Pretending to be a cat stalking prey

- Loud:
  Stamping feet
  Slapping the floor
  Marching
  Rocking forcefully
  Moving like a dinosaur

Exploring Continuums. To familiarize children with the concepts of accelerando and ritardando, tell them that they are going to play Follow the Leader, with you as leader. Then, accompanying yourself on a hand drum (one beat for every

Tapping out the beat with rhythm sticks.

© Cengage Learning 2013.

- Slow:
  Gentle swaying
  Walking as though through mud (or deep snow or peanut butter)
  Pretending to be a turtle or a snail
  Pretending to be on film that is being played in slow motion

- Fast:
  Running lightly (in place or around the room)
  Skipping
  Pretending to be a bumblebee
  Pretending to be a race car

step you take), begin to move very slowly. Gradually accelerate your tempo until you are going as fast as you want the children to go. Then begin to gradually slow down until you are back to the original speed. (Be sure to vary your movements by changing levels, directions, pathways, and, if possible, body shape.)

Once children are familiar and comfortable with this activity, try it to music that accelerates, retards, or does both. Eventually, choose children to act as leaders.

You can explore the concepts of crescendo and decrescendo with this same activity. To do so, your steps and

(Continued)

drumbeats will have to be very soft at first, gradually increasing (and then decreasing) in intensity.

Do-Re-Mi. Sing the scale to children, explaining how each successive note is higher in pitch than the previous one. (If possible, also demonstrate on a keyboard or show the scale written on a staff so children will see as well as hear the rising and descending pitches.)

Ask children to sing the scale with you. (Depending on your group, you may want to limit their initial experiences to a rising scale only and later explore it in both directions.) Then have them place their hands in their laps, raising their hands a little bit higher with each note you sing (and lowering them if you are singing the descending scale). Once children have grasped the concept, challenge them to demonstrate with their whole bodies, beginning close to the floor and getting as close to the ceiling as possible (and then the reverse).

You can vary this activity to explore other concepts. The simplest variation is to change the tempo at which you sing or play the scale. Or you can sing or play in staccato and legato styles. You can add the concepts of crescendo and decrescendo by beginning at either a soft or loud volume and gradually increasing or decreasing it. Eventually, if the children have become very familiar with the notes of the scale, you can sing them out of order, challenging children to demonstrate with their arms or whole bodies whether a note was higher or lower than the previous one.

Once children can successfully demonstrate pitch with their arms, challenge them to show you a rising or descending pitch with the whole body.

Body Sounds. Children love to make noise, and making noise with their bodies can be a great introduction to rhythm. Talk to the children about the sounds of a cough, sneeze, yawn, hiccup, giggle, and snore. Then ask them to show you how each sound makes their bodies move. You can ask them either to incorporate the sound into their movement or to perform silently. Challenge them to perform repetitions of each movement.

Next (or in another lesson), ask them to discover how many sounds they can create with different body parts (e.g., hands, feet, tongue, and teeth). Can they move about the room, accompanying themselves with any of these sounds?

Can they use different parts of the room—floor, walls, chalkboard—to create new sounds?

Identifying Household Sounds. Edwards et al. (2008) suggest making a recording of household sounds and then asking children to identify those sounds. To vary and extend this listening activity, ask children to show, rather than tell, you the source of the sound. In other words, they must depict, through movement, the item creating the sound.

Possibilities include keys rattling, a washing machine, an electric can opener, a blender, a broom sweeping, a clock ticking, toast popping out of the toaster, a vacuum cleaner, a door closing, a garbage disposal, a telephone ringing, and water running.

"If You're Happy." Teach children the first verse of "If You're Happy." Then ask them for suggestions of other movements to demonstrate happiness (e.g., tap your feet, wave hello, nod your head, etc.). Do they want to sing about other emotions (e.g., sad, tired, angry, hungry)? What motions and facial expressions go along with those emotions?

The lyrics of the first verse are provided here.

If you're happy and you know it
Clap your hands (clap, clap)
If you're happy and you know it
Clap your hands (clap, clap)
If you're happy and you know it
Then your face will surely show it
If you're happy and you know it
Clap your hands (clap, clap).

Introducing Instruments. Choose three or four instruments to introduce to children. Show each instrument, one at a time, demonstrating how it is held and played. After producing a sound with an instrument, ask children for suggestions of a movement to accompany the sound (e.g., they might suggest shaking for a maraca, tiptoeing for a triangle, or stamping feet for a drum). Select one movement for each instrument.

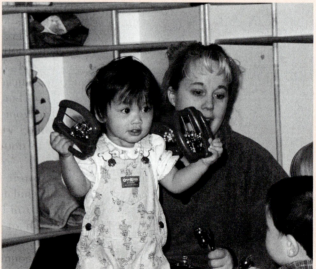

The younger the children, the simpler the instruments should be.

Randomly play the instruments one after another, challenging children to do the appropriate movement with each sound. Substitute and add instruments to keep increasing the challenge.

ASSIGNMENTS

1. List typical objects in children's environment that can serve as sound sources.

2. Research the music collection at your local library. What does it offer?

FIELD OBSERVATIONS

1. Watch a group of children during music activities and note your observations regarding the difference between hearing and listening.
2. Experiment with music of different textures and notice its effect on the movements of a child or group of children.

3. Introduce a new song or style of music to a group of children and note the effect of exposure and repetition upon several individuals.

REFERENCES

Achilles, E. (1992). Current perspectives on young children's thinking: Implications for preschool music education. In B. Andress (Ed.), *Readings in early childhood education* (pp. 67–74). Reston, VA: Music Educators National Conference.

Andress, B. (1973). *Music in early childhood*. Reston, VA: Music Educators National Conference.

Andress, B. (1991). From research to practice: Preschool children and their movement responses to music. *Young Children, 47,* 22–27.

Church, E. B. (1992). *Learning through play: Music and movement.* New York: Scholastic.

Edwards, L., Bayless, K. M., & Ramsey, M. E. (2008). *Music: A way of life for the young child.* Upper Saddle River, NJ: Prentice Hall.

Haines, B. J. E., & Gerber, L. L. (1999). *Leading young children to music.* Upper Saddle River, NJ: Prentice Hall.

Jarnow, J. (1991). *All ears.* New York: Penguin.

Wolf, J. (1992). Creating music with young children. *Young Children, 47,* 56–61.

RELEVANT WEBSITES

United States Copyright Office:
www.copyright.gov

To learn about and download classical music:
www.classical.com
www.bearshare.com
www.eclassical.com
www.classiccat.net

For children's music:

KIDiddles:
www.kididdles.com

Children's Music Web:
www.childrensmusic.org

Best Children's Music:
www.bestchildrensmusic.com

Songs for Teaching:
www.songsforteaching.com

To download free children's music:
http://freekidsmusic.com

KEY TERMS & DEFINITIONS

style of music The form, melody, harmony, sound, and rhythm of music.

texture In music, the instrumentation used to create sounds.

tempo The speed at which music is performed.

accelerando Describes music that begins slowly and gradually increases in tempo.

ritardando Indicates a gradually decreasing tempo.

volume Part of the broader category of dynamics, refers specifically to the loudness or softness of sounds.

crescendo Describes music that begins softly and gradually gets louder.

decrescendo/diminuendo Refers to a gradually decreasing volume.

staccato Notes are punctuated, like bound flow.

legato Indicates that music is to be played without any noticeable interruptions. The music flows smoothly, like free flow in movement.

pitch The highness or lowness of a musical tone.

phrase A division of a composition, commonly a four- to eight-measure phrase. Similar to a sentence in grammar.

form The overall design of the phrases that constitute a song's organization. Often designated by letters.

rhythm The organization of sounds, silences, and patterns into different groupings.

PART THREE

Facilitating Movement Experiences

8 Teaching Methods

9 Creating and Maintaining a Positive Learning Environment

© Cengage Learning 2013.

Teaching Methods

Learning Objectives

After completing this chapter, the student will be able to:

1 Describe and use the direct approach to teaching.

2 Describe and use guided discovery to facilitate children's movement education.

3 Describe and use exploration to facilitate children's movement education.

TERMS TO KNOW

direct approach

guided discovery

Spectrum of Teaching Styles

exploration

Traditionally, physical education has been taught with a command style of instruction. With this direct style, the teacher decides on the subject matter and how it is to be learned, and demonstration and imitation is the primary mode of instruction. When movement education, which calls for more indirect teaching styles, began gaining popularity, many traditional physical education specialists took exception to its philosophy. Thus, for a long while, the field consisted of two "warring" factions which each believed that its method was the only way physical education should be taught.

Today, as Gallahue and Cleland-Donnelly (2007) report, the focus has shifted from the method to the learner. As a result, specialists on both sides of this issue have come to realize the value to learners of both direct and indirect styles of instruction. The question is no longer, "Which is the best teaching style?" Rather, it is, "Which style is best for the subject matter being taught?" The two styles are now blended into most movement programs, and the striking difference between physical education and movement education no longer exists.

The Direct Approach

Some subjects simply lend themselves to a **direct approach** to teaching. In the human movement field, ballet is a prime example. This dance style consists of positions and steps that must be executed exactly; expecting students to "discover" these positions and steps through exploration is a preposterous notion. A command style that uses demonstration and imitation is the only teaching method that makes sense for ballet.

Standard 4b

Although movements as codified as ballet steps are developmentally inappropriate for young children, learning by imitation is sometimes appropriate and necessary. Modeling is often the best means of helping infants, toddlers, and some children with special needs achieve success. Likewise, as children mature, they have to learn to follow directions and to physically imitate what their eyes are seeing (e.g., when they must write the letters of the alphabet as seen in a book or on a chalkboard). According to Mosston and Ashworth (1990), "Emulating, repeating, copying, and responding to directions seem to be necessary ingredients of the early years" (p. 45). They cite Simon Says, Follow the Leader, and songs accompanied by unison clapping or movement as examples of command-style activities enjoyed by young children. Mirroring and fingerplays are among the other activities that fit into the same category.

MORE ABOUT THE ADVANTAGES AND DISADVANTAGES

Advantages of the Direct Approach
- Uses time efficiently
- Produces immediate results
- Produces uniform movement
- Teaches children to replicate movements
- Teaches children to follow directions
- Lends itself to immediate evaluation

(Continued)

Advantages of Indirect Approaches

- Stimulate cognitive processes and enhance critical thinking
- Develop self-responsibility
- Broaden the movement vocabulary
- Reduce fear of failure and produce a sense of security
- Allow for individual differences among children
- Allow for participation and success for all children
- Develop self-confidence
- Promote independence
- Develop patience with oneself and one's peers
- Lead to acceptance of others' ideas

Disadvantages of the Direct Approach

- Does not allow for creativity and self-expression
- Does not allow for individual differences in development and ability levels
- Focuses on the product versus the process

Disadvantages of Indirect Approaches

- Require more time
- Require patience and practice by the teacher

As mentioned, command-style teaching—the most direct approach—depends on the teacher making all or most of the decisions regarding what, how, and when the students are to perform (Gallahue & Cleland-Donnelly, 2007). This task-oriented approach requires the teacher to provide a brief explanation, often followed by a demonstration, of what is expected. Children then perform accordingly, usually by imitating what was demonstrated.

One advantage of this approach is that results are produced immediately. This, in turn, means teachers can instantly ascertain if a child is having difficulty following directions or producing the required response. For example, if the class is playing Simon Says and a child repeatedly touches the incorrect body part, the teacher is at once alerted to a potential problem, possibly with hearing, processing information, or simply identifying body parts.

One of the advantages of the direct approach is that results are produced immediately, allowing teachers to determine whether a child is having difficulty following directions or producing the required response.

© Cengage Learning 2013.

ABOUT TEACHER PARTICIPATION

Standard 4b

When conducting workshops, one of the most common questions I am asked by teachers and caregivers is, Should I participate in the movement activities myself? The question is a logical—and an important—one. After all, if diverse responses are the goal of exploration, teachers do not want children imitating them, which is exactly what children will do if the teacher models.

My answer, however, is, "Yes and no." As mentioned, modeling can be helpful (even necessary) with infants, toddlers, children with special needs, and some children who are reluctant to participate. And certain activities—like fingerplays and songs requiring identical responses from the children—are meant to be demonstrated.

However, when self-expression and inventiveness are sought—as when children are asked to assume crooked shapes—the teacher should refrain from participating so that children can find their own responses. Afterward, by providing feedback that welcomes a variety of responses to every challenge, a teacher can encourage diversity and ensure that even children who were initially afraid of "getting it wrong" or "looking foolish" will realize that it is okay to be themselves.

Exploration is not an invitation for teachers to simply sit back and issue challenges. They may not have to model, as required by the direct approach, but they should always enthusiastically participate in every activity—even if only with vocal and facial expression.

Efficient use of time is often seen as the most significant advantage of the direct approach. Naturally, it takes much less time to show children how movements are to be performed than to let them discover how. Lack of time is a common problem in early-childhood and elementary classrooms, where so many subjects must be covered, and in physical education classes, which often last only 30 to 40 minutes.

Mosston and Ashworth (1990) cite achieving conformity and uniformity as two of the behavior objectives of the command style. They also cite perpetuating traditional rituals as one of the subject-matter objectives. For example, if "rituals" like the "Mexican Hat Dance" and the "Hokey Pokey" are to be performed in a traditional manner, with all children doing the same thing at the same time, the only expedient way to teach these activities is with a direct approach, using demonstration and imitation. Although conformity and uniformity are not conducive to creativity and self-expression, they are necessary to the performance of certain activities. And because such activities are fun for young children and can produce a sense of belonging, these activities should play a role in the movement program.

Of course, the early-childhood years are commonly regarded as the best period for development of creativity. Thus, a major disadvantage of the direct approach is that it fails to allow for creativity and self-expression. Another disadvantage is its failure to recognize individual differences in development and ability among children. Finally, this style focuses on learning certain skills but not on the learning process itself (Gallahue & Cleland-Donnelly, 2007). The direct approach, therefore, is the teaching method least used in movement education programs.

Guided Discovery

Teaching methods that require students to problem solve are called indirect styles and are typically considered child centered, as opposed to teacher or task centered. Movement education incorporates two indirect styles: exploration, which involves divergent problem solving and is discussed in the next section; and guided discovery, which involves convergent problem solving. Whereas the direct approach is more appropriate for the youngest of young children, because it relies on convergent problem solving, guided discovery is most suitable for older preschoolers and primary-grade students.

With guided discovery, the teacher has a specific task or concept in mind (e.g., teaching children to perform a step-hop or explaining that a wide base of support provides the most stable balance). The teacher then leads children through a sequence of questions and challenges toward discovery of the task. This process, while still allowing for inventiveness and experimentation, guides children as they converge on the right answer.

One example of this style is a series of questions that leads children toward discovery of a forward roll (see Exploring Upside Down in Chapter 1). As another example, if a teacher wants primary-grade children to learn to execute a step-hop, she would first have to choose how to accomplish this. She would either use the direct approach and simply show children how to do it, or she would help children discover it for themselves. With the latter approach, the teacher might issue the following challenges:

● Practice walking forward and in place with short springy steps.
● Hop in place. Hop forward, first on one foot and then the other. Change feet often.
● Make up your own combination of walks and hops, using any number of each. Try it first in place and then moving forward.
● Make up a combination of walks and hops that fits into two counts, slightly accenting the first count.

The only correct response to the final challenge is a step-hop, as the step is more accented than the hop. Once some students have discovered this, the teacher can ask them to demonstrate, with the rest of the class asked to try it that way. The children will then have successfully "discovered" the step-hop.

Although guided discovery does take longer than the direct approach, many educators feel its benefits far outweigh the time factor. With problem solving in general (convergent or divergent), children are not only learning skills but also learning how to learn. Critical-thinking skills are enhanced as children make choices and decisions (Buschner, 1990; Kirchner, Cunningham, & Warrell, 1970). In addition, according to Klein (1990), "Most learning takes place when young children are actively engaged in ... experimenting, experiencing, and raising their own questions and finding answers" (p. 27).

Self-responsibility is another positive result of indirect teaching styles. Students are involved in the learning process and, therefore, acquire a sense of self-direction. They are able to take ownership of their responses and, ultimately, to develop confidence in their ability to discover and solve problems (Gallahue & Cleland-Donnelly, 2007; Klein, 1990; Pica, 1993).

Problem solving also helps broaden children's movement vocabulary. In addition, it reduces fear of failure and thus produces a sense of security that motivates them to continue experimenting and discovering. Guided discovery, specifically, enables children to find the interconnection of steps within a given task.

When using guided discovery with children, it is important to accept all responses—even those considered "incorrect." For example, if you have asked a series of questions designed to ultimately lead to execution of a forward roll and some children respond with other rolls, these responses must be recognized and validated. Children can then be given more time to "find another way," or you can continue the process, asking even more specific questions, until the desired outcome is achieved.

One important tip is that you should never provide the answer (Graham, 2008; Mosston & Ashworth, 1990). If the answer is given in the beginning, the discovery process is no longer possible (one cannot discover what one already knows). If after a convergent problem-solving process in which children do not

Occasionally selecting children to demonstrate can help lead toward the solution sought in guided discovery and offers them the opportunity to see movement.

© Cengage Learning 2013.

discover the expected solution, you give the answer anyway, children will expect this and will be less enthusiastic about exploring possible solutions themselves. Graham (2008) also maintains that because "wonder and curiosity are valuable mental processes," there is no harm in concluding a lesson in which children have yet to discover the solution.

Two valuable problem-solving tools (whether it be convergent or divergent problem solving) are demonstrations and verbalization, which give children two other ways to experience movement. Although demonstrations should not be overused, selecting some children to occasionally demonstrate or asking half the class to perform for the other half (thus alleviating self-consciousness) gives children the opportunity to see movement as well as experience it physically. In addition, as in the step-hop example, demonstrations can be used in guided discovery to help lead children toward the solution.

MORE ABOUT GUIDED DISCOVERY

In 2001, Mosston introduced the **Spectrum of Teaching Styles**, a model of instructional styles based on the premise that the teaching/learning process involves decisions made by the teacher and the learner before, during, and after learning (Mosston & Ashworth, 2001). Since then, he and his colleagues continued to expand, modify, and improve his original ideas (Franks, 1992). Mosston's spectrum is now accepted and applied throughout the United States and throughout the world in gymnasiums and classrooms and is the model for the teaching styles described in this chapter.

Mosston and Ashworth (1990) present an example of guided discovery that has become so well known that most physical educators need only to hear "slanted rope" to recognize the principle being discussed. The example is repeated here to help you better understand guided discovery.

In the episode cited, the "target," or the principle that the teacher wishes children to discover, is inclusion—that is, how to include everyone in the same task. The teacher begins by asking two children to hold a rope for the others to jump over. The two children respond by holding the rope horizontally at about hip level. The teacher then asks them to decrease the height so everyone can be successful.

(Continued)

When all children have jumped the rope, the teacher wonders aloud what they should do with the rope now. Inevitably, children clamor to raise it higher. The rope is raised a little, and the jumping resumes. Afterward, the teacher again asks what they should do, and again the answer is the same.

This process continues until some children become unable to clear the height of the rope. Instead of eliminating these children, as would have been the case in traditional situations, the teacher stops the process and explains that the result has been exclusion rather than inclusion. "What can we do with the rope," the teacher asks, "to include everyone?"

Usually, the children offer two possible solutions: (1) hold the rope high at the ends and let it dip in the middle; or (2) slant the rope so one end is high and the other is low. The teacher encourages them to try the second alternative. The rope is slanted, and the students prepare to jump over it, with each student selecting the height at which he or she can jump successfully. The guided discovery process has led children to the solution sought: inclusion for all.

© Cengage Learning 2013.

Verbalization is a tool you will use more often than children do, because you will be teaching them the names of the movements and the movement elements as they are experienced. However, you can also occasionally ask children to evaluate what they have seen during a demonstration (ensure a positive evaluation by asking what they liked about what they saw) or to describe a movement they have just performed or a body position they have just assumed (e.g., "I'm sitting cross-legged, and my hands are on my shoulders"). This technique gives them a chance to form mental images of what they are doing.

Children should occasionally be asked to describe a movement they have just performed or a body position assumed. This child might describe herself as being a small, round shape.

© Cengage Learning 2013.

For the teacher, of course, the most difficult part of guided discovery is designing questions and challenges that will lead children to the desired outcome. Mosston and Ashworth (1990) suggest two techniques for achieving this. One is to work backward, beginning with the final question—the one that will produce the targeted answer. The preceding question can then be identified, and so on, back to the first question. The second technique is to write a series of commands, as though a direct approach were going to be used. The commands can then be converted to questions.

Exploration

Exploration is developmentally appropriate for young children and, therefore, should be the teaching method most widely used in their movement programs. Because it results in a variety of responses to each challenge presented, it is also known as divergent problem solving. For example, a challenge to demonstrate crooked shapes could result in as many different crooked shapes as there are children responding. A challenge to balance on two body parts can result in one child balancing on the feet, another balancing on the knees, and still another—who may be enrolled in a gymnastics program—performing a handstand.

Standard 4b

This approach to instruction was perhaps best described by Halsey and Porter (1970):

> [Movement exploration] should follow such basic procedures as (1) setting the problem, (2) experimentation by the children, (3) observation and evaluation, (4) additional practice using points gained from evaluation. Answers to the problems, of course, are in movements rather than words. The movements will differ as individuals find the answer valid for each. The teacher does not demonstrate, encourage imitation, nor require any one best answer. Thus the children are not afraid to be different, and the teacher feels free to let them progress in their own way, each at his own rate. The result is a class atmosphere in which imagination has free play; invention becomes active and varied. (p. 76)

In other words, you will present children with a challenge (e.g., "Show me how tall you can be" or "Find three ways to move across the balance beam in a forward direction"), and children will offer their responses in movement. You can then issue additional challenges to continue with and vary the exploration (extending the activity), or you can issue follow-up questions and challenges intended to improve or correct what you have seen (refining responses).

Exploration or divergent problem solving results in a variety of responses being given to each challenge.

© Cengage Learning 2013.

Extending exploration is a technique that requires your time, patience, and practice—and therein lies one drawback to this instruction method. When teachers are not yet comfortable with all the aspects of exploration, they may hurry from one movement challenge to the next. Not only does this leave the class with too much time and nothing left to do, but it also fails to give children ample experience with the exploration process and with the movements being explored.

In general, three aspects make up extending activities. The first involves using the elements of movement to vary the way skills are performed. As discussed in Chapter 4, the elements of space, shape, time, force, flow, and rhythm are considered to be adverbs used to modify the skills, which are regarded as verbs. An example was given of using the movement elements to change the locomotor skill of walking. As another example, if children are asked to make themselves tall, you might challenge them to change the body's shape while still being tall. If children are challenged to move across the balance beam in a forward direction, you could suggest that they try it at different levels (the element of space) to encourage them to consider forms of locomotion other than walking.

The second way to extend movement experiences, as you might assume, entails reacting to children's responses. In the last example, you simply may have wanted children to experiment with different levels in space. Or you may have seen that they were walking across the beam, so you therefore chose that particular question to inspire other forms of locomotion. Another possible follow-up is the simple challenge to "find another way."

Mosston and Ashworth (1990) recommend that you continue to encourage children to find new ideas until a pause occurs. They assert that until then, even though participants are producing divergent responses, those responses are mainly "safe" or "common"—the product of recalling past experiences. Less common responses begin to appear after the first pause. If you persist in encouraging additional exploration beyond the second and third pauses, learners may appear physically uncomfortable but will eventually cross the "discovery" or "creativity" threshold. New solutions will evolve as divergent production continues.

The third aspect of extending responses puts parameters on the exercise. For instance, again using the example of children crossing the beam in a forward direction, you can further limit the possible responses by suggesting that children move with more than two body parts touching the beam or in a rounded shape. Mosston and Ashworth (1990) wrote,

> As the new combinations evolve, cognitive inhibition is reduced and often disappears in such episodes. It changes to joyful production. Episodes like this often evoke laughter, enjoyment, and intense interest in the process ... People realize

A challenge to move across the balance beam in a forward direction is likely to result first in a walk. Teachers can elicit more creative responses by suggesting that children find another way or by encouraging them to use specific elements of movement. For example, teachers might suggest that this child make a different body shape the next time she moves across the beam.

© Cengage Learning 2013.

ABOUT EXPECTING THE UNEXPECTED

Standard 1a

As pointed out in Chapter 3, children do not think the same way adults do. Not only do their cognitive processes differ from ours, but they also tend to be much more creative than we are— perhaps because their creativity has yet to be invalidated, or perhaps because they have yet to experience situations in life that limit their idea of how things should be. Whatever the reason, adults conducting movement activities with young children should be aware of this so they can expect the unexpected.

Graham (2008) offers examples of this. He warns teachers that while some children count a single foot as a one-part balance, others count each toe, meaning a balance on one foot is actually a balance on five body parts. Some children count the bottom as one body part; others count it as two.

He relates the story of asking a class to make narrow shapes with their bodies and questioning the response of one child who was standing with feet and arms spread wide. He was looking at it the wrong way, the child informed him, and instructed him to look at it from the side. He did and discovered that from the side, her shape was indeed narrow.

I once asked children in a class to make themselves as tall as possible. Some children stretched tall but did not rise onto the balls of their feet. I wanted to encourage them to try all of the possibilities but did not want to state specifically that they should get on tiptoe. Instead, I asked, "Is there some way you can use your feet to make yourself even taller?" In my mind, there was only one possible response to this question. But one little girl did not see it the way I did: She lifted her entire leg as high as she could and called out, "I don't think so!"

in a very short time that they can, indeed, produce new ideas in an area in which they were not accustomed to do so. (p. 252)

Of course, teachers must design problems and suggest extensions that are developmentally appropriate and relevant to the subject matter and to the children's lives (Cleland, 1990). They must also provide the encouragement that children need to continue producing divergent responses. Encouragement should consist of neutral feedback (e.g., "I see you're moving across the beam on your tummy" or "Your three-point balance uses two hands and a foot").

ABOUT OBSERVATION AND ASSESSMENT

Standard 3b

Because movement education primarily uses indirect approaches to instruction, teachers often believe that observation and evaluation are not critical because students have little chance of responding incorrectly. But the efficient execution of motor skills is the ultimate goal of any movement program and is the determining factor in deciding how far and how fast to progress through the program.

Assessment methods vary greatly and are essentially a matter of personal choice. Some teachers feel more comfortable with checklists; others, with rating scales. Most major physical education and motor development textbooks include descriptions and/or illustrations of the progression of motor skills from initial to elementary to mature stages. Using these resources as guides, you can devise your own checklists or rating scales to evaluate the motor patterns of children in your movement program. There are also motor assessment tests available that are fairly inexpensive and that do not require a lot of time to administer. Three are listed below, with addresses so you can receive additional information.

(Continued)

- The Denver Developmental Screening Test (DENVER II; www.denverii.com) is intended for use with children from birth to age 6 and is designed to quickly identify children with significant developmental delays.
- The Bruininks-Oseretsky Test of Motor Proficiency (BOT-2; http://ags .pearsonassessments.com; enter "BOT-2" in the search box) is a product-oriented assessment instrument for children aged 4½ to 14½. It provides a comprehensive index of motor proficiency in addition to separate measures of both gross and fine motor abilities. The entire battery of tests takes 45 minutes to an hour to complete; there is also a short form that can be administered in just 15 to 20 minutes.
- The Test of Gross Motor Development, 2nd edition (TGMD-2; http://www .theraproducts.com; enter "TGMD-2" in the search box) assesses the gross motor skill patterns of children aged 3 to 10. The test covers six locomotor skills (running, leaping, jumping, hopping, galloping, and sliding) and six manipulative skills (striking a stationary ball, stationary dribbling or bouncing, kicking, catching, overhand throwing, and underhand throwing. The test requires only about 15 minutes to administer and little special training. It is available from the same company as the Peabody Developmental Motor Scales, 2nd edition, which provides in-depth assessment and training or remediation of gross and fine motor skills of children from birth through 5 years old.

For most early-childhood professionals, observational assessment is often the best tool. With this method, you would choose two or three children and perhaps four skills per week to observe. This allows you to evaluate in a natural setting (authentic assessment) and in a manner that will not be overwhelming to you or the children.

Although you must be careful to accept all responses, there will come a time when you wish to help children improve or refine their solutions. If, for example, you have challenged children to make themselves as small as possible and some children respond by lying flat on the floor, you should not observe aloud that this response is incorrect. In fact, it is not necessarily incorrect; it is simply another way of looking at things (see "About Expecting the Unexpected"). However, if you want children to truly experience a small shape, you might issue the further question, "Is there a way you can be small in a rounded, or curled, shape?" Although you have helped children improve their responses, you have not stifled their individuality, because diverse solutions are still possible (e.g., some will make a small rounded shape in a sitting position, some will lie on their sides, others on their backs, etc.).

Too often in the past, physical education was taught "to the middle." In other words, teachers chose activities that could be handled by children of average ability. Although the system worked well for these children, students who were not as skilled were constantly lagging behind, resulting in a vicious cycle of failure that eroded their confidence and led to more failure. Highly skilled children, on the other hand, were not sufficiently challenged and became increasingly bored.

Exploration allows every child to participate and succeed at her or his own level of development and ability. In addition to the self-confidence and poise that continual success brings, this process promotes independence, helps develop patience with oneself and one's peers, and allows the acceptance of others' ideas. Perhaps most important for young children, exploration leads children to discover the richness of possibilities involved in the field of human movement.

ASSIGNMENTS

1. List at least five activities, in addition to those cited in this chapter, that are best presented with a direct approach. Write an explanation of why these particular activities lend themselves to a direct approach.

2. Choose a movement skill that could be taught with guided discovery to young children. Prepare a list of questions (working backward or beginning with commands, if necessary) that can guide children to the "discovery" of the skill. Justify in writing your choice of guided discovery as the method for teaching this skill.

3. Choose a movement theme that lends itself to exploration. Create a set of challenges and questions that encourage children to fully explore it. Justify your choice of exploration as the teaching method for this theme.

4. Imagine that you have asked children to explore moving through general space in a backward direction. Create a list of common responses and then devise follow-up questions and challenges that extend the activity and encourage uncommon solutions. What if some children were actually demonstrating sideward movement instead? What questions and challenges could you pose to correct (refine) that response?

FIELD OBSERVATION

1. Observe a teacher conducting a movement lesson. Note the teaching style or styles being used. Is it/are they the best for the subject matter being taught? Why, or why not?

REFERENCES

Buschner, C. A. (1990). Can we help children move and think critically? In W. J. Stinson (Ed.), *Moving and learning for the young child* (pp. 51–66). Reston, VA: AAHPERD.

Cleland, F. (1990). How many ways can I … ? Problem solving through movement. In W. J. Stinson (Ed.), *Moving and learning for the young child* (pp. 73–76). Reston, VA: AAHPERD.

Franks, B. D. (1992). The spectrum of teaching styles: A silver anniversary in physical education. *Journal of Physical Education, Recreation, and Dance, 63,* 25–26.

Gallahue, D. L., & Cleland-Donnelly, F. (2007). *Developmental physical education for all children.* Champaign, IL: Human Kinetics.

Graham, G. (2008). *Teaching children physical education.* Champaign, IL: Human Kinetics.

Halsey, E., & Porter, L. (1970). Movement exploration. In R. T. Sweeney (Ed.), *Selected readings in movement education* (pp. 71–77). Reading, MA: Addison-Wesley.

Kirchner, G., Cunningham, J., & Warrell, E. (1970). *Introduction to movement education.* Dubuque, IA: Brown.

Klein, J. (1990). Young children and learning. In W. J. Stinson (Ed.), *Moving and learning for the young child* (pp. 23–30). Reston, VA: AAHPERD.

Mosston, M., & Ashworth, S. (1990). *The spectrum of teaching styles: From command to discovery.* White Plains, NY: Longman.

Mosston, M., & Ashworth, S. (2001). *Teaching physical education.* San Francisco: Benjamin Cummings.

Pica, R. (1993). Responsibility and young children: What does physical education have to do with it? *Journal of Physical Education, Recreation, and Dance, 64,* 72–75.

RELEVANT WEBSITES

For information on Mosston's Spectrum of Teaching Styles:
www.spectrumofteachingstyles.org
www.sports-media.org/sportapolisnewsletter23newlook.htm

www.nipissingu.ca/education/barbo/resources/TEACHING_STYLES_IN_THE_GYM.doc
http://physicaleducationresources.com/teachingstylesmosstonpe.aspx

KEY TERMS & DEFINITIONS

direct approach A command style of teaching that uses demonstration and imitation.

guided discovery A teaching method using convergent problem solving.

Spectrum of Teaching Styles A model of instructional styles based on the premise that the teaching/learning process involves decisions made by the learner before, during, and after learning. Also referred to as Mosston's Spectrum, this model is now accepted and applied throughout the world.

exploration A teaching method employing divergent problem solving.

© Cengage Learning 2013.

Creating and Maintaining a Positive Learning Environment

Learning Objectives

After completing this chapter, the student will be able to:

1 Describe and use a variety of teaching tips to create and maintain a positive learning environment.

2 Specify a variety of reasons for nonparticipation.

3 Describe ways in which to handle disruptive behavior.

4 Describe the role of relaxation in a child's life and movement experiences.

TERMS TO KNOW

personal space
auditory or visual signal
boundary
positive challenge
praise addict
nonparticipant
disruptive behavior

Many teachers and caregivers hesitate to make movement part of their programs, because when they think of children and movement at the same time, they immediately form a mental image of children "bouncing off the walls." This is certainly a realistic concern. Movement activities can generate a lot of energy, and unless the instructor has some idea of what to expect and how to deal with all that potential energy, the "walls" will certainly see much action.

Managing the movement session must be handled with special care. You do, however, have a few factors in your favor from the outset. Most important, a success-oriented program is likely to have few behavioral problems. After all, a child who is experiencing success is not likely to want to wreak havoc on the class. The same is true of the child who is actively involved and interested. Thus, movement exploration lends itself to successful, active involvement.

Common sense also plays a vital role. Beginning at the beginning (wherever children are, developmentally) and building from there with a logical progression of skills will ensure that children are challenged but not overwhelmed. Not only can you expect greater success from children who are asked merely to build on their earlier successes, but also you can expect greater response from them.

Another common-sense guideline offered by Cherry (1971) is planning movement activities when children are well rested and not overstimulated from another activity. She suggests planning movement activities immediately following rest or story time or shortly after children's arrival in the morning.

Because success is always the goal in movement exploration, the class atmosphere is critical. As Miller (2009) points out, "It is more nurturing and less stressful for everyone involved if adults focus on setting the stage for proper behavior, rather than on reprimanding children after they behave improperly."

This chapter focuses on teaching tips that can help set the stage for what can be stress-free movement experiences. There are no surefire recipes for success, however. Should you find yourself doing everything right and still running into occasional stumbling blocks, this chapter also examines dealing with the nonparticipant and with disruptive behavior. Finally, it concludes with a discussion of the role of relaxation in the movement program.

Tried and Tested Teaching Tips

If you have conducted movement sessions with young children, you may have had an experience or two in which a group became so unmanageable, you wondered whether there was not an easier way to make a living. The following suggestions (offered in no particular order) cannot guarantee that you will never again be tempted to look for a less-challenging job, but they can help make the task easier and more satisfying for you and your young students.

Establish Rules

Creating and maintaining a positive learning environment does not mean an absence of ground rules. Children need rules and guidelines; once established, those rules must be enforced consistently. Most rules for young children are related to safety (Essa, 2010)—certainly true where movement is concerned. At the beginning of the movement program, you must determine what guidelines are needed to keep the children safe (e.g., no participating in stocking feet, no gum allowed during movement). However, you (with help from the children) may want to establish additional guidelines to ensure that movement activities run smoothly. Graham (2008) suggests that once you have outlined these "protocols," you practice them with children, just as you would practice other skills.

Standard 4b

The two following rules should have a place in every movement program.

Rule 1: We will respect one another's personal space. At first, this may be difficult to enforce, especially with the youngest students, because they usually enjoy bumping into each other. So it is your challenge to make it a goal for children to avoid colliding or interfering with one another.

You can accomplish this goal by practicing the personal space activities outlined in Chapter 4. In addition, at the beginning of every movement class, you can ask children to space themselves evenly. Reinforce the idea of personal space, encouraging children to imagine they are each surrounded by a giant bubble. Whether standing still or moving, they should avoid causing any bubbles to burst.

Another image that works quite successfully is that of dolphins swimming. Children who have seen these creatures in action, whether at an aquarium or on television, will be able to relate to the fact that dolphins swim side by side but never get close enough to touch one another. The goal, then, is for children to behave similarly. (Showing pictures of dolphins swimming together could be helpful.)

Hoops provide tangible evidence of personal space. When placed strategically throughout the area, they can help children develop a respect for one another's space.

© Cengage Learning 2013.

Rule 2: We will participate with as little noise as possible. Naturally, you cannot expect movement exploration to take place in silence. But you should not have to raise your voice or shout to have your challenges, directions, and follow-up questions heard.

Establish an **auditory or visual signal** to indicate that it is time to stop, look, and listen ("Stop, look at me, and listen for what comes next."). Choose a signal that children have to watch for (two fingers held in the air or the time-out sign from sports) or something they must listen for (a hand clap, a strike on a triangle, or two taps on a drum).

With some classes, either possibility works well. With more challenging groups of children, you will probably find that an audible signal is more effective than a visual one. After all, children can avoid looking if they want to, but they cannot avoid hearing. If you do choose an audible signal, you should be aware that your voice may not be the best choice, because it is heard so often by the children. Also, be sure your signal is a quiet one. A whistle, for example, is usually not suitable, because it can be heard above a great deal of noise. (It also has certain authoritarian connotations.)

Whatever the signal, it is not unreasonable to expect children to be stopped, looking, and listening within two to four seconds of having seen or heard it. You should have to give the signal only once (Graham, 2008). This, however, will also require practice.

Children are usually willing to follow rules as long as they know what is expected of them and they know that the rules have significance for them (Essa, 2010; Miller, 2009; Woods, 1993). Do not simply tell children what the rules are; tell them why the rules are necessary. Or, better yet, create the rules together.

Establish Boundaries

A movement space needs to be open and uncluttered if children are to participate without distraction or injury. Although a spacious gymnasium is the ideal location for movement, such a space is not always (or even often) available.

If you are working in a classroom, the space must be prepared in advance and clearly defined. Helping prepare the space can be part of the protocol you

Use items like plastic cones to mark boundaries in an especially large area. Do not hesitate to ask children to assist you in preparing the space.

© Cengage Learning 2013.

establish with children, who are usually quite happy to lend a hand. (Clements and Schiemer [1993] suggest asking children to pretend to be construction workers, Santa's elves, or Snow White's dwarves as they help rearrange the furniture.) Certain areas and objects (the art corner or the piano, for instance) should be designated as off-limits.

Boundaries are still required, even if you have access to a gym or an exceptionally large room; too much space can be overwhelming to some children. You also do not want children roaming so far from you and the group that they are either unable to hear you or no longer seem to be part of the activity. Masking tape, rope, or plastic cones (available from suppliers like Flaghouse and Play with a Purpose [see Appendix 2]) are examples of materials that can be used to outline the boundaries.

Use Positive Challenges

If you assume that children are capable of handling your challenges, they are more likely to *be* capable. For example, "Find four ways to …" assumes that students can find several ways to respond. Similarly, "Show me you can …" implies that you know they can. Conversely, if you present challenges by asking, "Can you … ?" you are implying a choice, and many preschoolers will simply say no.

Standard 4b

Standard 1a

In addition, young children love to show off—to display their abilities—especially for their teachers. Therefore, if you introduce challenges with phrases like "Let me see you …" or "Show me you can …", children will want to show you they can. Although positive challenges are a simple technique, they are amazingly effective, especially when used in tandem with positive reinforcement.

Make Corrections Creatively

Singling out children who have responded incorrectly (for example, hopping when the challenge was to skip) causes embarrassment and self-consciousness. Those feelings do not lead to future success. On the other hand, you cannot help children improve if you simply ignore their incorrect responses. The alternatives are

Standard 4b

to (1) ask children responding correctly to demonstrate, (2) describe the differences between skipping and hopping, or (3) reissue the challenge to give them another chance to succeed. If the same children still respond incorrectly, you are alerted to an area requiring attention. However, you should offer the attention when it is possible to provide it privately and positively. (Do not forget that some children will be unable to perform certain skills because they are not developmentally ready.)

Not squelching children's creativity and self-expression is also extremely important. When you have asked children to create new words to a song, for example, you must accept their creations, even if they do not rhyme or fit the rhythm of the melody. Correcting and adjusting their lyrics will invalidate their offerings and give the sense that they can succeed only with adult intervention.

In a similar vein, Sullivan (1982) gives the example of a child who responds to a challenge to make a high shape by climbing onto a table. She suggests, "Rather than negate the inventiveness, you can acknowledge the cleverness and add '… with both feet on the ground' to the next instruction" (p. 18).

Standard 4b

Use Honest Praise and Positive Reinforcement

Praise children, but only when it is deserved. Children can sense when adults are not being honest; praise will cease to have any meaning for them if it is not sincere. On the other hand, an overabundance of praise can turn children into praise addicts who need more and more every day to maintain their self-esteem (Miller, 2009).

Perhaps one of the most difficult habits to overcome is moralizing. We often say, "Good girl" or "Good boy," which implies the child is good because she or he is doing what we asked. We might also say, "That was a good jump," when it would be more appropriate to describe the jump as high, low, light, or heavy.

Miller (2009) suggests recognition and encouragement as alternatives to false praise and value judgments. By describing children's responses with enthusiasm and respect, we validate them and encourage original solutions.

Use Your Voice as a Tool

This is a straightforward, commonsense suggestion. If you want children to move slowly, then you should speak slowly. If you want them to move quietly, speak quietly. In addition, just as you can catch more flies with honey than vinegar, you can attract and maintain more attention with a lower volume than with a higher one. Children are far more likely to react to a whisper than to a yell. Remember, too, although you should present your challenges enthusiastically (and with the proper facial expressions), if you maintain a fever pitch of enthusiasm, children will become overstimulated.

One additional thing you can do with your voice is to say the children's names often. A child's name is special; when a child hears it being said in a positive way by an adult, he or she receives recognition and reassurance (Essa, 2003).

Use Familiar Imagery

If you ask a group of 4-year-olds to walk as though anxious or disillusioned, you will probably get puzzled looks as a response. But if you ask them to walk as though mad or sad, you know they will be able to respond, because every 4-year-old has felt those emotions. Similarly, if you ask preschoolers to walk like different animals, you know that an elephant will be more familiar to them than, for instance, an anteater. This is not to say, however, that children must be personally acquainted with every object, creature, or situation you ask them to portray. Young children enjoy pretending to walk weightlessly on the moon because they have witnessed such scenes on television and in the movies, they have heard about it in books and discussions with their teachers, and they have wonderful, vivid imaginations. So if you want to use imagery with which children are not personally familiar, you must first make it familiar to them. Otherwise, your challenges will be met with blank stares.

© Cengage Learning 2013.

ABOUT POSITIVE REINFORCEMENT

Alfie Kohn (1999), author of *Punished by Rewards: The Trouble with Gold Stars, Incentive Plans, A's, Praise, and Other Bribes,* expresses strong feelings about the use of positive reinforcement to manipulate children. Instead of using praise,

(Continued)

rewards, or punishment, Kohn suggests that teachers ask children to look at the effects of their actions on others. In addition, he suggests modeling appropriate behavior, planning activities that make children feel connected to one another, and giving them lots of opportunity for choice.

Kohn's controversial book will engender strong feelings in readers—and unqualified agreement with the author is unlikely. But I found that it raised many questions for me, and, therefore, I feel it should be read by anyone who spends time with, and serves as an influence upon, children.

Monitor Energy Levels

As mentioned, movement activities can generate an abundance of energy, and too much energy can result in frustrating, unproductive, unmanageable movement sessions. Too little energy, however, can have comparable results, as tired children tend to display irritability and off-task behavior.

Standard 4b

Alternating lively and quieter activities is usually enough to prevent frenzy and fatigue. Sullivan (1982) suggests other contrasts: difficult movements with easy movements, high with low, loose with tight, and big with little to keep everyone involved. She also proposes bringing children to the ground with commands to freeze and collapse or to sit in order to achieve a calming effect.

Whether you choose to alternate contrasting activities, channel excess energy into gross motor activities (Cherry, 1971), use grounding techniques, or simply stop at the first sign of fatigue, having some plan beforehand can help guarantee you will not have to end your movement sessions abruptly, feeling helpless and frustrated.

Be Flexible

Dancers and gymnasts, of course, are known for the flexibility of their bodies, but that is not the flexibility being referred to here. Rather, you need a flexibility of mind and spirit to accept that your lessons will not always go exactly as you have outlined them on

Standard 4b

paper. We are, after all, talking about young children and movement exploration.

In monitoring children's energy levels, for instance, you may suddenly find it necessary to veer from your original course to either excite or calm the class. Perhaps nothing you planned is interesting to a particular class on a particular day, forcing you to either improvise or go to another lesson plan entirely. Young children also have wonderful ideas of their own—ideas that would never occur to you. If you can be flexible enough to sometimes explore the possibilities presented by children, not only will this help personalize the lessons for them, but they will also gain greater confidence in their creative abilities.

What about the Nonparticipant?

Sometimes, especially at the beginning, some children do not want to participate in the movement program. There can be several reasons for this, and you must determine why a **nonparticipant** chooses to sit out—initially by eliminating any physical problems as the cause.

Standard 4b

Although sad, some children refuse to take part out of a fear of looking foolish or "being wrong." Even at a very young age, this fear is not only instilled in some preschoolers but can also be quite powerful.

For these children, observing your success-oriented movement experiences is the key to unlocking their fear. They will notice, for example, that eight of their classmates have responded to your challenge in eight different ways—and you are validating each and every response. They will begin to realize that there is no right or wrong. With a bit of gentle coaxing and positive reinforcement, these children can eventually be encouraged to join in.

Some children are genuinely shy and only need time to get used to the idea of moving with the rest of the group, while others will require specific encouragement from you or another adult. Essa (2010) outlines a series of steps to help children overcome shyness at group time:

1. Sit with the child for a few minutes at least once a day and read her a story.
2. Invite another child to join the activity.
3. Gradually add more children to the small group.
4. Continue the daily small-group activities while also making an effort to involve the child in total group times.
5. Reinforce any involvement in group activities.

Sometimes merely standing near the shy child as you facilitate movement activities, offering occasional smiles or gentle touches, is the only encouragement you need to offer. At other times, you may have to physically (but gently) initiate the child's participation by taking his hands in yours and moving them accordingly or by sitting behind the child and rocking him with you to the rhythm of the music. Positive reinforcement of any level of participation will do much to contribute to the shy child's confidence. For example, if you have asked children to freeze and the nonparticipant is sitting particularly still, you can use him as an example of stillness. If you have asked children to move just one body part and the nonparticipant raises an eyebrow, you can acknowledge his "response."

At the other extreme is the child who uses nonparticipation as a way of getting adult attention. If that is the case, Essa (2010) suggests ignoring all nonparticipation and offering reinforcement only when the child is involved in group activity, using a process of "successive approximations." At first, reinforce the child when she is observing the activity of others. When the child consistently watches, you move on to the next step, which is reinforcement as the child moves physically closer to the group. Once the child is fully involved, you can gradually decrease the amount of reinforcement, offering only as much as you offer children who are participating.

Whatever the reason for the lack of involvement, nonparticipants must not be forced to join in, as this can place undue emotional stress on them. You can insist, however, that they not be allowed to do other classroom activities, like reading or playing with blocks, during the movement session. Instead, they must take on the role of audience. Not only does this involve them to a certain extent, but it also ensures that they are gaining something from the experience, as children can absorb much from watching movement. Occasionally, you may even be pleasantly surprised to learn from a parent that a child who is merely watching at school or child care is imitating everything in the privacy of her own home.

What about Disruptive Behavior?

Disruptive behavior is another tactic children use to receive attention from adults; for some children, even negative attention is better than none at all. Unfortunately, because disruptions are annoying, distracting, and sometimes harmful, children causing
Standard 4b

them often do get more attention than those who are behaving well. But you should never let a class fall apart in order to respond to one child.

Essa (2010) and Miller (2009) agree that, in general, ignoring the behavior is an effective policy when that behavior is simply annoying or mildly distracting.

Because the child does not receive the attention he is seeking, there is no longer any need to continue the behavior. Sometimes the child's focus can be redirected elsewhere; for instance, a child making noise stamping his feet can be asked to demonstrate tiptoeing or other substitutes for the stamping.

Both Essa and Miller believe, however, that when the disruptive behavior is harmful to the child or others, it must be stopped immediately. Sometimes a single warning, issued firmly but gently, is enough to end the behavior. Miller (2009) suggests undivided attention involving eye contact, a body position at the child's level, appropriate touch, and use of the child's name: "A half-hour of nagging and threatening from across the room will not have the impact of one quiet statement made eye-to-eye, using the child's name." If after one such warning, the harmful behavior continues, the child should be removed from the group (calmly and without anger) to allow for a cooling-off period—for both the child and the teacher.

Philosophies regarding time-out specifics vary. Graham, Holt-Hale, and Parker (2009) suggest that the time-out last until the child comes to you and explains why she was asked to sit out; Gallahue & Cleland-Donnelly (2007) suggest questioning the child about the reason for the isolation and how it can be prevented in the future. Essa (2010), on the other hand, contends that the child knows the reason and that no further discussion is necessary. Graham et al. (2009) also recommend time-out for the remainder of the class should the child misbehave again, but French, Silliman, and Henderson (1990) feel that exclusion for longer than five minutes is less effective than are shorter periods. (Be aware that some children will be disruptive to get out of class; thus, time-out gives them exactly what they wanted.)

How you handle time-out has to be a personal choice. Most experts tend to agree, however, that once a child is asked to sit out, she should be ignored. Also, time-out must be used sparingly; otherwise it will become an ineffective management technique.

BAM! radio

PODCAST: *Go to www. bamradionetwork.com and search for the podcast "Time to Give 'Time Out' a Time Out".*

- *In what way does Dr. Haiman believe that time out causes harm?*
- *What is Amy McCready's advice concerning the use of a new "t" word?*
- *Has your position on time outs changed as a result of listening to this segment? Why or why not?*

Although philosophies regarding the use and specifics of time-out vary widely, the experts all agree that this management technique must be used sparingly.

© Cengage Learning 2013.

The Role of Relaxation

Teachers are often surprised by the idea of relaxation as part of a movement program. But there are many good reasons why every movement session should include relaxation exercises.

When used alternately with vigorous activities, quieter activities can help establish a pace that assures there will be no "wall bouncing." Relaxation gives children the opportunity to experience motionlessness and an understanding of its contrast to movement. It helps prepare children for slow and sustained movement, which requires greater control than does fast movement. In addition, whether children are going to another subject, to lunch, or home at the end of your movement session, it is always a good idea to wind them down a bit before sending them on their way.

Relaxation exercises offer many other benefits to young children. If you use imagery to promote relaxation, you enhance their ability to imagine. If you use music, you expose them to the world of quiet, peaceful music. Most important, relaxation is a learned skill. With stress being so much a part of our society and our children's lives, it is a greatly needed skill. Jacobsen (1973), a leading authority in relaxation techniques, believes that tension control can help children learn better. Cherry (1981) says simply that relaxing can make "serenity" a part of children's lives, helping them learn that "they can be in control of their own bodies and feelings rather than having to let their bodies and feelings control them."

Following are five suggestions for promoting relaxation. Cherry (1981) offers dozens of others.

Images

What comes to mind when you think of rag dolls, cooked spaghetti, or soggy dishcloths? Limp! Show children a rag doll or a wet dishcloth. Talk to them about the difference between uncooked and cooked spaghetti. Then ask them to pretend to be one of these objects.

You can also paint a picture in their minds. Ask them to lie on the floor and imagine, for example, they are at the beach. Talk to them softly about the warmth of the sun, the cool breeze, and the gentle sounds of the waves and the gulls circling overhead. Do not be surprised if a few of them drop off to sleep.

Melting

Melting is a wonderful slow-motion activity with which to end a movement session. Discuss how slowly ice cream cones, snow sculptures, or ice cubes melt. Then ask children to stand and demonstrate one of these possibilities.

Relaxation exercises will benefit both the children and the movement program.

© Cengage Learning 2013.

Balloons

To promote deep breathing, you can ask children to expand (by inhaling) and contract (by exhaling) like balloons, alternately and slowly inflating and deflating. Initially, you can demonstrate with an actual balloon to help make this image more vivid.

Feeling Calm/Feeling Nervous

This activity (adapted from Pica, 2001, pp. 28–29), which focuses on contracting and relaxing the muscles, is appropriate for early-elementary children.

Background Information. Calm is a very relaxed feeling, like that experienced just before falling asleep at night. At those times, muscles feel loose and "liquid." Other times when children might have experienced calmness include while sitting by a lake, observing a bird soar through the sky, or watching the sun set.

What are some times when children have felt nervous? Nervous is a combination of scared and worried. Have they ever worried it might rain on the day of a big outing? Have they ever lost sight of their parents in a big store and felt nervous until spotting them again? How did their muscles and bodies feel at those times? Were their muscles loose or tense? Ask them to show you.

Calm and Nervous. Children are going to experience the differences between feeling calm and feeling nervous at various levels in space. They begin standing. When you say "Calm," children should make their bodies as relaxed as possible. When you say "Nervous," they should tense up. (Vary the time between verbal cues. Also, remember that the quality of your voice is very important; it should sound like the word you are saying.) Repeat this process with children kneeling, sitting, and finally lying down.

Using Music

Because music is mood altering, it offers wonderful possibilities for relaxation. Chapter 7 lists examples of slow and soft pieces, as well as children's recordings made especially for resting or quiet times. These are some of your best choices for relaxation, along with certain other classical and new age compositions.

Choose only those selections that you have previously heard and found to be suitably relaxing. Ask children to lie or sit comfortably with eyes closed, sometimes listening to the music in general and other times listening specifically for sounds or elements you have asked them to identify. You can also use peaceful music in conjunction with imagery or deep-breathing exercises.

ASSIGNMENTS

1. List the rules you feel would be especially important in conducting a successful movement program. Provide justification for each.

2. Determine a policy for time-out. Cite the reasons behind your decision.

3. Create four or five activities you could use to promote relaxation.

FIELD OBSERVATION

1. Observe a movement session, noting the pace and the participation level. Are all children taking part? If there are nonparticipants, are they observing? Can you get a sense of the reason(s) for their lack of participation? Are some children displaying disruptive behavior? What do you think is the cause? How does the instructor handle it?

REFERENCES

Cherry, C. (1971). Creative movement for the developing child. Carthage, IL: Fearon.

Cherry, C. (1981). *Think of something quiet*. Carthage, IL: Fearon.

Clements, R. L., & Schiemer, S. (1993). *Let's move, let's play: Developmentally appropriate movement activities for preschool children*. Montgomery, AL: KinderCare Learning Centers.

Essa, E. (2010). *A practical guide to solving preschool behavior problems*. Belmont, CA: Cengage Learning.

French, R., Silliman, L., & Henderson, H. (1990). Too much time out. *Strategies, 3*, 5–7.

Gallahue, D. L., & Cleland-Donnelly, F. (2007). *Developmental physical education for all children*. Champaign, IL: Human Kinetics.

Graham, G. (2008). *Teaching children physical education*. Champaign, IL: Human Kinetics.

Graham, G., Holt-Hale, S., & Parker, M. (2009). *Children moving: A reflective approach to teaching physical education*. Mountain View, CA: Mayfield.

Jacobsen, E. (1973). *Teaching and learning new methods for old arts*. Chicago: National Foundation for Progressive Relaxation.

Kohn, Alfie. (1999). *Punished by rewards: The trouble with gold stars, incentive plans, A's, praise, and other bribes*. New York: Houghton Mifflin.

Miller, D. F. (2009). *Positive child guidance*. Belmont, CA: Cengage Learning.

Pica, R. (2001). *Wiggle, giggle, & shake: 200 ways to move & learn*. Silver Spring, MD: Gryphon House.

Sullivan, M. (1982). *Feeling strong, feeling free: Movement exploration for young children*. Washington, DC: National Association for the Education of Young Children.

Woods, A. M. (1993). Off to a good start: Establishing a productive learning environment. *Teaching Elementary Physical Education, 4*, 8–9, 11.

RELEVANT WEBSITES

For articles from Alfie Kohn:

Alfie Kohn:
www.alfiekohn.org

For classroom management techniques:

National Education Association:
http://www.nea.org/tools/ClassroomManagement.html

The Teacher's Guide
http://www.theteachersguide.com/ClassManagement.htm

For physical education management techniques:

P.E. Central:
www.pecentral.org

KEY TERMS & DEFINITIONS

auditory or visual signal Something children must be listening or watching for indicating that it is time to "stop, look, and listen" to the teacher.

boundary Limitation placed on the movement area; objects the children cannot move beyond or on.

positive challenge Introductory phrase to a movement challenge, indicating a belief that children can do what's being asked of them.

praise addict Child who needs more and more praise from adults to maintain self-esteem.

nonparticipant Child who refuses to take part in movement activities.

disruptive behavior Acting out in order to receive attention from adults.

personal space The area immediately surrounding the body. It includes whatever can be reached while remaining in one spot and can be likened to a large bubble surrounding the body.

PART FOUR

Movement and Music Through the Day

10 Movement Across the Curriculum

11 Using Movement and Music for Transitions

12 Bringing Movement Education Outdoors

© Cengage Learning 2013.

CHAPTER
10

Movement Across the Curriculum

Learning Objectives

After completing this chapter, the student will be able to:

1 Describe the connections between movement and art and create appropriate movement experiences that enhance understanding of art concepts.

2 Describe the connections between movement and language arts and create appropriate movement experiences that enhance understanding of language arts concepts.

3 Describe the connections between movement and mathematics and create appropriate movement experiences that enhance understanding of mathematics concepts.

4 Describe the connections between movement and science and create appropriate movement experiences that enhance understanding of science concepts.

5 Describe the connections between movement and social studies and create appropriate movement experiences that enhance understanding of social studies concepts.

TERMS TO KNOW

whole child

kinesthetic mode

bodily/kinesthetic intelligence

content area

integrated approach to literacy

fingerplay

quantitative idea

Unfortunately, although the concept of the whole (thinking, feeling, moving) child has existed for years, many teachers still fail to acknowledge the moving part of the child—the **kinesthetic mode** of learning, or the **bodily/kinesthetic intelligence**. Methods abound for learning through the eyes and ears—discussion, books, chalkboards, audiovisual equipment, and, more recently, videos and computers. But little planning and few equipment purchases serve the physical senses (Hendricks & Hendricks, 1983; Rowen, 1982; Werner & Burton, 1979). As Hendricks and Hendricks (1983) aptly put it, "Kinesthetic learners have typically gotten the short end of the slide rule in schooling" (p. 4).

Children are not known for their ability to sit still, yet in most elementary schools (and, increasingly, even in preschools), they are expected to remain motionless at desks for lengthy periods. Not only does this make concentration difficult, but it also often causes children to act out—if not in the classroom then on the playground, when the long-awaited recess presents an opportunity to break free. At the other end of the spectrum, Hendricks and Hendricks (1983) and Gilbert (2002) attest to the sense of community and the atmosphere of cooperation generated by allowing children to move in the classroom.

naeyc
Standard 3b

Furthermore, movement activities provide teachers with an effective means of evaluation. The traditional question-and-answer method does not always reveal those students who have failed to grasp the concept under discussion; movement experiences,

ABOUT MULTIPLE INTELLIGENCES

An excellent resource for educators wanting to know more about Howard Gardner's (1993) theory of multiple intelligences is Thomas Armstrong's *Multiple Intelligences in the Classroom*. Armstrong's easy-to-read book defines the eight primary intelligences first identified by Gardner and describes how educators can bring multiple intelligences into the classroom every day. (At the time Armstrong's book was written, Gardner had just suggested the possibility of a ninth intelligence—the existentialist intelligence. Armstrong takes only a brief look at that intelligence at the end of his book. Gardner has since included the existentialist intelligence in his multiple intelligences theory.) Armstrong's book also includes checklists for determining strongest and weakest intelligences in both adults and children, as well as practical suggestions for further developing those intelligences.

In the preface of an earlier book, *Seven Kinds of Smart,* Armstrong (2000) explained that his interest in exploring the multiple intelligences began after he had worked for several years as an elementary-school teacher and became "disenchanted with the way parents and teachers all too often plucked the learning potential from blossoming children by focusing too much attention on words and numbers at the expense of other gifts and talents" (p. 5). It is Armstrong's hope that knowledge of the various intelligences can help prevent the loss of further potential.

FIGURE **10.1** Model of early-childhood curriculum, demonstrating seven major content areas.
From J. E. Fox & R. Schirrmacher, **Art and Creative Development for Young Children**. *Copyright 2011 by Cengage Learning.*

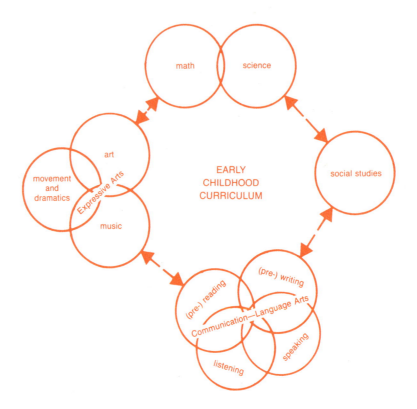

however, allow teachers to immediately detect those students who do not understand (Gilbert, 2002).

Standard 4b

Whether incorporating into the curriculum full-fledged movement sessions that require desks to be pushed aside, short movement breaks at desks, or occasional physical demonstrations to help make concepts clearer, classroom teachers can use the activities that follow—and others like them—to enhance learning, to develop rapport among children, to gain immediate feedback, and to promote a positive attitude toward education that can influence future learning. Similarly, physical education specialists can use these activities to augment the cognitive and affective aspects of physical activity and relate their programs to those taking place in the classroom. When both classroom and physical education teachers decide to use a multisensory approach that has an impact on the cognitive, affective, and physical domains, then—and only then—can we truly educate the whole child.

Art

Art and movement have a number of things in common, particularly where young children are concerned. Art, because it involves movement, helps develop motor skills. Gross motor skills are used in such art activities as painting on an easel, creating murals, body tracing, and working with clay. Fine motor control, which is refined later than gross motor control, is practiced during such art activities as working with small paintbrushes, cutting with scissors, and pasting.

Both art and movement also help develop eye–hand coordination (Mayesky, 2008; Fox & Schirrmacher, 2011).

Perhaps the most significant common factor between art and movement is that self-expression is encouraged. When given ample opportunity to explore possibilities—whether through movement or a variety of art materials—children make nonverbal statements about who they are and what is important to them. Through both media, they can express emotions and work out issues of concern to them, while also achieving the satisfaction that comes from experiencing success. These results can occur, however, only when the child's movement responses and artwork are not censored by adults and when they are accepted and valued as evidence of the child's individuality. With such acceptance, children gain confidence in their abilities to express themselves, solve problems, and use their creativity. (See "About Self-Expression" in Chapter 2 for examples of what happens when adults invalidate children's artistic efforts.)

Finally, concepts like shape, size, spatial relationships, and line are also part of art and movement education. Even such artistic concepts as color and texture can be explored and expressed through movement. It makes sense, therefore, to explore these concepts through both media.

Adding Literature and Music

Many children's books deal with artistic concepts. Tana Hoban's books, for instance, include *Circles, Triangles, and Squares* (also appropriate for mathematics); *Round, Round, Round; Is It Larger? Is It Smaller?* (also appropriate for mathematics); *Shapes, Shapes, Shapes;* and *Is It Red? Is It Yellow? Is It Blue?* Other possibilities are Eric Carle's *My First Book of Colors* and *My First Book of Shapes;* John Reiss's *Colors and Shapes;* and Joanne and David Wylie's *A Fishy Color Story* (also appropriate for science).

To make music part of the experience, you can ask children to paint to the accompaniment of different styles of music, perhaps suggesting that they change colors every time the music changes. In addition, many songs relate to the

Whenever children arrange their bodies in the space around them, it can be said that they are exploring artistic concepts as well as physical ones.

© Cengage Learning 2013.

Sample Activities

Whenever children arrange their bodies in the space around them, they are exploring artistic, as well as physical, concepts. With their bodies, they are creating lines and shapes. When they move into different levels, in different directions, along different pathways, and in relation to others and to objects, they are increasing their spatial awareness. All these concepts are ingredients of art and movement education—and of bodily/kinesthetic and spatial intelligences.

Making Straight and Round. To explore shape with the youngest children, begin with simple comparisons between straight and round. Show children straight objects (e.g., rulers or the lines on ruled paper) and round objects (e.g., a ball or a globe). Then ask them to create these opposite shapes with their bodies. Later, you can ask them to form bridges and tunnels with their bodies or body parts. Play a mirror game: Face them and create different shapes and challenge them to match each shape, as though they were your mirror reflection.

Making Shapes. When children are developmentally ready, challenge them with an activity like Making Shapes (see Chapter 2), eventually adding more difficult shapes (e.g., pointed, angular, or oval). With older children, explore the possibilities for symmetrical and asymmetrical shapes.

Exploring Line. To focus on the concept of lines, use a jump rope or something similar to demonstrate the differences among vertical, horizontal, diagonal, curved, and crooked lines. Can children use their bodies to replicate the lines you create with the rope?

Shapes and Colors. Shapes and colors can be explored in tandem by providing pictures or examples of objects in various colors (e.g., a yellow banana, a red apple, a green plant) and asking children to demonstrate the shape of each object. An alternative is to mention a color and ask children what it brings to mind. Children can then either take on the shape of the objects mentioned or become them (e.g., if the color green reminded some children of frogs, they could depict the movement of frogs).

Primary Colors. An appropriate activity for early-elementary children is Primary Colors (Pica, 2001, pp. 196–197). For this activity, discuss—or, better still, demonstrate—the primary colors red, yellow, and blue. Children should know that red and yellow combine to make orange; yellow and blue combine to make green; and red and blue create purple.

Divide your class into three groups and assign each group a primary color. Ask the members of each group to pretend to be as many different things in their color that they can think of. (They can perform these examples either individually or with others in the group.)

In the next phase, have one child from each group pair with a child from a different group. Each pair must then depict something in the color they have created with their joining. For example, if a child from the red group and a child from the blue form a pair, they should create something purple. You can ask the pairs to work simultaneously, or you can ask one pair at a time for a solution, which they will demonstrate for the rest of the class for the class to guess.

Exploring Texture. You can even explore the concept of texture through movement by gathering items of various textures (e.g., rope, satin, burlap, feathers, a beach ball, seashells, a stuffed animal, a carpet square) for children to see and feel (Figure 10.2). Talk to them about how each item feels or makes them feel (i.e., feathers might make them feel ticklish). Then ask them to demonstrate their feelings through movement.

FIGURE **10.2** A feather, a seashell, and a stuffed animal all have different textures.

Art and Movement. Of course, the simplest combination of art and movement is to ask children to draw pictures of something they experienced during a movement session. Immediately following the session is best, while the images are still fresh in their minds. Figures 10.3 and 10.4 are examples of drawings from kindergartners and second-graders, respectively, following movement sessions.

FIGURE **10.3** The kindergartners who drew these two pictures especially enjoyed moving to the song "Robots and Astronauts."

FIGURE **10.4** Second-graders created thank-you cards for me after I visited their school for a special movement session on Earth Day. The combined activities integrated physical education, music, science, art, and language arts.

FIGURE **10.4** (Continued)

Incorporating Other Senses. Because these activities involve more than one sense, they are valuable learning experiences for young children. You can incorporate other senses by using books and/or recordings to expand these experiences.

For example, after reading a story to children, ask them to draw something related to the story and to act out or dance about what they drew. (You can extend the experience even further by asking older children to write about what they drew.)

concepts of color and shape. Among them are Hap Palmer's "Colors" from Volume I of *Learning Basic Skills Through Music*. From Volume II of the same recording are "Parade of Colors," "Triangle, Circle, or Square" (also for mathematics), and "One Shape, Three Shapes." Derrie Frost's *Color Me a Rainbow* and Mr. Al's *Mr. Al Sings Colors and Shapes* are both devoted to artistic concepts.

Language Arts

Because the language arts include listening, speaking, reading, and writing, this content area is an intrinsic part of every individual's life. It is about communication—imparted or received. It is tied to linguistic intelligence, which has enormous validation in our society. And it is part of every curriculum, in one form or another, from preschool through advanced education.

naeyc
Standard 5a

In early-childhood programs, language arts traditionally receive the greatest concentration during daily group or circle times. During these periods, teachers and caregivers read stories or poems to children, who sit and listen. Sometimes discussion precedes or follows the reading. In elementary schools, reading and writing have commonly been handled as separate studies, with children focusing on topics like phonics, spelling, and grammar.

Recent approaches to children's emerging literacy have recognized that listening, speaking, reading, and writing overlap and interrelate, each contributing to the growth of the others. These approaches also acknowledge that children best learn those concepts that are relevant to them; therefore, their language acquisition and development must be a natural process that occurs over time and that relates to all aspects of their lives (Raines & Canady, 1990; Sawyer & Sawyer, 1993).

Movement and language both play essential roles in life and are both forms of communication. Rhythm is also an integral part of both language and movement. There is a rhythm to words and sentences, and we develop an internal rhythm when we read and write. Similarly, individuals have personalized rhythms for movement. When a teacher asks children to get into small body shapes, for example, each child responds at his or her own pace—some quickly and some slowly. Moreover, as children acquire and refine their motor skills, they learn subconscious lessons about rhythm. Finally, movement and language are both abstract, consisting as they do of symbols and ideas. The word *quick*, for example, has only so much meaning to a child when she reads it or spells it. However, when she moves quickly, the meaning is definitive in both mind and body (Pica, 2007a).

Movement and language, therefore, are naturally linked. Teachers who adopt an integrated approach to literacy soon realize that movement is a vital tool in the acquisition and development of the language arts.

Mathematics

To many adults, math is the most abstract of the content areas. We may have an aversion to this content area because we failed to do well in subjects like algebra and calculus or on standardized tests (IQ tests or SATs), which

Sample Activities

The possibilities for exploring language arts through movement are inexhaustible. Beginning in infancy, when we label a baby's actions ("You're making your arms go up and down!"), we are making vital connections. Consider the simple act of children forming letters of the alphabet with their bodies or body parts, individually or with a partner. Such an activity leads to greater awareness of the straight and curving lines that make up each letter and the difference between upper- and lowercase letters. It also leads to greater awareness of directionality. Olds (1994) contends that such spatial orientation is necessary for letter identification and the orientation of symbols on a page. She explains that a lowercase *b* and a lowercase *d,* for example, are the same—both composed of a line and a circle. The only difference is in their spatial orientation—that is, which side of the line the circle is on.

Talking about experiences, depicting them through movement, and then discussing the movement contribute to language development by requiring children to make essential connections among their cognitive, affective, and physical domains.

Rhythm. Rhythm is an essential ingredient in words and movement. The rhythmic patterns of poetry, in fact, often make it difficult for young children to just sit and listen (Rowen, 1982). Therefore, when children clap the rhythm of words or rhymes or move to the rhythm of a poem, they are increasing their knowledge of both rhythm and language.

Clapping, stamping, or stepping to the rhythms of words can also familiarize children with syllables.

Fingerplays. Fingerplays are basically poems or wordplays in which movement has a critical function—that is, to make the words more meaningful. Raines and Canady (1990) write, "The complementary rhythms and movements of fingerplays and action songs incorporate language, symbolism, and perception, which help children to remember them" (p. 178). Omitting lines from familiar fingerplays (while still performing the actions) tests children's memories and listening abilities. (See Chapter 11 for more about fingerplays.)

Sound Identification. Any listening or sound identification activity (see suggestions in Chapter 7) helps develop auditory discrimination. Auditory sequential memory can be improved by giving children a sequence of movement instructions to follow. You might, for example, present a challenge to clap twice, blink eyes, and turn around, lengthening the sequence as children are developmentally ready. (Begin by performing the actions as you say the words; as children progress, eliminate the actions.)

Obstacle Courses. Obstacle courses provide recognition of and practice with prepositions. As children move over, under, around, through, beside, and near objects (for example, under the tree branch, through the hoop, over the jump rope), these words take on significance (Pica, 2007a).

(Continued)

Take the children for a listening walk during which they are asked to listen for either manmade or natural sounds.

Acting Out. Acting out fairy tales and nursery rhymes increases children's comprehension and helps them recall the order of events (Rowen, 1982). And it is fun! Nursery rhymes like "Jack and Jill," "Humpty Dumpty," and "Jack Be Nimble" (the last of which also provides practice with jumping) are perfect for dramatization, as are such classic tales as *Jack and the Beanstalk, Henny Penny, Hansel and Gretel, The Three Billy Goats Gruff,* and *Goldilocks and the Three Bears.*

Children's stories like *The Little Engine That Could* and *Rosie's Walk* are among those that also lend themselves to movement. Raines and Canady's (1990) series of Story S-t-r-e-t-c-h-e-r-s books offer hundreds of activities—among them movement and music activities—for "expanding" children's favorite books. Or you can simply ask children to show you their interpretations of the story's characters and action. Rowen (1982) suggests the following criteria for determining whether a story is appropriate for dramatization:

1. The story must have action.
2. There must be changes in feeling.
3. It can have many characters, but only two or three should be involved in the action at the same time.
4. Characters with differing qualities make good dramatization. (p. 43)

Acting out the meaning of individual words from stories, poems, or even spelling lists can also lead to greater understanding.

Understanding Words. Through movement, children can begin to comprehend suffixes and, thus, the distinction between words like *frightened* and *frightening.* They can better grasp the meaning of action words like *slither, stalk, pounce,* and *stomp* or descriptive words like *graceful, smooth,* and *forceful.* Preschool children can work in pairs to demonstrate the meanings of simple opposites like sad and happy or up and down, whereas primary-grade partners can be challenged to demonstrate possibilities like tight versus loose or open versus closed.

Reading-Readiness Activities. Gilbert (2002) suggests reading-readiness activities involving movements that go from left to right, such as turning the head slowly and quickly or drawing a line on the floor with a leg.

Adding Music. Music can also become a component in an integrated language arts approach. Songs like "Eensy Weensy Spider" and "Where Is Thumbkin?" can sometimes be substituted for nonmusical fingerplays. Familiarize children with the lyrics of songs by introducing the lyrics without music first—as though they were poems. As you say the words, ask children to depict the actions suggested by the lyrics or the meaning of individual words. Also available are song picture books—illustrated versions of children's songs—some with the music notation and some with a recording. (Two examples are Merle Peek's *Roll Over: A Counting Song* and *The Cat Came Back: A Traditional Song,* illustrated by Bill Slavin.)

Musical Storytelling. Isenberg and Jalongo (2002) recommend musical storytelling—for example, using a slide whistle to represent Jack's ascent and descent of the beanstalk and drums of different sizes to depict Jack's and the giant's footsteps. When children are developmentally ready, challenge them to use rhythm sticks or other instruments to mark the rhythms of words, rhymes, or poems. Children should also be encouraged to invent new lyrics to familiar melodies—with or without your help, depending on their level of development.

Songs and Albums. Songs and albums are also available that emphasize the language arts. Hap Palmer's *Ideas, Thoughts, and Feelings* includes "Letter Sounds (A–M) and (N–Z)," and Volume I of Palmer's *Learning Basic Skills Through Music* contains "Marching Around the Alphabet." Palmer also has an album called *Classic Nursery Rhymes,* and Rosemary Hallum and Henry "Buzz" Glass offer *Children's All-Time Mother Goose Favorites,* both of which are available from Educational Activities. Available from Kimbo are *Alphabet Jam, Alphabet Animal Songs,* and *Singable Nursery Rhymes.*

© Cengage Learning 2013.

BAM! radio

PODCAST: *Go to www. bamradionetwork.com and search for the podcast "What Is Developmentally Appropriate Math for Very Young Children?".*

- *What is Juanita Copley's definition of "more math?"*
- *What concepts fall under the content area of math in early childhood?*
- *Why should math not be taught using worksheets?*

concentrate heavily on areas related to logical/mathematical intelligence (Armstrong, 2009; Gardner, 1993). Or we may consider balancing a checkbook or staying within a budget complicated processes.

But children do not view math the same way we do. For them, it is not abstract. As Essa (2010) explains, "The foundations of math are grounded in concrete experience such as the exploration of objects and gradual understanding of their properties and relationships. The cognitive concepts … of classification, seriation (ordering), numbers, time, and space all contribute to the gradual acquisition of math concepts."

Thus, children are acquiring mathematical knowledge (Essa, 2010; Mayesky, 2008) when they sort, stack, and compare manipulatives; play with sand and water; measure or set the table in the housekeeping center; or learn nursery rhymes and stories such as "The Three Little Kittens" and *Goldilocks and the Three Bears*.

Quantitative ideas are also part of the language of mathematics. Mayesky (2008) recommends that the following words be incorporated into children's daily routines:

big and little	pair	highest
few	wide and narrow	most
bunch	together	middle
long and short	many	lowest
tall and short	late and early	twice
group	same length	once
high and low	more	longer than
light and heavy	first and last	

Obviously, physically experiencing these words can help children attach meaning to them, as well as to numerals and other mathematical concepts. This will make math a concrete, rather than an abstract, subject.

The mathematical concepts appropriate for exploration with young children include quantitative ideas, number awareness and recognition, counting, basic geometry, and simple addition and subtraction.

When children sort, stack, and compare manipulatives, they are acquiring mathematical knowledge.

© Cengage Learning 2013.

Sample Activities

With one look at the list of quantitative words, it is easy to see that movement is an ideal, tangible means of conveying most of these ideas to children.

Quantitative Concepts. Activities involving levels and body shapes can demonstrate the concepts of big and little, long and short, high and low, wide and narrow, tall and short, highest and lowest, and even same length and longer than. The movement element of force is about light and heavy. Children can form pairs and groups, or a few children can work together. Throughout the movement activities, teachers can pose questions and challenges: "Which body part has the *most* possibilities?" "*How many* ways can you find to …?" "Show me you can do it *twice*." "Repeat the action *once more*."

The poem "Giants and Elves" (Pica, 2000a) is an example of quantitative concepts in action:

See the giants, great and tall
Hear them bellow, hear them call
Life looks different from up so high
With head and shoulders clear to the sky
And at their feet they can barely see
The little people so very tiny
Who scurry about with hardly a care
Avoiding enormous feet placed here and there
But together they dwell, the giants and elves
In peace and harmony, amongst themselves.

Positional Concepts. Positional concepts can be demonstrated by asking the first or last child in line to perform an action. You can ask children to stand in front of or behind a person or object or between or in the middle of others. Props and obstacle courses are excellent for demonstrating such positional concepts as over, under, around, and through.

Blast Off! To develop number awareness and recognition, children must hear the numerals often. The simple activity Blast Off! is appropriate for even the youngest children and can help them advance from rote memorization of numbers to actual comprehension. With this activity, children squat low, pretending to be spaceships on their launching pads as you count backward from 10 (with as much drama as you can muster). When you say, "Blast off!" children "launch" themselves upward.

Forming Number Shapes. Children can form the shapes of numbers with their bodies or body parts. To begin, assign numbers that they must replicate, challenging them to try it at varying levels (i.e., standing, kneeling, sitting, lying). When children are developmentally ready, ask them to choose numbers—say, between 0 and 4 or between 5 and 9. Ask them to form the shapes of numbers with jump ropes and to trace those shapes with locomotor skills. Challenge them to show you their ages with their bodies, to form numbers in

pairs or trios, or to draw invisible numbers in the air or on the floor with different body parts. Can their classmates guess the numbers drawn?

Movement activities can help children attach meaning to quantitative concepts. The child in this photo is demonstrating high, long, and tall, while the child in the lower photo displays an example of low, long, and wide.

Counting and Movement. Although an activity like Blast Off! can begin to familiarize children with counting backward, the process will have little meaning for them until they fully understand how to count forward. Help them develop this understanding by counting beats clapped (e.g., clapping and counting 1–2–3 and asking them to echo), steps taken (giving the class a number and asking children to take that many steps or hop that many hops), or repetitions performed (asking children to repeat a movement two more times).

Other possibilities include asking children to place a certain number of body parts on the floor or to balance on so many parts. Challenge them to count the number of times they are able to bounce a ball, the number of seconds they can hold a static balance, or the number of ways they can find to move the head, for example. With all these activities, you can instantly ascertain which children are having trouble counting.

This chapter has already discussed shape as part of the subject of art, but shape is also a component of math—especially geometry (Figure 10.5). Simple geometry includes straight, curved, vertical, horizontal, crossed, and diagonal lines, as well as circles, squares, triangles, and rectangles (Werner & Burton, 1979).

FIGURE 10.5 Simple geometry includes vertical, horizontal, diagonal, curved, and crooked lines. Children can be challenged to replicate these lines with their bodies and body parts.

contains foam wedges, cubes, balls, crawl-through boards with geometric shapes cut out, or geometrically shaped beanbags to throw through geometrically shaped holes in target boards, they will begin to attach meaning to such words as *circle, square, triangle,* and *rectangle.*

More Geometry. Children can form lines, curves, points, and angles with the body or body parts and later advance to forming geometric shapes—alone or with others—at various levels in space. They can move in straight, curving, zigzag, and diagonal lines and advance to moving in circular, square, rectangular, and triangular patterns on the floor.

Geometric Shapes. You can begin acquainting children with geometric shapes by giving them blocks, puzzles, and other manipulative materials. If the children's environment

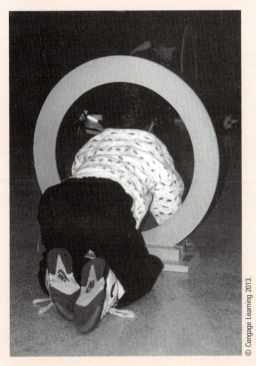

By creeping through geometric cutouts, children begin to attach meaning to such words as circle and rectangle.

FIGURE 10.6 The arms can be used to help children remember the difference between plus and minus signs.

(Continued)

Adding and Subtracting. Computation is much less abstract when human bodies are used for addition and subtraction. Fingers and toes have always been the perfect tools for adding and subtracting, but whole bodies can also be used. Acting out the song "Roll Over" ("There were 10 in the bed, and the little one said …") makes subtraction very clear—and lots of fun. (Merle Peek illustrated this song in the book *Roll Over: A Counting Song*.) By asking one child to stand at the front of the room and then adding (then later subtracting) one child at a time, you can help children learn both processes. Similarly, when three bodies are lying on the floor and one rolls away, it is quite easy to see three minus one leaves two.

Plus and Minus Signs. Cambigue (1981) suggests using the arms as a means of helping children understand the plus and minus signs (Figure 10.6). When the children form a plus sign with their arms, you should point out they are putting two things together; and whenever they see this sign, they should remember to put the things or numbers together (addition). Then ask them to take away the vertical arm and put it behind the back. This leaves the horizontal arm demonstrating the minus sign, which should remind them they must always take something away from something else when they see this sign (subtraction).

Adding Literature and Music

Children's books that emphasize early mathematics and can serve as jumping-off points for movement activities include Molly Bang's *Ten, Nine, Eight* (counting backward from 10); Laurent de Brunhoff's *Babar's Counting Book*; Susanna Gretz's *Teddy Bears One to Ten*; Tana Hoban's *1, 2, 3*; Lois Ehlert's *Fish Eyes*; and Scholastic's *My First Look at Sorting*.

As with art and the language arts, you can purchase musical selections to help make mathematics more concrete and enjoyable for children. Among these selections are the shape songs mentioned under "Art," as well as "The Number March" from Volume I of Hap Palmer's *Learning Basic Skills Through Music* and "Lucky Numbers" from Volume II. He also has three albums dedicated to mathematics: *Math Readiness: Vocabulary and Concepts*; *Math Readiness: Addition and Subtraction*; and *Singing Multiplication Tables*, all available from Educational Activities. Alan Stern's *Sing a Sum … or a Remainder*, for first and second grades, is also available from Educational Activities. Melody House offers an album called *Number Fun*.

Science

The word *science* reminds us of such topics as chemistry, physics, biology, botany, and astronomy. We can imagine men and women in lab coats, poring over facts and figures or measuring strange concoctions into test tubes and beakers. Because none of this is relevant in the lives of young children, you might wonder—rightly—how science fits into the early-childhood curriculum. Science, however, is also about exploration, investigation, problem solving, and discovery—all of which are relevant for young children. A child's whole life, from its very beginning, is exploring, investigating, solving problems, and discovering!

Standard 5a

The principal difference between these two views of science is that much of the former deals with the theoretical and the abstract, while the latter, as far as young children are concerned, deals with the concrete and the tangible—with what can be easily observed. For example, children discover what objects will float or sink by actually placing objects in water. They discover a different kind of floating by blowing bubbles through a wand and watching them drift through the air. Balls, however, will not float when sent into the air; this is due to gravity, a concept the children may not grasp but one they can witness firsthand. In other words, science for young children is learning by doing—just as movement is.

Naturally, this text cannot begin to cover the endless possibilities for exploring science themes through movement. For a multitude of ideas and activities, you should refer to the many excellent resources cited at the end of the chapter. Remember, too, that almost every theme and movement activity has corresponding music; it is just a matter of looking for it.

BAM! radio

PODCAST: Go to www. bamradionetwork.com and search for the podcast "Teaching Physics in Early Childhood".

- *What does physics "look like" in early childhood education?*
- *What is the connection between play and the exploration of physics concepts?*

Sample Activities

Many themes typically explored in classrooms and child care centers fall under the science category, including such themes as the human body (body parts and their functions, the senses, hygiene, and nutrition), seasons, and other topics related to nature, including weather, animals, plants, and the ocean.

Body-Part Identification. Body-part identification, with activities like Simon Says and Head, Shoulders, Knees, and Toes, is where the connection between movement and science begins for young children. You can even address body-part identification with infants by labeling each body part as you touch it ("We're going to put your shoe on your foot now") and playing such games as "This Little Piggy" and I've Got Your Nose.

Functions of the Human Body. Of course, every time children perform movements—locomotor, nonlocomotor, manipulative, gymnastic, and dance—they are learning something about the functions of the human body. However, you can be more specific simply by focusing on certain functions. You can ask children to concentrate on the muscles, for example, by suggesting that they think about the amount of muscle tension used to perform a movement or the shape of the muscles when they freeze in different positions.

Relaxation Exercises. Relaxation exercises that require children to contract and relax muscles are also excellent for developing an awareness of these important body parts. Similarly, relaxation exercises focusing on the breath can create an awareness of the lungs.

Function of the Heart. You can introduce the function of the heart by asking children to find their pulse at rest and after strenuous activity. Can they match their pulse's rhythm with the tapping of a hand or foot?

Exploring the Senses. Listening activities focus on the sense of hearing. Asking children to try various nonlocomotor movements with their eyes closed draws attention to the sense of sight. The texture activity suggested under "Art" can be used to concentrate on the sense of touch. Taste and smell, which are also part of a nutrition unit, can be explored by challenging children to demonstrate with faces or bodies how various flavors and odors make them feel.

Exploring Nutrition. Nutrition can be further explored by challenging children to take on the shapes of various fruits and vegetables. You can also ask them to show you the difference between, say, an apple hanging from a tree and applesauce simmering on the stove (especially if the class has visited an orchard and then made applesauce). Cathy Slonecki's album *Eat Well! Feel Well!* (available from Educational Activities) is

dedicated to nutrition and includes such songs as "The Vegetable Rock" and "I Am What I Eat."

Every time children move, they are learning something about the functions of the human body. Here they are also learning about shadows.

© Cengage Learning 2013.

Exploring Hygiene. Even hygiene can be less abstract and more fun by exploring it through movement and music. Children can pretend to perform many hygienic activities—brushing teeth, washing hair, bathing, and caring for clothes. Nursery rhymes like "Rub-a-Dub-Dub, Three Men in a Tub" can also lead in to such activities. A number of musical selections can also accompany your explorations, including "Take a Bath," "Cover Your Mouth," "Keep the Germs Away," and "Brush Away" from Volume II of Hap Palmer's

(Continued)

Learning Basic Skills Through Music. Joe Scruggs offers "Even Dragons Brush Their Teeth" on his album *Even Trolls Have Moms;* Raffi sings "Brush Your Teeth" on *Singable Songs for the Very Young* and "Bathtime" on *Everything Grows;* and "The Wash Song" can be found in Rae Pica's (2000b) *Moving & Learning Series: Toddlers.*

Moving Like Animals. Animals are tremendously appealing—and therefore relevant—to young children. Moving like different animals can contribute not only to knowledge about the animals but also to the development of empathy and proficiency with various movement skills and elements. It is not enough, however, to merely ask children to pretend to be different animals. You must also create a greater awareness by discussing pertinent characteristics of the animals they are to portray. Cats, for example, can move very slowly and

quietly. What is it about the way cats use their muscles and paws that makes this possible? What is it about their spines that makes them able to twist, stretch, and arch so easily?

Numerous possibilities for exploring the study of animals with music are available. Educational Activities offers *Animal Antics;* Kimbo, *Animal Walks* and *Walk Like the Animals;* and Derrie Frost presents *A Zippity Zoo Day,* available from Melody House.

The Environment. Virtually every aspect of nature can be explored in innumerable ways through movement and music. You can even promote an early and much-needed awareness of the environment by asking children to portray insects, ocean creatures, plants, weather conditions, and more.

Exploring Scientific Concepts

Specific scientific concepts appropriate for exploration with early-elementary children include flotation, gravity, balance and stability, action and reaction, magnetics, machinery, and electricity. Balance and stability, gravity, and even flotation, in particular, are naturals for exploring through movement. For example, children can watch bubbles, feathers, and chiffon scarves drift through the air and then attempt to simulate the movement. Does floating require light or strong movement? Little or much muscle tension?

naeyc
Standard 5a

Is it possible for human beings to really float in air? No—because of gravity. When we jump, hop, or leap in the air, the force of gravity pulls us back down, just as it pulls down any object (e.g., a beanbag or ball) we toss in the air. But the higher we toss the object, the longer it takes to reach the ground. Challenge children to discover how many times they can clap or turn around before the beanbag or ball returns to their hands or to the ground.

Gravity is also a factor when we attempt to balance. Challenge children to balance on their knees or seat, lean in any direction as far as they can before falling over, and then return to their original positions. This is called balance and recovery. Now ask them to lean again, this time going beyond the point of recovery. What happens? Gravity causes them to fall over. You can also help children discover that balance is easier when the body's center of gravity is lowered and there is a large, rather than a narrow, base of support.

Weightlessness (lack of gravity) is a concept you cannot actually explore, but it is one children love to imagine. Children are fascinated by outer space—a topic that "addresses the child's innate sense of wonder at the universe … [and] promotes a better understanding of our own planet" (Weimer, 1999). Weimer, at the encouragement of NASA, created *Space Songs for Children,* a cassette with 12 songs written from a child's perspective, with an accompanying 104-page book with lyrics and suggestions for related activities to extend the ideas in each song. The project was created for children ages 3 to 8.

Other scientific concepts may be less-obvious candidates for movement exploration, but that does not mean movement cannot be used—or that movement cannot make these ideas less abstract. For example, children are familiar with most, if not all, of the six simple machines: lever, wheel, pulley, inclined plane, screw, and wedge (Gilbert, 2002). They can roll like wheels and twist like screwdrivers, and they may have had experience with inclined planes and wedges meant specifically for movement. Levers with which children are familiar—and which they can imitate—include scissors, wheelbarrows, and seesaws.

A lesson in gravity.

© Cengage Learning 2013.

Children can also depict the movement of such household machines as washing machines, dryers, vacuum cleaners, dishwashers, and blenders. An activity called The Machine not only can begin to develop their understanding of machinery but is also an excellent exercise in cooperation. In this activity, one child begins by repeatedly performing a movement that can be executed in one spot. A second child then stands near the first and contributes a second movement that relates in some way to the first. For example, if the first child is performing an up–down motion by bending and stretching, the second child might choose to do the reverse, standing beside his or her classmate. A third child might choose an arm or leg motion timed to move between the two bodies bending and stretching. As these movements continue, each remaining student adds a functioning part to the machine. They may choose any movements, as long as they do not interfere with the actions of others and they contribute in some way to the machine. Once all the parts are functioning, you can ask each child to make a corresponding sound.

All the aforementioned household machines require electricity to operate. What other machines or appliances can children think of—and show you—that use electricity? You can also introduce the idea of electricity being conducted by asking children to hold hands in a line or a circle and pretend electricity is flowing from one body to the next.

Rowen (1982) suggests that children discover action and reaction (every action force has an equal and opposite reaction force) by sitting on the floor in pairs with legs straddled, feet touching, and hands held. As one child pushes forward, the other pulls back—and then the reverse. (Remind children to move slowly for this activity to avoid hurting one another.)

Magnets are always fascinating for children. Once you have demonstrated that opposite poles attract (stick together) and identical poles repel, have the children pretend to be magnets. Ask them to move around the room as though they were magnets with only north or south poles. What happens when two such magnets (children) approach each other? Then assign half of the class to act as north poles and the other half as south poles (or ask them to decide themselves which they would like to be). The "north poles" should point a finger or hand toward the ceiling, as the "south poles" point toward the floor. Now what happens when two magnets get close to each other? (If two identical poles meet, they repel; if opposite poles meet, they stick together.)

To add a literature component to science/movement activities, you can choose from a great many children's books focusing on early science concepts.

In addition to the seemingly endless number of books about animals and seasons, many science series are available. Among them are Scholastic's First Discovery Books, which include *Weather* and *The Ladybug and Other Insects,* and David Evans and Claudette Williams's Let's Explore Science series, *Make It Balance, Make It Go, Make It Change,* and *Me and My Body.* And do not forget Eric Carle's *The Very Hungry Caterpillar, The Very Busy Spider,* and *The Tiny Seed.*

This is only a small sample of the possibilities for exploring science concepts. Any teacher with a little imagination and a strong desire to educate the whole child can devise countless others.

Social Studies

Lessons in social studies for young children begin with the children themselves, because that is where their world begins. Self-concept, therefore, is a logical starting point in the early-childhood social studies curriculum. The child's world then extends to family, friends, neighborhood, and the community in general (Mayesky, 2008; Raines & Canady, 1990).

Standard 5a

As children learn about themselves and about each other, they discover how they are alike and different. They explore feelings, rules for living (particularly with regard to safety), holidays and celebrations, traditions and cultures, and the jobs that keep a community functioning. In early-childhood settings, these topics usually fall under the themes of self-awareness, families and friends, holidays and celebrations, occupations, transportation, and multicultural education/diversity.

These children are demonstrating what their bodies look like when they are feeling cold.

© Cengage Learning 2013.

Ask children to demonstrate various emotions with faces or hands alone before challenging them to show you with the whole body. This preschooler is displaying his best "angry" face.

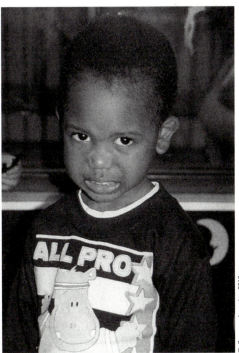

© Cengage Learning 2013.

Under "Science," we considered how movement develops an understanding of the body and its parts, functions, senses, and care. Obviously, movement contributes greatly to self-awareness. In addition, a positive self-concept is promoted through the successful experiences that movement education offers. In Chapter 1, we looked at some ways social development, in general, is enhanced through movement. Based on the information in Chapters 1 and 9 alone, we can easily argue that every movement activity is an exercise in social studies. However, the following section will offer specific recommendations for exploring topics that typically come under the heading of social studies with young children.

Self-Concept

Emotion is one aspect of self-awareness that fits better under social studies than under science. If a young child is to have a positive self-concept, she needs to accept her feelings as a part of herself to later gain greater understanding of them. She must also learn that others have feelings, too.

Activities in which children pretend to walk as though sad, mad, proud, scared, tired, or happy are a good place to start because they give children permission to express themselves. Children can also show you with their hands or faces alone how these emotions look (see "A Face Has Many Roles in Life" in Chapter 2).

Songs like "If You're Happy" can get children thinking about their feelings, especially if you add other emotions to the lyrics. Some children's albums dedicated to self-concept are *Mr. Al Sings Friends and Feelings* and Hap Palmer's *Getting to Know Myself* and *Ideas, Thoughts, and Feelings*. Children's books related to self-concept include Nancy Carlson's *I Like Me*, Marissa Moss's *Regina's Big Mistake*, Norma Simon's *I Was So Mad!*, and Aliki's *Feelings*.

Families and Friends

The concepts of families and friends are explored in such children's books as James Marshall's *George and Martha One Fine Day*; Jackie Carter's *Knock, Knock*; Harriet Hains's *My Baby Brother*; Anne and Harlow Rockwell's *When*

ABOUT CELEBRATIONS

Because I'm always looking for a reason to celebrate (and because children love a celebration, too), it has saddened me to see so many early-childhood programs eliminating holiday celebrations. That's why I was thrilled to find *Celebrate! An Anti-Bias Guide to Enjoying Holidays in Early Childhood Programs*. This book, written by Julie Bisson and published by Redleaf Press in 2002, guides teachers through the sensitive issues concerning holidays and offers plenty of strategies for implementing holiday activities that are both developmentally and culturally appropriate.

I Go Visiting; and many more. Tonja Evetts Weimer's two-volume set *Fingerplays* and *Action Chants* comes with accompanying cassettes, the second volume of which is *Family and Friends*. All these materials can be lead-ins to activities in which children demonstrate what it means to have a younger or older sibling, pretend to be a parent or grandparent, or depict some things they do with family and friends.

Holidays and Celebrations

Possibilities abound for exploring holidays and celebrations through movement, music, and literature. Catherine Stock's *Christmas Time*, Jeanne Titherington's *Pumpkin Pumpkin* (also science), Thacher Hurd's *Little Mouse's Big Valentine*, and Jean Marzollo's *In 1492* are just a tiny sample of the variety of children's books about holidays and celebrations. Musical selections include Steve and Greg's *Holidays and Special Times*, Jill Gallina's *Holiday Songs for All Occasions*, Tickle Tune Typhoon's *Keep the Spirit*, and Hap Palmer's *Holiday Songs and Rhythms* and *Holiday Magic*.

Holidays offer a multitude of images that inspire movement. Children can move like black cats and ghosts at Halloween, turkeys at Thanksgiving, flickering flames and melting candles at Hanukah, elves and reindeer at Christmas, and on and on. For specific ideas, refer to Pica (2001, 2007), Wnek (1992, 2006), and thematically organized curriculum resources that include movement.

Occupations and Transportation

Field trips, in conjunction with books like Rachel Field's *General Store* and Margret Rey and H. A. Rey's *Curious George at the Fire Station*, are perfect for stimulating movement experiences related to occupations. Children can impersonate everyone and everything they have seen and heard. You can also inspire discussion and movement experiences about lesser-known occupations. Or ask early-elementary children to demonstrate three actions performed by someone in the occupation of their choice, with the rest of the class challenged to guess the occupation.

Naturally, because transportation is specifically about movement, there is no lack of ideas for matching these two fields. (Several activities related to transportation can be found in Chapter 11.) To make problem solving part of your exercises, ask children to think of and depict modes of transportation found mainly in cities, on water, and in the sky, or ones that work without motors. To add a literature component to the activities, incorporate books like Donald Crews's *Flying* and *Freight Train*, Helen Oxenbury's *The Car Trip*, and Diane Siebert's *Truck Song*.

Under transportation, you may also want to deal with traffic safety. *Safe Not Sorry* is an album from Melody House that deals with safety, including traffic. Volume III of Hap Palmer's *Learning Basic Skills Through Music* has a song called "Buckle Your Seat Belt." You can also introduce children to traffic lights by playing a movement game with three sheets of paper—one red, one yellow, and one green. When you hold up the green sheet, children walk. They walk in place when they see the yellow sheet and come to a complete stop when you hold up the red.

Multicultural Education/Diversity

As mentioned in Chapter 2, using the music and learning the dances of other cultures and countries can aid in multicultural education, but only if the activities are accompanied by discussion and related learning experiences. A good first step is inviting family members of children representing various cultures to visit the classroom and share something of their heritage—particularly as it relates to movement and music.

Introduce children to instruments of different cultures. What sounds do these instruments make? What images do the sounds create in the children's minds? How do the instruments inspire children to move?

What games, songs, dances, and other physical activities do children of different cultures participate in? What cultures are represented in the families of the children in your group or in your community? By incorporating ethnic foods, language phrases, and other cultural experiences (both contemporary and traditional) into your studies—and creating movement experiences related to them—you can integrate social studies, language arts, science, and physical education.

Use books like Marie Hall Ets's *Gilberto and the Wind*, Phil Mendez's *The Black Snowman*, Verna Aardema's *Bringing the Rain to Kapiti Plain,* and Tomie dePaola's *The Legend of the Indian Paintbrush* to stimulate discussion and movement activities. Children's recordings of multicultural music include Georgiana Stewart's *Children of the World: Multicultural Rhythmic Activities,* available from Kimbo; Cathy Slonecki's *Children's Songs around the World,* available from Educational Activities; Putumayo's *World Playground: A Musical Adventure for Kids;* and Ella Jenkins's *Multicultural Children's Songs. Let's Make Music: An Interactive Musical Trip around the World,* by Jessica Baron Turner, is a book/audio package that lets children sing and play songs from around the world by making their own musical instruments (instructions are included). Remember that you can also find collections of folk songs at your local public library. These may not specifically be intended for children, but they are still perfectly suitable for listening and moving.

Sources for multicultural children's games include:

- *Children's Games from Around the World* by Glenn Kirchner
- *Multicultural Games* by Lorraine Barbarash
- *Play with Us: 100 Games from Around the World* by Oriol Ripoll
- International Games: Building Skills Through Multicultural Play by Gayle Horowitz

Putting It All Together

Throughout Chapter 10, suggestions have been made as to how you can use movement, music, and literature to explore the major content areas of art, language arts, mathematics, science, and social studies. These suggestions have specifically linked the content area under discussion with the three content areas of physical education (movement), music, and language arts (literature). However, there is no need to stop there if you want a truly integrated, cross-curricular program.

An example of how one topic can be studied through experiences covering all seven content areas follows. We will use a nutrition theme, which falls under the general heading of science. If nutrition were the weekly, monthly, or quarterly unit, it would be logical to spend some time studying breads.

Scientific explorations concerning bread would, of course, depend on the developmental stage of the children. However, an explanation that breads and grains are one of the food groups would be appropriate for all stages. The basic ingredients of bread should be discussed, as well as the various kinds of bread and their common elements. An excursion to a local bakery would be an appropriate and enlightening field trip. Naturally, at some point, the class would make some bread—and sorting and measuring the ingredients would fall under the content area of mathematics.

Ann Morris's *Bread, Bread, Bread,* with photos by Ken Heyman, adds literature, art, and multicultural (social studies) components to this hypothetical study. Published by Scholastic and suitable for children ages 3 to 8, this book contains photographs of people throughout the world eating different breads. The index identifies the countries and breads shown in the photographs. Because bread is something every child is familiar with, this multicultural aspect of nutrition is relevant to them. Children can then talk or write about the bread their families eat (language arts) and draw pictures of their favorite bread (art).

You could choose a familiar melody and create new lyrics about, for example, kneading bread to add a musical component (also language arts). Or you could select from the surprising number of bread-related songs on children's recordings. Possibilities include the following, which are available from the Educational Record Center:

- "Biscuits in the Oven" on Raffi's *Baby Beluga*
- "Peanut Butter Sandwich" on Raffi's *Singable Songs for the Very Young*

Sample Activities

Baking Bread. Tell children you are going to be the baker and they are going to be the ingredients. When you are through with them, they are going to be loaves of bread all ready to eat.

Use the appropriate hand and arm movements for each step of the process as you pretend to do to the children the steps listed. They, in turn, will pretend to have the following done to them. The process is as follows:

1. Stir the flour and water and yeast together.
2. Knead the dough.
3. Cover the dough with a cloth and let it rise.
4. Punch down the dough.
5. Roll out the dough.
6. Shape the dough into a loaf.
7. Let the dough rise again.
8. Bake the dough; it rises even more and becomes firm.
9. Remove the bread from the pan.
10. Slice the bread and eat it!

All That Dough. As an alternative activity, ask children to take on the shapes of other types of dough, including the following:

pretzel
gingerbread man
muffin
round loaf

- "The Muffin Man" on Steve & Greg's *We All Live Together #2* and Sharon, Lois, & Bram's *Singing 'n Swinging*
- "Pizza" on Rosenshontz's *Family Vacation*
- "Animal Crackers" on Ann Murray's *There's a Hippo in My Tub*

Of course, our study would be incomplete if we failed to incorporate movement (physical education) into the "recipe." Bread making can become much more understandable—and memorable—to children if they themselves depict the ingredients and then the bread itself. Following is an activity adapted from Pica (2001, p. 32).

Background Information

Where does bread come from? The supermarket of course—although some "enlightened" children might say the bakery. But back in the "olden days," children knew where bread really came from: Their mothers made it from flour and water and yeast, and it filled the house with a most wonderful aroma.

Talk to children about this basic food, explaining that it does not originate on the grocer's shelves. Describe the process of mixing flour and water and yeast into dough, kneading the dough, letting it rise, rolling it out with a rolling pin, shaping it to fit a bread pan, and baking it.

In Summary

There you have it: one topic explored through experiences covering all seven major content areas. And this is just one possibility. In the words of Susan Griss (1994):

> Children exposed to creative movement as a language for learning are becoming more aware of their own natural resources. They are expanding their concepts of

INTEGRATION IS EASY

Integrating content areas is easier than you might imagine. Take for example, a simple activity like Ducks, Cows, Cats, and Dogs, adapted from Docheff (1992).

This activity, which is fun for groups of all ages, requires children to close their eyes. Once all eyes are closed, the teacher whispers the name of an animal in each player's ear. For the youngest children, the animals should be limited to two or three of those cited in the title of the game, because their sounds are most familiar to young children. To make the activity more challenging for older children, use all four animals. If the group is large enough, add other animals that have familiar sounds, such as pigs, chickens, donkeys, or birds.

When each child has been assigned an animal, he or she gets on hands and knees and, at the teacher's start signal, begins to move, making the sound of his or her animal. The object of the game is for like animals to find one another. When they have done so, they stop making their sounds and sit and watch the others who are still trying. (Once the teacher sees that all the dogs, for example, have found each other, he can let that group know they have succeeded in their goal.)

Obviously, this exercise provides experience with the locomotor skill of creeping, making it a physical education activity. However, because it is also a listening—or sound discrimination—activity, it falls under the headings of music and language arts; by requiring cooperation, it is also in the category of social studies. Because the topic of animals and the sense of hearing are emphasized, the content area of science is involved. Children can even be asked to count the number of animals in each group, making it a mathematics experience as well. To put a finishing touch on the experience, invite children to draw their animals.

creativity and of how they can use their own bodies. They are learning through their own creations. The combination of discipline and imagination is an invaluable foundation for creative thinking. Encouraging children to work both alone and with others, to give and to take, to evaluate and to edit, to feel and to think, proves to be empowering to students, and ultimately, therefore, to teachers. (p. 80)

ASSIGNMENTS

1. Based on the information in this chapter, write a rationale of why movement, when used as a teaching tool, can promote a more positive attitude toward learning.
2. Find at least four poems and/or stories not cited in this chapter that lend themselves to movement experiences. Write brief descriptions of the movement activities that could accompany the literature.
3. List action and/or descriptive words that movement can help young children better comprehend.
4. Provide at least one additional example of how movement can help children better understand quantitative ideas.
5. Find five songs or albums not cited in this chapter appropriate for use in studying aspects of art, language arts, math, science, and social studies.
6. Choose a topic (like the nutrition/bread example) and describe experiences that cover the seven major content areas.

FIELD OBSERVATION

1. Create at least one movement activity for each of the five content areas covered in this chapter. Test them on a group of children. Did you see evidence that they aided comprehension?

REFERENCES

Armstrong, T. (2000). *Seven kinds of smart*. New York: Penguin.

Armstrong, T. (2009). *Multiple intelligences in the classroom*. Alexandria, VA: Association for Supervision and Curriculum Development.

Cambigue, S. (1981). *Learning through dance/movement*. Los Angeles: Performing Tree.

Docheff, D. M. (1992). *Hey, let's play! A collection of P. E. games and activities for the classroom teacher*. Elma, WA: Dodge R Productions.

Essa, E. (2011). *Introduction to early childhood education*. Belmont, CA: Cengage Learning.

Fox, J. E., & Schirrmacher, R. (2011). *Art and creative development for young children*. Belmont, CA: Cengage Learning.

Gardner, H. (1993). *Frames of mind: The theory of multiple intelligences*. New York: Basic Books.

Gilbert, A. G. (2002). *Teaching the three Rs through movement experiences*. Reston, VA: National Dance Association.

Griss, S. (1994). Creative movement: A language for learning. *Educational Leadership, 51*, 78–80.

Hendricks, G., & Hendricks, K. (1983). *The moving center: Exploring movement activities for the classroom*. Englewood Cliffs, NJ: Prentice Hall.

Isenberg, J. P., & Jalongo, M. R. (2002). *Creative expression and play in the early childhood curriculum*. New York: Merrill.

Mayesky, M. (2008). *Creative activities for young children*. Belmont, CA: Cengage Learning.

Olds, A. R. (1994). From cartwheels to caterpillars: Children's need to move indoors and out. *Child Care Exchange*, 32–36.

Pica, R. (2000a). *Moving & learning series: Preschoolers & kindergartners*. Belmont, CA: Cengage Learning.

Pica, R. (2000b). *Moving & learning series: Toddlers*. Belmont, CA: Cengage Learning.

Pica, R. (2001). *Wiggle, giggle & shake: 200 ways to move & learn*. Silver Spring, MD: Gryphon House.

Pica, R. (2007a). *Jump into literacy: Active learning for preschool children*. Silver Spring, MD: Gryphon House.

Pica, R. (2007b). *Moving & learning across the curriculum*. Belmont, CA: Cengage Learning.

Raines, S. C., & Canady, R. J. (1990). *The whole language kindergarten*. New York: Teachers College.

Rowen, B. (1982). *Learning through movement*. New York: Teachers College.

Sawyer, W. E., & Sawyer, J. C. (1993). *Integrated language arts for emerging literacy*. Clifton Park, NY: Delmar Learning.

Weimer, T. E. (1999). *Space songs for children*. Pittsburgh: Pearce-Evetts.

Werner, P. H., & Burton, E. C. (1979). *Learning through movement*. St. Louis, MO: Mosby.

Wnek, B. (1992). *Holiday games and activities*. Champaign, IL: Human Kinetics.

Wnek, B. (2006). *Celebration games*. Champaign, IL: Human Kinetics.

RELEVANT WEBSITES

For children's literature:

The Children's Literature Web Guide:
www.ucalgary.ca/~dKbrown/

Children's Literature Comprehensive Database:
www.childrenslit.com

Database of Award-Winning Children's Literature
www.dawcl.com

KEY TERMS & DEFINITIONS

whole child The concept of children as thinking, feeling, moving human beings who learn through all their senses.

kinesthetic mode A way of learning that involves physically experiencing concepts.

bodily/kinesthetic intelligence Strongest in individuals who are able to solve problems or create with their bodies or body parts.

content area A subject or discipline that is part of the curriculum—typically art, language arts, mathematics, music, physical education, science, and social studies.

integrated approach to literacy Recognition that listening, speaking, reading, and writing overlap and interrelate, each contributing to the growth of the others.

fingerplay Poem or wordplay in which movement has a critical function. Originally used only the hands and fingers to teach concepts but now sometimes employs the whole body.

quantitative idea Mathematical concepts related to size, quantity, or relationships that should be part of children's daily lives.

© Cengage Learning 2013.

Using Movement and Music for Transitions

Learning Objectives

After completing this chapter, the student will be able to:

1 Describe how movement and music can be used upon the children's arrival and create appropriate activities for this transition.

2 Describe how movement and music can be used for transitions within the classroom and create appropriate activities.

3 Describe how movement and music can be used for transitions to outside the classroom and create appropriate activities.

4 Describe how movement and music can be used for cleanup and create appropriate activities for this transition.

5 Describe how movement and music can be used for nap time and create appropriate activities for this transition.

6 Describe how movement and music can be used for the children's departure and create appropriate activities for this transition.

TERMS TO KNOW

transitions

creativity question

closure

Although usually not given as much thought as other facets of the curriculum, **transitions** absorb a good part of each child's day, especially in early-childhood settings. Therefore, they merit equal consideration (Allen & Hart, 1984; Essa, 2010; Feldman, 1991; Hearron & Hildebrand, 2008; Isenberg & Jalongo, 2000). If transitions are to take place without chaos—another goal—they must be planned, just as other daily components of the program are planned.

naeyc
Standard 4b

General tips for ensuring smooth transitions include the following:

- Remain calm and collected. If you appear unhinged during transitions, children will become unhinged, too. On the other hand, if you move slowly and speak softly, children will respond in kind.
- Make necessary preparations in advance. If children are transitioning to lunch, for instance, they should not have to sit at the table waiting; the meal should be ready as they are concluding their prior activity.
- If the transition involves taking turns (as do those involving toileting or putting on outerwear), be sure that the same children are not always chosen to go first. Hearron and Hildebrand (2004) write, "Children learn to wait their turns when they know from experience that they'll get a turn." One day, you can assign brown-eyed children to go to the coatroom first. The next day, all children wearing blue shirts can go first, with children born in January asked to lead on the following day.

An important benefit of planning transitions, which often represent an accumulation of wasted time (Davidson, 1982), is that they can be used as yet another opportunity for learning. Not only will children learn to bring satisfactory closure to activities, but also successful transitioning teaches them to move easily into and out of group situations. These dynamics naturally entail cooperation and consideration. Furthermore, children learn to follow directions "from the simple to the complex and concerned with locations, object descriptions, and sequences of actions" (Allen & Hart, 1984, p. 104). Transitions can also be linked to curriculum content, adding continuity and more opportunity for learning to the day's components. (This chapter uses a transportation theme to show how transitions can be connected to the curriculum.)

Because transitions usually require moving from one place to another—and music is a common partner of movement, as well as being mood altering—movement and music are the perfect instruments for transition times. Children naturally enjoy movement and music, so transitions can become pleasurable experiences—even something to be looked forward to. Movement activities, songs, and fingerplays (all of which should be in a teacher's ready repertoire) provide a focus for children during transitions, hold the attention of waiting children, and are easily tied to curriculum content. In addition, transitions present opportunities for additional experience with movement and music—two subjects that teachers often have trouble finding ample time for.

Arrival

Standard 1a

Everybody, at any age, likes to be welcomed; it makes people feel special. Teachers and caregivers can make the children in their programs feel special—and get the day started right—by providing a warm welcome for each arriving child.

Especially warming is the sound of one's own name, which children love to hear. However, simply saying, "Good morning, [Tony]" may not be enough to generate enthusiasm and make the child feel glad to be there. Instead, adults greeting children at the door can use songs or chants that include the names of the children. One possibility is simply to sing, "Good morning to you ..." to the tune of "Happy Birthday." Another example, sung to the tune of "London Bridge," is

[Marianne] is here today

Here today, here today

[Marianne] is here today

[I'm] [We're] so glad to see you!

FIGURE **11.1** These sample schedules show the many transitions that occur during a typical day.

Excerpted from A. Gordon and K. W. Browne, **Beginnings and Beyond: Foundations in Early Childhood Education.** Copyright 2010 by Cengage Learning.

Half-Day Toddler Program

9:00–9:30	Greet children
	Inside activities
	• play dough and art/easel
	• home living
	• blocks and manipulatives
	• books
9:30	Door to outdoors opens
9:45–10:20	Outdoor play
	• large motor
	• social play
10:20	Music/movement outdoors
10:30	Snack/"Here We Are Together" song
	• washing hands
	• eating/pouring/cleanup
10:45–11:15	Outside
11:15	"Time to Put Our Toys Away" song
	• all encouraged to participate in cleanup
11:20	Closure (indoors)
	• parent-child together
	• story or flannelboard

Full-Day Program for Preschoolers

7:00	Arrival, breakfast
7:30	Inside free play
	• arts/easels
	• table toys/games/blocks
	• dramatic play center; house, grocery store, etc.

(Continued)

9:00	Cleanup
9:15	Group time: songs/fingerplays and small-group choices
9:30	Choice time/small groups

- discover/math lab/science activity
- cooking for morning or afternoon snack
- language art/prereading choice

10:00	Snack (at outside tables/cloths on warm days) or snack center during free play
10:15	Outside free play

- climbing, swinging; sand and water, wheel toys, group games

12:00	Handwash and lunch
12:45	Get ready: toileting, handwashing, toothbrushing, prepare beds
1:15	Bedtime story
1:30	Rest time
2:30	Outdoors for those awake
3:30	Cleanup outdoors and singing time
4:00	Snacktime
4:15	Learning centers; some outdoor/indoor choices, field trips, storyteller
5:30	Cleanup and read books until going home

Half-Day Kindergarten Plan

8:15–8:30	Arrival
	Getting ready to start

- checking in library books, lunch money, etc.

8:30	Newstelling

- "anything you want to tell for news"
- newsletter written weekly

9:00	Work assignment

- write a story about your news or
- make a page in your book (topic assigned) or
- work in math lab

9:30–10:15	Choice of indoors (paints, blocks, computer, table toys) or second-grade tutors read books to children

- when finished, play in loft or read books until recess

10:15	Snack
10:30	Recess
10:45	Language: chapter in novel read or other language activity
11:15	Dance or game or visitor and snack
11:45	Ending: getting ready to leave

- check out library books
- gather art and other projects

12:00–1:30	For part of group each day Lunch, then

- field trips
- writing lesson
- math or science lab

Performing fingerplays is a pleasant way to come together and to transition into the rest of the day. Teachers should acquire a collection of fingerplays, keep a card file of favorites (the teacher's enjoyment will help ensure that of the children), and memorize several for use whenever the need or opportunity arises. Because children love and need repetition, it is not necessary to learn dozens of fingerplays. Hamilton and Flemming (1990) suggest the following guidelines for choosing the most appropriate fingerplays:

naeyc
Standard 4b

1. Select one or two fingerplays for each subject, making certain they teach best the concept to be learned.
2. As with books, poems, and songs, watch for difficult vocabulary, the length of verse, the concept to be learned, and the maturity level of your group.
3. Use the simplest fingerplays with the youngest or least mature group; increase the complexity as the group shows readiness.
4. Select fingerplays carefully with a sensitivity for all people. Consider your group's age, understanding, and experience and the appropriateness for its use that day.
5. Adapt when one word, adjective, or action spoils an otherwise good rhyme or action game. Some descriptive words can be alternately exchanged. "Boys" or "girls" or a nonsexist term can be exchanged for one given in a book. Verses that stereotype or ridicule a race, cultural group, type of physical disability or refer to violence (guns, soldiers) in any form should be avoided. For example, a military reference in a fingerplay to soldiers marching in a parade can be replaced by the words "gymnasts" or "band."
6. Fingerplays at best can be vehicles for teaching good English. Watch out for misuse of verbs and adverbs. Books such as *Move Over, Mother Goose* offer imaginative fingerplays and poems that consider the broader need to explore language while many other books of fingerplays only rhyme.* (p. 50)

Books of fingerplays include

- *Move Over, Mother Goose* by Ruth Dowell (available from Gryphon House)
- *Finger Frolics: Fingerplays for Young Children* by Liz Cromwell and Dixie Hibner (published by Partner Press and available from Gryphon House)
- *Ring a Ring o' Roses* by Flint Public Library (Redleaf Press)
- *Little Hands Fingerplays and Action Songs* by Emily Stetson and Vicky Condon (Williamson Publishing)
- *The Complete Book of Rhymes, Songs, Poems, Fingerplays, and Chants: Over 700 Selections* by Jackie Silberg, Pam Schiller, and Deborah Wright (Gryphon House)

Musical versions of fingerplays can be found on the following recordings:

- *PreSchool Action Time* by Carol Hammett (Kimbo)
- *Fingerplay Fun!* by Rosemary Hallum (Educational Activities)
- *Fingerplays and Footplays for Fun and Learning* by Rosemary Hallum and Henry "Buzz" Glass (Educational Activities)
- *Clap, Snap, and Tap* by Ambrose Brazelton (Educational Activities)
- *Let's Sing Fingerplays,* a collection from Tom Glazer's book *Eye Winker, Tom Tinker, Chin Chopper* (Educational Record Center)

Video

VIDEO: *ECE/Child Development: "Infants & Toddlers: Emotional Development" (Child Care in Action)*

According to Hamilton and Flemming (1990), some fingerplays date back almost 2,000 years. Although fingerplays originally used only the fingers and hands to teach various concepts (including the most famous musical fingerplay,

---

*Note: *A Few Guidelines When Selecting Fingerplays.* Copyright © 1990 by Harcourt Brace & Co., reprinted by permission of the publisher.

Performing fingerplays is a pleasant way to come together and to transition into the rest of the day.

"Where Is Thumbkin?"), today's fingerplays sometimes use the entire body. Hamilton and Flemming suggest teaching fingerplays to children by demonstrating the actions while speaking or singing the words. The process is then repeated, with children being encouraged to perform only the actions. On the next repetition, children who want to can participate with both actions and words. As children arrive at the school or center, one adult could serve as the official greeter, while a second adult sits on the floor and performs fingerplays with those children who have shed their outerwear and are ready to begin their day.

When all the children have arrived and are gathered together, an activity like This Is My Friend (adapted from Orlick, 2006) is a wonderful way for children to welcome one another. In this activity, children stand in a circle holding hands. One child raises the arm of the child to his or her right or left, saying "This is my friend, [Ahmad]." The process continues around the circle, in the same direction, until each child has been introduced and all arms are in the air. Children can then take a deep bow for a job well done.

An activity like This Is My Friend is a wonderful way for teachers and children to welcome each other.

Finally, before proceeding, you can talk with children about what to expect throughout the day and then perform a relevant song or movement activity. If you are working with a theme, the song or activity should definitely be related to it. For instance, if the theme is transportation, you might sing "Wheels on the Bus," with or without the accompaniment of a recording. (For those who want to use a recording, this song is on Raffi's *Rise and Shine;* Hammett and Bueffel's *Toddlers on Parade;* and Sharon, Lois, and Bram's *Elephant Show.*)

Transitions within the Classroom

Among transitions within the classroom are moving from group time to free time, from free time to group time, and to snacks or lunch—all of which can easily be tied into the current classroom theme.

Continuing with the transportation theme, you might ask children to move from place to place as though rowing a boat, riding a horse, or using another familiar mode of transportation. Children can sing an appropriate song (e.g., "Row, Row, Row Your Boat"), or you could create and teach them a short chant involving a form of transportation.

Transitions within the classroom also offer a means to reinforce something experienced during a movement session. Children can be asked to perform their favorite movement from the most recent session or to execute a specific skill—locomotor, non-locomotor (e.g., turns), or manipulative (e.g., pretending to pull something)—as they move from place to place. Movement elements can also be explored. For example, if you have been working on the element of force, you could ask children to make the transition as lightly as possible, like a butterfly, or as though weightless in outer space.

Opportunities for problem solving also present themselves here. Gordon and Browne (2010), referring to problem solving as a creativity question, suggest asking children to move while using only one foot and one hand in some way. Other possibilities include asking them to move like any four-legged animal, in a particular shape, at the highest or lowest level, in a backward or sideward direction, using only curving or zigzag pathways, or using any locomotor skill but walking or running.

If children are going to or from snack or lunch, you can ask them to move like juice being poured, as if moving through peanut butter or marshmallow

Use transitions to reinforce something experienced during a movement session. These children have been asked to move like robots.

© Cengage Learning 2013.

fluff, as if they were floating through the air like the odor of food, or in the shape of a food served—perhaps, a carrot stick or a cookie. In keeping with the transportation theme, ask them to move like trucks, trains, tractors, grocery carts, or wheelbarrows transporting food.

When leaving story time, children can pretend to move like their favorite character in the story. A song performed to the tune of "London Bridge" can help transition children from other group times to free time:

> Now we go our separate ways, separate ways, separate ways
> Now we go our separate ways
> We'll come back together soon.

To dismiss a few children at a time from the group, you could point to individual children as you sing the following, to the tune of "Ten Little Indians":

> One little, two little, three little children
> Four little, five little, six little children
> Seven little, eight little, nine little children
> Off to learning centers [Leaving from our circle].

If you want children to transition from free to group time and to form a circle, you can ask every child to take the hands of two other children, with all tummies facing the center of the room, and to meet in the middle of the room (or the movement space, etc.). Or you could use the following chant:

> Come together, come together
> Come together now
> Stand together in a circle
> Take a great big bow!

Transitions to Outside the Classroom

This section discusses transitions that involve, among others, going outdoors for play time or recess, leaving for field trips, or simply going to another area within the building (e.g., the gym, library, or cafeteria).

When preparing to leave the room in single file, you might use some of the suggestions mentioned earlier, such as asking all children wearing a certain color shirt to line up at the door, followed by all those whose names begin with the letter B, and so forth. Or, if children have been working individually at learning centers, you can move from center to center, inviting children to join you with a chant such as the following:

> Take my hand
> Come take my hand
> We're going on a journey.

You can then lead children, with a spirit of adventure, toward the door. Follow the Leader is an excellent activity for these transitions. Leaders should use the elements of movement to vary how they transport the group (e.g., slowly, quickly, lightly, strongly, at various levels, in different shapes). Or they can relate the activity to the current theme. Using transportation, for instance, the leader can pretend to be flying in an airplane, riding on a train engine, riding a horse, or rowing a boat. Initially, adults should act as leaders, but once children have gained ample experience, they can take turns handling the responsibility.

Problem solving is also appropriate here. You can use the examples given in "Transitions Within the Classroom," as well as the following possibilities:

- Move to the playground (library or cafeteria) like the occupation (character, animal) you would most like to be.
- Find a way to move using only one foot (or three body parts, etc.).
- Move in the most crooked shape possible.
- Move in a sideward direction, using any method of locomotion other than walking or running.
- Find a way to move that involves a preposition (e.g., over, under, around, between, or through).

Children are willing to wait their turn as long as they know they will get one. Vary the methods you use to form lines so the same children are not always first or last.

© Cengage Learning 2013.

If you need to be especially quiet during a transition, as when going down a hallway when other classes are in session, ask children to pretend to be turtles, weightless astronauts, butterflies, eagles soaring, or mimes. They can also imagine they are moving through peanut butter, deep snow, or waist-high water.

Finally, if your class is going on or coming from a field trip, you can make the transition more relevant by relating it in some way to the trip. If, for example, the field trip was to the fire station, ask children to move like water flowing through a hose or the hose being unwound from the truck and stretched out. (Can they create a single hose with their bodies?) If the field trip was to the public library, they can pretend to move like a bookworm, a quiet librarian, or a whisper.

Cleanup

Cleaning up is a fact of life for adults. Many do it grudgingly, only because it must be done. But perhaps that would not be true if cleanup had been an enjoyable experience during early childhood. Teachers and caregivers can ensure that cleanup is pleasant for young children. By making it agreeable and a necessary routine, they can help children learn self-responsibility.

naeyc
Standard 4c

Although experts vary in their suggestions regarding the length of notice to be given prior to cleanup time, they agree it is important to give children notice of forthcoming shifts in activity. Isenberg and Jalongo (2000) suggest 10-, 5-, and 1-minute warnings before beginning cleanup; Gordon and Browne (2010) suggest a five-minute warning; and Essa (2010)—because older children are more product-oriented—recommends one minute of warning for each year of the child's age (e.g., three minutes for 3-year-olds). Whatever time that you determine to be most appropriate, you should establish a signal, such as a flick of the lights, to indicate it is time to begin wrapping up. A chant can also serve as a signal that warning time has elapsed and the actual cleanup must begin.

It's time to clean up
It's time to clean up
It's time to clean up right now.

Experts agree that it is important to give children notice of forthcoming shifts in activity.

Once cleanup starts, a number of possibilities can make it both fun and expedient. Music can certainly be valuable. Beaty (2007) suggests playing a favorite recording and challenging children to finish cleaning up before the song ends. You might choose Mr. Al's "It's Clean-Up Time" from *Sing Me Some Sanity,* a collection of transition songs available from Melody House. Any lively song is fine as long as it is one with which children are very familiar, so that they can anticipate the ending.

You can also encourage children to sing or hum "Whistle While You Work." For recorded accompaniment, this song can be found on *Homemade Games and Activities,* available from Kimbo. Or you could put your own words to the melody.

> Singing while we work
> We're happy to be neat
> We pick up here and pick up there
> Until our job's complete.

Imagery can also do the job. Children enjoy pretending to be vacuum cleaners, elves, robots, construction workers, homemakers, and custodians. Other images, again using the transportation theme, include pretending to be trains or garbage trucks transporting materials to where they belong. Children should also learn that walking while carrying things is a form of transportation.

Nap Time

As mentioned in Chapter 9, relaxation is a learned skill. Nap time offers a daily opportunity to help children acquire this skill.

To bring closure to any activity and to alert children that nap time has arrived, dim or turn off the lights and play a recording of some soft, slow, instrumental music. Several possibilities, including children's recordings for quiet times, are listed in Chapter 7. To help children make the transition from activity to inactivity, ask them to move to their mats or cots in any of the following ways:

- balloons deflating and coming down from the sky
- wind-up toys winding down
- the melting witch in *The Wizard of Oz*
- turtles
- snails
- bears lumbering to their caves for hibernation

If you are using a theme, incorporate it into the imagery. For a transportation theme, you could ask children to imagine they are hot air balloons or planes coming in for a gentle landing, motorboats or cars running out of gas, or trains chugging into the station.

Once children are in their places, some of the relaxation exercises suggested in Chapter 9 can help them unwind. You could sing a favorite, slow-paced song or do a fingerplay. "Tony Chestnut" and "Eensy Weensy Spider" cover both bases and should be familiar enough to children to be relaxing. Or teach children a fingerplay specifically related to rest that can become part of their naptime routine. One example is the following fingerplay, excerpted from Cherry (1981):

> It's time to rest, to rest your head
> (Put right forefinger in left palm.)
> Snuggled down in your own little bed.
> (Rock finger back and forth.)
> Covered up tight in blankets so warm
> (Cover with left fingers.)
> Safe and cozy and away from all harm.
> (Bring hands to cheek, bend head against hands, close eyes.) (p. 79)

Create chants and songs using children's names. Sing these songs from your place in the center of the group, looking at each child as you sing his or her name. Or sing the song as you quietly move from cot to cot. The following is one possibility, sung to the tune of Brahms's "Lullaby":

> Rest your eyes, rest your eyes
> Rest your eyes, little [Sarah]
> Let your body relax
> Feel the peace that it brings.

Later, waking children can stretch like waking cats or bears coming out of hibernation. They can then go quietly to prepared learning centers or into a group led by a teacher doing fingerplays, songs, or quiet movement activities. Because children (all people, in fact) have varying body rhythms, they should be allowed 15 to 20 minutes following nap time for quiet activities (Cherry, 1981).

Children who are still asleep after most others have gotten up should be woken gently. You might place a hand on the sleeping child, quietly singing "Are You Sleeping?" and substituting the child's name for Brother John.

Create quiet chants and songs using children's names. The personal touch is always appropriate.

© Cengage Learning 2013.

Departure

Because achieving closure brings such satisfaction, the transition to departure is an important one. It can help children feel good about their day, good about you, and good about returning in the morning.

"Ring Around the Rosie" is a fun, familiar activity to bring children together in a circle on the floor. Once they are sitting down, you can sing an uplifting song like "If You're Happy," asking those who are developmentally ready to suggest motions, in addition to clapping, that demonstrate happiness.

An activity that reviews what was experienced or learned during the day (about transportation, for example) is appropriate for closing the day. "Punchinello," for instance, is an excellent end-of-the-day activity. Children form a circle, with one child ("Punchinello") in the center. They all chant or sing, "What can you do, Punchinello, funny fellow? What can you do, Punchinello, funny you?" The child in the center chooses one of the day's activities to demonstrate. When she is through, the group sings, "We can do it, too, Punchinello, funny fellow. We can do it, too, Punchinello, funny you." And they do. Each child, in turn, has a chance to be Punchinello.

Finally, just as each arriving child was welcomed individually, so should each departing one be individually acknowledged. The following is a chant you and the remaining children can offer to each child as he or she leaves:

> It was good to have you with us today
> It was good to have you, [Kara]
> It was good to have you with us today
> I'll (we'll) see you in the morning.

Or you and the children could sing the following song to the tune of "Goodnight, Ladies":

> Goodbye, [Michael], goodbye, [Michael]
> Goodbye, [Michael]
> We'll see you tomorrow.

Obviously, many activities suggested in this chapter, though listed under one category, can work equally well for other transitions. Use these examples as a starting point, creating and collecting other ideas as you work with the children. If you plan transitions and use movement and music to add personality, warmth, learning opportunities, and fun to parts of the day that might otherwise be routine and dull, you will know that you and the children are making the most of every day.

ASSIGNMENTS

1. Create at least one original activity with movement and/or music for each transition described in this chapter.
2. Choose a well-known song and write new lyrics that can help bring children from free time to group time.
3. Write a rationale for planning transitions in the same manner that other parts of the daily program are planned.
4. Produce a collection of at least eight songs, movement activities, and fingerplays (not including those you created for assignment 1) that could be routinely used for transitions.

FIELD OBSERVATION

1. Spend enough time in an early childhood classroom to observe at least two transitions. Did they extend the learning in any way? Was movement incorporated? Describe what you saw and what changes if any you would like to see made.

REFERENCES

Allen, K. E., & Hart, B. (1984). *The early years: Arrangements for learning.* Englewood Cliffs, NJ: Prentice Hall.

Beaty, J. J. (2007). *Skills for preschool teachers.* Upper Saddle River, NJ: Prentice Hall.

Cherry, C. (1981). *Think of something quiet.* Carthage, IL: Fearon.

Davidson, J. (1982). Wasted time: The ignored dilemma. In J. F. Brown (Ed.), *Curriculum planning for young children* (pp. 196–204). Washington, DC: National Association for the Education of Young Children.

Essa, E. (2010). *Introduction to early childhood education.* Belmont, CA: Cengage Learning.

Feldman, J. R. (1991). *A survival guide for the preschool teacher.* West Nyack, NY: Center for Applied Research in Education.

Gordon, A., & Browne, K. W. (2010). *Beginnings and beyond.* Belmont, CA: Cengage Learning.

Hamilton, D. S., & Flemming, B. M. (1990). *Resources for creative teaching in early childhood education,* 2nd ed. Fort Worth, TX: Harcourt Brace Jovanovich.

Hearron, P. F., & Hildebrand, V. (2008). *Guiding young children.* Upper Saddle River, NJ: Prentice Hall.

Isenberg, J. P., & Jalongo, M. R. (2000). *Creative expression and play in the early childhood curriculum.* New York: Merrill.

Orlick, T. (2006). *Cooperative games and sports: Joyful activities for everyone.* Champaign, IL: Human Kinetics.

RELEVANT WEBSITES

For transition activities:

Gayle's Preschool Rainbow:
www.preschoolrainbow.org/transition-rhymes.htm

Perpetual Preschool:
www.perpetualpreschool.com/transitions.html

Songs for Teaching:
www.songsforteaching.com/transitions.htm

KEY TERMS & DEFINITIONS

transitions Passages or movement from one state, condition, or place to another. Also passing from one subject to another.

creativity question An opportunity for children to problem solve.

closure Bringing an activity or a period of time (e.g., the day) to a satisfactory conclusion.

© Cengage Learning 2013.

Bringing Movement Education Outdoors

Learning Objectives

After completing this chapter, the student will be able to:

1 Describe how the play space can be used for movement education.

2 Describe how climbing structures, balance beams, tunnels, platforms, tires, sand, riding toys, and swings can be used for movement education.

3 Explain ways in which the playground can be a place of learning.

TERMS TO KNOW

play leader

static playgrounds

divergent play experiences

Time spent outdoors has traditionally been considered "break" time—an opportunity for children to play without interference from adults and for teachers and caregivers to relax a bit. However, more and more, early-childhood professionals are realizing the potential of the outdoors as an extension of the indoor setting, with that time viewed as yet another opportunity to enhance children's development. And the experts agree. Gordon and Browne (2010), Isenberg and Jalongo (2000), Shipley (1998), Essa (2010), and Frost (1992) are just some of the authors who maintain that outdoor space should be used not only for the enhancement of physical skills but also for children's social, emotional, creative, and cognitive development.

This is not to say that teachers must go to the extreme of preparing structured lesson plans for every outdoor session. But many activities begun indoors can certainly be continued and extended outdoors, including movement activities. (Batteries in the CD player and handheld instruments, like guitars, recorders, and autoharps, even allow music to be part of outdoor movement experiences.) During free play time, adults can and should interact naturally and informally with children, offering guidance and suggestions that extend children's play.*

Frost (1996, p. 27) tells us that the role of the teacher in supporting outdoor play is that of a **play leader**, whom he defines as someone who interacts with children by asking leading questions and providing guidance for certain skills. A play leader also does the following:

> Helps children plan where they will go to play, helps them deal with problems that come up, and talks with them about their play. Through her example, she teaches children to plan and evaluate their play. Chiefly, she is willing, available, and able to assist the children in their play without taking charge. (p. 27)

When dealing with children with special needs, Capt (1996) asserts that it is imperative for teachers to

> take an active role in encouraging children to explore the equipment by planning specific activities during the playground time. For example, a game of "follow the leader" around an obstacle course you designed can motivate a child with a disability to challenge his body with new experiences, to master directional concepts, and to practice balance. (p. 14)

For children with motor impairments, Capt suggests offering extra physical support to enable them to use equipment. She recommends tactile markers or assistance to help a child with visual impairments find her way to, from, and around equipment. For a child with hearing impairments, remaining in the child's field of vision will ensure that he can get your attention if necessary.

BAM! radio

PODCAST: *Go to www. bamradionetwork.com and search for the podcast "Why Kids Aren't Going Out to Play - Why They Should".*

- *What are some ways to get around the obstacle of children not coming dressed for weather?*
- *Name some alternatives to expensive outdoor play equipment.*
- *Outline an argument for parents and/or early childhood professionals as to why children can meet academic requirements outdoors.*

naeyc
Standard 4c

---

*Note: Portions of were adapted from Pica, R. (1991). On the playground: Bringing movement education outdoors. *Early Childhood News, 3*, 1, 13. By permission of *Early Childhood News.*

And for children with emotional problems, Capt advises setting clear physical and behavioral boundaries.

Unfortunately, traditional **static playgrounds** and their traditional uses do little to stimulate children's development. Curtis (1982) says, "[Playgrounds] fall short of providing the impetus for movement that is essential to a child's development because they are static. Children cannot change the equipment to challenge themselves and practice specific movements" (p. 107). Bowers (1992) concurs with Curtis, stating:

> The natural play of all young children, which is characterized by exploration, creativity, and gaining mastery over new physical challenges, is in direct conflict with the limited ways traditional play equipment can be used. Play equipment which … demands that these activities be performed in a singular prescribed way severely limits the imaginative play of children. (p. 158)

Although some modern, multiple-function structures (both wooden and modular plastic ones) lend themselves to **divergent play experiences**, not every playground has such equipment. Even on those playgrounds that do, children may still view these structures as having limited uses and thus require adult assistance in discovering more creative possibilities.

The playground is the obvious and natural choice for many facets of the movement program. Unless you are fortunate enough to have the necessary equipment indoors, such gymnastic skills as climbing, hanging and swinging, and balancing can be experienced best on outdoor equipment. The playground can be the most appropriate area for the practice of manipulative skills—not only is it conducive to the performance of such ball-handling skills as throwing, catching, and striking, but also on the playground, children have opportunities to perform such actions as pushing a swing, pulling a wagon, and lifting and carrying movable objects. Of course, it is also in the outdoors that children can fully and freely experience gross motor skills such as running, leaping, and jumping (including jumping off things).

Some modern, multifunction playground structures lend themselves to divergent play experiences, but children may still require adult assistance in discovering creative uses for the equipment.

© Cengage Learning 2013.

Creeping becomes a whole new experience when performed outdoors.

© Cengage Learning 2013.

The remainder of this chapter looks at how teachers and caregivers can encourage children to use the playground space and typical equipment in varied and creative ways. Not only do the suggested activities promote motor learning in ways the basic, obvious uses of swings, slides, and sandboxes simply cannot, but they also provide children with a much-needed outlet for creativity, self-expression, and problem solving. In other words, the playground—an area already synonymous with movement—can become an arena for movement education.

Note that some of the following activities require adult supervision and/or assistance. Caution the children that they should have an adult helper if they try these activities at home or at the park.

Playground Space

As mentioned, the playground is a great place to practice manipulative skills. On paved areas, children can work on their bouncing and ball-rolling abilities. Grassy areas are perfect for practicing dribbling (the grass helps keep the ball under control). And any open area is great for throwing, catching, kicking, volleying, and striking.

These, of course, are typical playground activities. However, you may not have considered the open areas of your playground for movement experiences—like large-group activities—that are inconvenient or impossible indoors due to lack of space. Games like Follow the Leader can be more challenging and more appealing when there is ample space to explore and obstacles that have an impact on the courses taken. Shipley (1998, pp. 346–347) suggests a game called Cross Over, in which children form a large circle, without holding hands, and note the two children standing on either side of them. On a signal from the teacher, the children try to cross through the circle to the opposite side without bumping into or touching one another. When they have crossed over, they should be standing next to the same children as they were when on the other side. This excellent activity reinforces the concept of personal space. In addition, whole-group activities such as this further social development.

Open areas naturally lend themselves to the practice of a number of manipulative skills.

© Cengage Learning 2013.

Cherry (1976) proposes that teachers construct "skinny paths" by laying "unit blocks or pieces of rope, wood, or board in parallel rows that allow just enough space for the children to move cautiously between them" (p. 71). These narrow walkways provide balancing challenges unlike those fostered by beams or planks raised off the ground.

Parachute, hoop, and ribbon activities are often more practical outdoors (ribbon activities are certainly safer in a large, open area). And the possibilities for obstacle courses, using small and large equipment, are endless. Start small, changing the course often (even daily) and gradually increasing the challenge. The course should give children a great deal of experience with such concepts as over, under, through, around, and between. Eventually, children can even help you design the courses.

Climbing Structures

Cherry (1976) notes that if she had room for only one piece of equipment, it would definitely be something to climb on. In addition to the physical benefits derived from the practice of climbing (and hanging and swinging), she believes, "Few experiences can make a child feel so important as sitting on top of a jungle gym" (p. 53).

Sample Activities

Pretending to Be ... Children can pretend they are ivy growing and spreading, snakes slithering and wrapping themselves around tree limbs, clothes hanging on a line and drying in the breeze, Tarzan, mountain climbers, squirrels, firefighters at work, birds perched on branches, lookouts in a watchtower, or chimps and gorillas.

Questions and Challenges to Pose. The following are possible ways to challenge children as they play on the climbing equipment:

- Can you climb using just one leg and one arm?
- Can you climb up by rocking from one foot to the other?
- Can you climb up and down on tiptoe?
- Climb up quickly and down slowly.
- Add pauses to your climbing (climb and pause, etc.).

Climbing, hanging, and swinging are the obvious possibilities for climbing structures, but teachers can also help children view them in new ways.

Whether your climbing equipment consists of a jungle gym, monkey bars, or cargo nets, you can help children view it in new and exciting ways. Suggestions for exploring climbing structures by using imagery and elements of movement are provided in the "Sample Activities."

Balance Beams

Balancing is a skill that children simply cannot practice too often. You can purchase a commercial balance beam from suppliers like Flaghouse and Kaplan (Appendix 2), or ask a parent to construct one for you. Another option is to use narrow planks that are placed either on or slightly above the ground, depending on the children's developmental levels. The edge of a sandbox, if wide enough, can also encourage other balancing activities (Figure 12.1).

FIGURE **12.1** The edge of a sandbox, if wide enough, can be used in place of a balance beam.

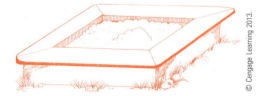

Sample Activities

Traveling Along the Beam. To explore travel along the beam, challenge children to move across like a tightrope walker; a gymnast (can they make up Olympic routines?); a butterfly, inchworm, spider, or bumblebee; a cat stalking its prey; or an elephant, penguin, turtle, kangaroo, or snake. How might a circus clown move from one end to the other? A ballet dancer? A giant or an elf?

Different Ways to Travel. Possibilities for travel along the beam include moving forward, backward, and sideward (trying it with right and left sides leading); on one foot; in slow motion and as quickly as possible; being as tall (small) as possible; on tiptoe or heels; taking tiny or giant steps; and moving as lightly or strongly as possible.

Other Locomotor Skills. Walking is not the only locomotor skill that should be practiced. How many other locomotor skills can children execute on a balance beam? Which are the easiest? Which are the hardest? How many of these skills can be performed backward or sideward?

Balancing, however, is not the only function of a balance beam. You can also explore the concept of over by asking children to find how many ways they can get over the beam. (Possibilities include jumping, hopping, leaping, and crawling.) Then challenge children to discover how many ways they can get onto and off the beam.

Tunnels

Most children love tunnels. When concrete conduits, plastic culverts, or modular playground structures are not readily available, children will create them from rows of upright tires, wooden crates, or large cardboard boxes (Figure 12.2). Tunnels are especially suitable for exploring the concepts of through and inside, but they can also be used for experiencing over, around, and under. (When inside the tunnel, children are also under the roof of the tunnel.)

FIGURE **12.2** Large, empty appliance boxes and rows of upright tires can be used to create tunnels.

© Cengage Learning 2013.

Sample Activities

Imagine That You Are ... Children can imagine they are hiding from someone or looking for buried treasure. They can also pretend that they are water flowing through the tunnel, space travelers, cave dwellers, bears in hibernation, and trains or subway cars.

Travel Like This ... Challenge children to travel through the tunnels in the following ways:

Backward
Being as round (flat) as possible

On hands and feet
On feet and bottom and hands (or in an upside-down way)
Slowly (quickly)
Lightly (heavily)
Occasionally pausing to look back over the shoulder
Using the arm and leg on one side of the body only

Platforms

Platforms can be part of playground superstructures or constructed with upright telephone cable spools, sturdy tables (e.g., picnic tables), solid wooden crates, or large tree stumps—all of which can also serve as support for bridges or high-wire acts for those children developmentally ready to move above the ground (Figure 12.3).

FIGURE **12.3** Telephone cable spools and large tree stumps can serve as platforms or "stages."

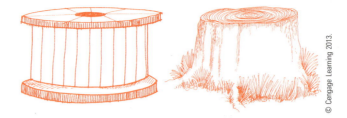

© Cengage Learning 2013.

Sample Activities

Children can use their imaginations to move on top of whatever platforms are available.

Being "On Stage." Frost (1992) describes the playground as a "stage where children can act out, spontaneously and freely, the events that touch their lives" (p. 106). When children are on outdoor platforms, encourage them to think specifically of being "on stage." Ask them to imagine they are any of the following:

    a singer
    a dancer
    someone making a speech
    a model in a fashion show
    an actor
    a performing seal
    a musician playing an instrument
    a magician

Being Above the Ground. Just being above the ground—even on a wide, stable base—can add an extra challenge to balance activities. Ask children to try balancing on tiptoes, one (and then the other) foot, one foot on tiptoe, one foot while leaning in different directions, one hand and one foot, one hand and one knee, one knee only, bottom only, and tummy only.

Personal Space. Imagining the platform is their very own personal space, how many ways can children find to move in that space? (This can lead to a thorough exploration of nonlocomotor skills.) How many body shapes can children find to fill the space? How many ways can they find to fill very little of the space? How many ways can they find to move around the space?

Tires

Tires have so many uses. (Just be sure to keep them free of standing water, which attracts mosquitoes. An easy way to do this is to drill holes in the sides of the tires facing the ground.) As mentioned earlier, tires can be placed upright in rows to create tunnels. They can also be stacked, rolled, crawled through, or

Sample Activities

Using a Tire: The Many Imaginative Possibilities. An automobile or bicycle tire lying flat on the ground can be a small boat being tossed at sea; a flying carpet; a cloud floating across the sky; a sled sliding down a steep, snowy hill; a hot air balloon; or any mode of transportation children can imagine.

Tires also make excellent cauldrons for stirring up a witch's brew, a giant pot for cooking a crowd-size batch of spaghetti, or the world's largest bowl of cereal. When children are done "cooking," they can pretend it is a pool and wade in it.

Moving In, On, and Around the Tire. Many of the activities described for platforms can be explored inside a tire. Because the area is smaller, the challenge of finding diverse ways to move can be even greater. Moving forward, backward, and sideward around the edge of the tire provides additional practice with balance. Challenge children to find as many ways as possible to get into and out of the tire. (Possibilities include jumping, hopping, and leaping.) Can they get into and out of the tire in forward, backward, and sideward directions? Quickly and slowly? Lightly and heavily?

Among other things, tires make great swings.

© Cengage Learning 2013.

used as targets for throwing balls and beanbags through. When laid flat, they can be grouped in different patterns (e.g., in a single-file line or in a pattern resembling hopscotch). In this case, you can invite children to explore possibilities for moving from one end to the other (e.g., by stepping either inside or on top of the tires). Tires also make great swings.

Sand

First and foremost, sand, with digging and pouring materials, is great for constructive play. It also lends itself to science experiments. What happens when a little water is added to sand? How about a lot of water? Does dry or wet sand weigh more? What would happen if a tunnel were dug into the sand and water poured into the tunnel? Does the water follow the path of the tunnel? Can children show you with their bodies what water looks like when it travels through a tunnel?

To incorporate art experiences, what shapes can the children mold with sand? Can they show you those shapes with their bodies?

Sand is also effective for fantasy play. Ask children to pretend to be digging for buried treasure at the beach or in the desert, to be chefs or bakers mixing a famous recipe, to be scientists working on an experiment, or to be gophers burrowing or dogs burying bones.

Riding Toys

Maneuvering a riding toy along pathways and around corners and obstacles does much to develop visual motor skill and laterality. But riding itself may not be enough of a challenge for some children. The following recommendations can add to the challenge.

Riding toys are great for promoting developmentally appropriate fitness.

© Cengage Learning 2013.

Sample Activities

Santa on His Sleigh, or ... Children can pretend to be absolutely anyone they would like to be, traveling on anything they would like transporting them. Possibilities include Santa on his sleigh, cowhands riding the range, a circus acrobat atop an elephant, an astronaut in a spaceship, a jockey, or a race car driver.

Riding a ... Less dramatic but equally valid are situations in which they pretend the riding toy is a tractor, bulldozer, fire engine, or police car. Perhaps it is a tow truck. What can the children find to tow? If it were a piece of construction equipment, what could they find to haul?

Let's Have a Parade. What if several children formed a parade with a line of riding toys? What modes of transportation are often seen in parades? (Possibilities include floats, fire engines, cars with convertible tops, and horses.)

Maneuvering. Challenge children to ride in straight, curving, and zigzag pathways. Set up an obstacle course with these three pathways. Can children ride first quickly and then slowly? (Which requires the most force?) Can children ride backward?

Slides

Slides are perhaps the most static pieces of equipment on a typical playground; they have so few functions. But you can introduce children to some nontraditional ways to use this traditional piece of equipment, opening their minds to the possibilities brought about through imagination and problem solving.

Swings

Shipley (1998) contends that swings promote "coordination, muscle development, and a sense of freedom and emotional release. Through learning to pump the swing to gain momentum, children develop a sense of the midline of the body" (p. 339). You can ensure that the swing sets on your playground have even more to offer the children.

Sample Activities

Using the Ladder. Children can use the ladder of the slide as a piece of climbing equipment and thus imagine they are all the people and things listed earlier. They can also pretend that the ladder is part of a hook-and-ladder truck, a piece of equipment used by a painter or carpenter, or a lifesaving fire escape.

Using the Slide. The slide itself does not have to be only a slide. It can be a laundry chute, a water slide, or the side of a steep mountain that must be climbed. Challenge children to climb the ladder in the same ways suggested for the climbing structures.

Moving on the Slide. For the slide itself, the possibilities include going down backward; lying on the tummy; or sliding in the smallest shape possible, as flat as possible, as crooked as possible, with one leg bent and the other straight, and with both legs bent. (Most of these require adult supervision to prevent mishaps.)

© Cengage Learning 2013.

A slide is perhaps the most static piece of equipment on a typical playground, but you can introduce children to some nontraditional ways of using it.

Sample Activities

Flying Like ... Swinging is probably the closest to flying that most children will ever get. Ask them to imagine they are on a flying trapeze or are any flying creature or superhero they would like to be.

Swinging Like ... Children can pretend to be the pendulum on a grandfather clock, a windshield wiper, or a tolling bell. The swing can be any mode of transportation imaginable, from a covered wagon to a space shuttle.

Swinging in Different Ways. Challenge children to swing with one leg bent and the other straight, with both legs remaining straight, with both legs bent, as slowly (quickly) as possible, gradually increasing speed and then gradually slowing, while nodding the head up and down or turning it from side to side, while kneeling, stopping on cue and starting again, or with as much force as possible.

The Playground: A Place of Learning

Although the ideas presented in this chapter certainly do not cover the full range of possibilities, they can begin to help you—and, in turn, your children—view some common playground equipment in uncommon ways. Children are naturally inventive and, with some initial enthusiasm from you, can create uses for the equipment beyond your wildest imaginings.

Frost (1992) asserts, "[The] adult who remains aloof from play misses opportunities for engaging with and learning from children" (p. 336). Furthermore, such an adult will be unable to enrich the children's outdoor experiences, and will thus be unable to offer them opportunities to express themselves creatively, stretch their imaginations, and be continually challenged. On the other hand, teachers and caregivers who interact with children on the playground can help make certain that the outdoors becomes an extension of the indoors and that movement education is taking place in both settings.

MORE ABOUT PLAYGROUND EQUIPMENT

When selecting playground equipment for children, teachers and caregivers must choose only those materials that are age appropriate and safe. For example, the American Academy of Pediatrics (AAP) states that trampolines have no place in outdoor playgrounds and should never be regarded as play equipment. In addition, if items like rakes, spades, and hoes are not child-size, they should be used only by adults and kept in storage, inaccessible to children.

The following is excerpted from Shipley (1998, pp. 344–345) and reprinted by permission of Nelson Education.

Large Muscle

climbing structure or A-frame

jungle gym

securely suspended rope to climb and
   swing on

tire or bucket swings

rope ladder

firefighter's pole

triangular ladder

slide with 15- to 20-inch drop at end

spring-based seesaw

trampoline (see AAP warning, above)

ramps for sliding and jumping

bowling set

snow shovels

baseball bat and ball

7-, 10-, and 18-inch balls

large hoops

punching ball or bag

skipping ropes and hoops

rowboat

beanbags and target

balance beams or interlocking boards

balance blocks

stilts

pogo stick

skateboards with helmets and shin pads

stationary-spring riding animals

horizontal ladder

simple playhouse or house frame

stick horses

tree house

steering wheel on wooden frame

large, hollow wooden building blocks

Vehicles and Accessories

gas station fuel pump

tricycles

wagons or carts

pedal cars

wheelbarrow

tractor

bicycle pump

hard hats

cargo for wagons and carts

Loose Materials

painted wooden boxes

barrels and kegs

large packing boxes and crates (e.g., appliance cartons)

sawhorses

short wooden ladders

lumber in 2- and 1-yards lengths

rocks and boulders

workbench

softwood supplies

tool kit and tools

tires

logs

tree stump

telephone cable spools

weather-treated large blocks

rope

milk crates

tarpaulins

clotheslines and pulleys

large and small paint brushes

pails

water-soluble paint

old shirts and drop sheets

surplus building materials

Gardening

hose and tap or pump

rakes

spades

hoes

hand shovels

claws

bags and baskets

sprinkler

watering cans

seed packets

flats for seeds

sterilized manure

string or rope

peat moss

wooden stakes

rubber gloves

gardening gloves (for the teacher)

overalls

old fabric and rags (for a scarecrow)

jiffy starter kits

gardening books

Sand and Water

buckets

scoops

shovels

sieves

steam shovels

heavy-duty trucks and cars

hose and tap

construction hats

camp stools

fishing rods and nets

tackle box

plastic wading pool

air mattress

diving mask

paddles

small sailing boats

inflatable raft

jugs and plastic pails

funnels and siphons

pup tent

flashlight

sleeping bag

knapsack

tin lunch boxes

canteen

tin pots and pans

saddle bags

Storage and Furniture

storage sheds with locks

benches

picnic table and umbrella

lawn chairs

barbecue or hibachi

firewood and grate

fire pit

prop box

ASSIGNMENTS

1. Think about your beliefs regarding the adult's role on the playground. Explain your position and justify it in writing.
2. Using early-childhood catalogs, create your own wish list of playground equipment and materials. Justify your choices in writing, keeping in mind creativity and safety.
3. Design an obstacle course. Determine how it can be made both less and more challenging to suit different developmental levels.
4. Using imagery and the elements of movement, create new uses for two pieces of equipment not described in this chapter.

FIELD OBSERVATIONS

1. Visit an early-childhood center and observe children playing outdoors. Are the teachers acting as play leaders, facilitating play? Describe what you see.
2. Cite examples of ways in which the outdoor setting enriched learning begun indoors, particularly in regard to movement education.

REFERENCES

Bowers, L. (1992). Playground management and safety. In C. M. Hendricks (Ed.), *Young children on the grow: Health, activity, and education in the preschool setting* (pp. 157–165). Washington, DC: ERIC.

Capt, B. (1996). Adapting the outdoor environment. *Scholastic Early Childhood Today, 10,* 14, 17.

Cherry, C. (1976). *Creative play for the developing child.* Carthage, IL: Fearon.

Curtis, S. R. (1982). *The joy of movement in early childhood.* New York: Teachers College.

Essa, E. (2010). *Introduction to early childhood education.* Belmont, CA: Cengage Learning.

Frost, J. L. (1992). *Play and playscapes.* Belmont, CA: Cengage Learning.

Frost, J. L. (1996). Joe Frost on playing outdoors. *Scholastic Early Childhood Today, 10,* 26–28.

Gordon, A., & Browne, K. W. (2010). *Beginnings and beyond.* Belmont, CA: Cengage Learning.

Isenberg, J. P., & Jalongo, M. R. (2000). *Creative expression and play in the early childhood curriculum.* Upper Saddle River, NJ: Prentice Hall.

Pica, R. (1991). On the playground: Bringing movement education outdoors. *Early Childhood News, 3,* 1, 13.

Shipley, D. (1998). *Empowering children: Play-based curriculum for lifelong learning.* Scarborough, Ontario: Nelson Education.

RELEVANT WEBSITES

For information on outdoor play, playgrounds, and playground safety:

Children & Nature Network
www.childrenandnature.org

National Program for Playground Safety
www.uni.edu/playground

Safe Kids USA
http://www.safekids.org/safety-basics/safety-resources-by-risk-area/playground/

Peaceful Playgrounds:
www.peacefulplaygrounds.com

S.A.F.E. Playground Supervision Kit:
http://www.uni.edu/playground/supervision/

KaBOOM!
www.kaboom.org

KEY TERMS & DEFINITIONS

play leader Someone who interacts with children in a play situation by asking leading questions and providing guidance for certain skills.

static playground Playground on which children cannot change the equipment to challenge themselves or stimulate their development.

divergent play experience Activity in which children have options, whether for uses of the play equipment or in how they choose to move or play.

Appendix

Sources and Resources

Professional Organizations and Publications

American Alliance for Health, Physical Education, Recreation, and Dance (AAHPERD):
> www.aahperd.org
> Journal: *Journal of Physical Education, Recreation, and Dance*
> Associations under the AAHPERD umbrella include National Association for Sport and Physical Education (NASPE) and National Dance Association (NDA)

American Association for the Child's Right to Play (IPA/USA):
> www.ipausa.org
> Journal: *PlayRights*

Association for Childhood Education International (ACEI):
> www.acei.org
> Journal: *Childhood Education*

Early Childhood Music and Movement Association (ECMMA):
> www.ecmma.org
> Journal: *Perspectives*

Music Teachers National Association (MTNA):
> www.mtna.org
> Journal: *American Music Teacher*

National Association for the Education of Young Children (NAEYC):
> www.naeyc.org
> Journal: *Young Children*

National Association for Music Education (MENC):
> www.menc.org
> Journal: *Music Educators Journal*

Relevant Sources for Articles

Earlychildhood NEWS: www.earlychildhoodnews.com
Scholastic Early Childhood Today: http://teacher.scholastic.com/products/ect
Scholastic Instructor: www.scholastic.com/instructor

Relevant Blogs

Early Ed Watch: http://earlyed.newamerica.net/blogmain
EarlyStories: http://earlystories.org/
Early Years: http://blogs.edweek.org/edweek/early_years/
Teach Preschool: www.teachpreschool.org/

Movement and Physical Education Book Publishers

American Alliance for Health, Physical Education, Recreation, and Dance (AAHPERD)
    800-213-7193
    www.aahperd.org
Gryphon House, Inc.
    800-638-0928
    www.gryphonhouse.com
HighScope Educational Research Foundation
    734-485-2000
    www.highscope.org
Human Kinetics
    800-747-4457
    www.humankinetics.com

Sources for Ordering Instruments

Childcraft
    888-388-3224
    www.childcrafteducation.com
Constructive Playthings
    800-448-1412
    www.constructiveplaythings.com
Lakeshore Learning
    800-428-4414
    www.lakeshorelearning.com
MMB Music
    800-543-3771
    www.mmbmusic.com
Music in Motion
    800-807-3520
    www.musicmotion.com
Rhythm Band Instruments
    800-424-4724
    www.rhythmband.com

Sources for Ordering Recordings

Educational Activities, Inc.
    800-797-3223
    www.edact.com

Kimbo Educational
    800-631-2187
    www.kimboed.com

Melody House
    800-234-9228
    www.melodyhousemusic.com

Sources for Ordering Equipment and Props

Constructive Playthings
    800-448-1412
    www.constructiveplaythings.com

Flaghouse, Inc.
    800-793-7900
    www.flaghouse.com

Kaplan Early Learning Company
    800-334-2014
    www.kaplanco.com

Lakeshore Learning
    800-428-4414
    www.lakeshorelearning.com

Play with a Purpose
    888-330-1826
    www.pwaponline.com

Glossary

A

Accelerando Music that begins slowly and gradually increases in tempo.

Aesthetic sense With regard to music, the development of sensitivity for the feelings, impressions, and images music can convey.

Auditory or visual signal Something children must be listening or watching for, indicating that it is time to "stop, look, and listen" to the teacher.

B

Bodily/kinesthetic intelligence Strongest in individuals who are able to solve problems or create with their bodies or body parts.

Bound flow Movement that is punctuated or halting, such as the movements of a robot.

Boundary Limitation placed on the movement area. Objects that children cannot move beyond or on.

C

Closure Bringing an activity or a period of time (e.g., the day) to a satisfactory conclusion.

Common meter The meters of 2/4, 3/4, 4/4, and 6/8 are the most commonly used in Western music. A meter indicates the distribution of beats in a measure of music.

Content area A subject or discipline that is part of the curriculum—typically art, language arts, mathematics, music, physical education, science, and social studies.

Creative dance An art form based on natural movement rather than the stylized movements used in ballet or other forms of theatrical dancing.

Creativity Not necessarily related to academic intelligence. The potential for creativity exists in all people, but the greatest chance for its development exists in children between the ages of 3 and 5 years old. See "Creativity and the Young Child" (Chapter 2) for multiple perspectives and definitions of creativity.

Creativity question An opportunity for children to problem solve.

Crescendo Music that begins softly and that gradually gets louder.

Cross-lateral movement Movement, such as crawling or creeping, in which limbs move in opposition. This type of movement helps children cross the body's midline and activates both hemispheres of the brain in a balanced way.

D

Decrescendo A gradually decreasing volume. Sometimes called *diminuendo*.

Developmental appropriateness Age appropriateness and individual appropriateness—the former reminds us that there are universal, predictable sequences of development in all domains, while the latter indicates that all children are individuals who develop according to their own timetables.

Developmental progression Beginning at the beginning and proceeding from there in a logical, developmental order.

Direct approach A command style of teaching that uses demonstration and imitation.

Disruptive behavior Acting out in order to receive attention from adults.

Divergent play experience Activity in which children have options, whether for uses of play equipment or in how they choose to move or play.

E

Educational gymnastics A child-oriented, natural progression of the exploration of fundamental movement skills that teaches body management—on the floor and with small and large apparatus—and develops strength, stamina, and flexibility through exploration and discovery. Educational gymnastics are not similar to Olympic gymnastics, where the student's ability to execute stunts determines success or failure.

Elements of movement How a movement is performed. If movement education is likened to the study of grammar, the skills themselves can be considered verbs, while the six movement elements (space, shape, time, force, flow, and rhythm) are the adverbs modifying them.

Emotional development How children feel about other people and things, and the way they express their feelings.

Emotional disability A disability that affects a child's ability to learn and that is not related to sensory, health, or intellectual problems. Such children are often depressed, have difficulties with social relationships, and demonstrate inappropriate behavior.

Emotionally handicapped Often used to describe children with emotional disabilities.

Two of the most common behaviors ascribed to emotionally handicapped children are a lack of self-control and a refusal to participate.

Exploration A teaching method employing divergent problem solving.

F

Fingerplay Poem or wordplay in which movement has a critical function. Originally used only the hands and fingers to teach concepts, fingerplays now sometimes employ the whole body.

Form The overall design of the phrases that constitute a song's organization. Often designated by letters.

Free flow Uninterrupted movement, such as is visible in ice skating.

G

General space Space that is usually limited only by floors, walls, and ceilings. It may also be referred to as *shared space*.

Group size The ratio of adults to children. Experts suggest one adult for every five 3- to 4-year-olds and one adult for every 10 to 15 older children.

Group time Period set aside for large-group activity that can be used for movement experiences.

Guided discovery A teaching method using convergent problem solving.

H

Health-related fitness One of the two components of physical fitness. Consists of cardiovascular endurance, muscular strength, muscular endurance, flexibility, and body composition.

Hearing impairment The malfunctioning of the auditory mechanism. Unless there is damage to the semicircular canals, which causes problems with balance, the major challenges for children with hearing impairments in movement programs are related to the use of music and the presentation of instructions.

I

Individual Education Plan (IEP) Plan developed for school-aged children who qualify for special services. Teachers, parents, and service providers work together to create short- and long-term goals in one or more developmental areas.

Integrated approach to literacy Recognition that listening, speaking, reading, and writing overlap and interrelate, each contributing to the growth of the others.

Intelligence According to Howard Gardner, the capacity to solve problems or make things that are valued in a culture.

K

Kinesthetic mode A way of learning that involves physically experiencing concepts.

L

Learning disabled Children who possess average or above-average intelligence but have difficulty in using written or spoken language.

Legato Music played without any noticeable interruptions; the music flows smoothly, like free flow in movement.

Lesson plan Usually detailed procedure for teaching one class period of a learning unit.

Limited understanding In this text, children with learning disabilities as well as those with mild or moderate retardation. In general, children with limited understanding have a short attention span and tend to become easily discouraged.

Locomotor skill Transports the body as a whole from one point to another. Although it is commonly believed that children acquire and develop locomotor skills automatically, children are in fact unable to reach a mature stage of development without practice, encouragement, and instruction.

M

Manipulative skill In this text, any gross motor skill that usually involves an object being manipulated.

Mental retardation Most commonly refers to below-average intellectual functioning concurrent with an inability to mature personally and socially with age. Mentally retarded children usually are below average in motor development as well, possibly because of cognitive difficulties or a lack of opportunities for physical activity.

Modalities of knowledge acquisition Types of knowledge acquisition that are divided into four basic groups: visual, auditory, tactile, and kinesthetic.

Movement education A success-oriented, child-centered form of physical education emphasizing fundamental movements and the discovery of their variations, which can later be used in games, sports, dance, gymnastics, and life itself.

Movement theme Unlike a classroom or unit theme, this theme is based on a movement element or skill.

N

Nonlocomotor skill Movement performed in place, usually while standing, kneeling, sitting, or lying. Involves the axis of the body

rotating around a fixed point. Some textbooks refer to this as a *nonmanipulative skill*.

Nonparticipant A child who refuses to take part in movement activities.

O

Object permanence The realization that something that has been hidden still exists.

Objective Intended goal to be accomplished over a period of time (e.g., by the end of a lesson or by the end of the school year).

Observation cue Question asked to help analyze and refine children's movements.

P

Perceptual-motor theorist Person who believes that movement is essential to a child's learning process. Unlike cognitive development, which requires children to use and process abstract information (using words and/or numbers), perceptual-motor development relies on the concrete, physical dimensions of the environment.

Personal space The area immediately surrounding the body. It includes whatever can be reached while remaining in one spot and can be likened to a large bubble surrounding the body.

Phrase A division of a composition; commonly a four- to eight-measure phrase. Similar to a sentence in grammar.

Physical fitness According to the American Alliance for Health, Physical Education, Recreation, and Dance, a physical state of well-being that allows people to perform daily activities with vigor, reduce their risk of health problems relative to lack of exercise, and establish a fitness base for participation in a variety of physical activities.

Physically challenged These children are the fastest-growing population of children receiving special education services. Among these children are those with disabilities caused by birth defects, accidents, or illness. In one way or another, the mobility of these children is restricted.

Pitch The highness or lowness of a musical tone.

Play leader Someone who interacts with children in a play situation by asking leading questions and providing guidance for certain skills.

Positive challenge Introductory phrase to a movement challenge, indicating a belief that the children can do what is being asked of them.

Praise addict Child who needs more and more praise from adults to maintain his or her self-esteem.

Primary theme The main focus of a lesson.

Q

Qualities of movement Divided into six categories: sustained, suspended, swinging, percussive, vibratory, and collapsing.

Quantitative idea Mathematical concept related to size, quantity, or relationships that should be part of children's daily lives.

R

Rhythm The organization of sounds, silences, and patterns into different groupings.

Ritardando A gradually decreasing tempo.

S

Self-expression The expression of one's personality; an integral part of the creative process.

Social development A long, continuous process that begins with self-discovery and results in the ability to interact with others.

Social play Divided into six categories: unoccupied behavior, onlooker behavior, solitary play, parallel play, associative play, and cooperative play.

Spectrum of Teaching Styles A model of instructional styles based on the premise that the teaching/learning process involves decisions made by the learner before, during, and after learning. Also referred to as Mosston's Spectrum, this model is now accepted and applied throughout the world.

Staccato Notes of music are punctuated, like bound flow.

Static playground Playground on which children cannot change the equipment to challenge themselves or stimulate their development.

Styles of music Differ in how they treat form, melody, harmony, sound, and rhythm.

T

Tempo The speed at which music is performed.

Texture In music, the instrumentation used to create the sounds.

Transition A passage of movement from one state, condition, or place to another. Also a passing from one subject to another.

U

Unit theme A classroom topic explored over a period of time (e.g., a week or a month).

Unrestrictive clothing Attire that allows for freedom of movement and lessens the possibility of injury.

V

Visually challenged Those whose visual impairments, even when corrected, adversely affect their learning. With minor modifications, a movement education program can meet the needs of children who are visually impaired.

Volume Part of the broader category of dynamics; refers specifically to the loudness or softness of sounds.

W

Whole child The concept of a child as a thinking, feeling, moving human being who learns through all the senses.

Index

Note: Page numbers referencing figures are italicized and followed by "*f*".

A

AAHPERD (American Alliance for Health, Physical Education, Recreation, and Dance), 237, 238
Abilities, creative thinking, 29
Academic achievements, 30
Accelerando, 149, 150
ACEI (Association for Childhood Education International), 237
Acting out, 194
Action and reaction, 201
Active listening, 147
Activities. *See* Individual activities by name
Act Out Fears activity, 57
Adding activities, 198
Adults
  effect of childhood habits in, 5
  reactions to infants, 40
  role in physical activity of children, 5
Aerobic exercise, 5–6
Aesthetic sense, 24
Affective development
  activities, 42
  early-elementary children, 64–66
  infants, 41–42
  preschoolers, 56–58
  toddlers, 48–51
Age appropriateness, 38. *See also* Developmentally appropriate movement programs
Aims of Education, The, book, 15
Albrecht, K., 40, 42
Alternating activities, 112, 178
Amabile, T. M., 29, 30–31
American Alliance for Health, Physical Education, Recreation, and Dance (AAHPERD), 237, 238
American Association for the Child's Right to Play (IPA/USA), 237
American Flag activity, 17
American music periods, 143
Andress, B., 144
Animal movement activities, 13, 50–51, 200
Arm movements, 135
Armstrong, Thomas, 187
Arrival transitions, 212–216
Art
  cross-curricular movement programs, 188–192
  experiences with sand, 231
"Art and Movement" activity, 190
Ashworth, S.
  command-style teaching, 162
  divergent problem solving, 168–170

  results of problem solving, 11
  The Slanted Rope, 165
Assessment, 169–170
Association for Childhood Education International (ACEI), 237
Associative play, 49
Attention spans
  of preschoolers, 55
  of toddlers, 44, 47
"At the Zoo" poem, 33
Attire, for movement sessions, 129–130
Auditory modality of knowledge acquisition, 12
Auditory signals, 175
Automatic phase of skill development, 88
Axial movements, 88

B

Back to Sleep campaign, AAP, 43
"Baking Bread" activity, 206
Balance
  in children with hearing impairments, 70
  in movement programs, 101–102
  during preschool years, 58
  and recovery, 200
Balance beams, 228–229
Balancing Beanbags Activity, 133
Ballistic stretching, 7
Balloons, 182
Balls
  activities for infants, 44
  equipment, 131
  rolling
    in movement programs, 97–98
    toddler activities, 53
Bare feet, 129
Batting Challenges activity, 99
Bayless, K. M., 68–69
Beanbags, 133
Becker, J. E., 29, 30–31
Being Above the Ground activity, 230
Being "On Stage" activity, 230
Benard, B., 9
Bending, 90
Bisson, Julie, 204
Blast Off! activity, 48, 196
Blowing bubbles activity, 41
Bodily/kinesthetic intelligence, 14, 18, 187
Body awareness activities, 44, 47
  preschooler, 55–56
Body composition, 7–9

Body functions activities, 199
Body-Part Identification activities, 199
Body parts activities, 17
Body Percussion activity, 47
"Body Poem, The," 55–56
Body Sounds activity, 156
Body-space awareness, 16
Books
  fingerplay, 214
  song picture, 194
BOT-2 (Bruininks-Oseretsky Test of Motor Proficiency), 170
Bouncing, 98–99
Boundaries, establishing, 175–176
Bound flow, 80
Bowers, L., 225
Boys
  competitiveness of, 57
  flexibility in, 7
Brain
  effect of music on, 24
  movement experiences in development of, 38–39
Bread, Bread, Bread book, 206
Bread-baking activity, 206
Bredekamp, S., 38
Bridges and Tunnels activity, 17
Browne, K. W., 216, 218
Bruininks-Oseretsky Test of Motor Proficiency (BOT-2), 170
Bubble activities, 41

C

Cambigue, S., 198
Canady, R. J., 193, 194
Cardiovascular disease, 5
Cardiovascular endurance, 5–6
Careers, 13, 119
Castle, K., 48
Catching, 99, 135
Catch It! activity, 99
Cats activity, 120
Celebrate! An Anti-Bias Guide to Enjoying Holidays in Early Childhood Programs book, 204
Celebrations, 204
Centers for Disease Control (CDC), 4
Challenges, positive, 176
Charlesworth, R., 49
Cherry, C., 173, 181, 220, 227
Childcraft, 239
Child-directed activities, 11
Children's Activity and Movement in Preschools Study (CHAMPS), 4

Circling With the Chute activity, 138
Clapping rhythms, 28, 81
Classical music periods, 143
Classroom
 transitions to outside, 217–218
 transitions within, 216–217
Cleanup periods, 218–219
Cleland-Donnelly, F., 72, 109, 161, 180
Climbing skills, 52, 67, 102–103
Climbing structures, 227–228
Clock activity, 64
Closure, 219
Clouds activity, *121f*
Cognitive development, 54–56
 early-elementary children, 62–64
 future implications, 15
 infants, 39–41
 overview, 12–15
 role of movement, 15–18
 toddlers, 45–48
Collapsing movement, 82
Combined movement activities, 56,
 60–61, 67
Command-style teaching, 162
Common meters, 28
Common sense, 173
Communication
 with hearing-impaired children, 70
 and language arts, 192, 193
 role of music in, 23
Competition, 11, 57, 65–66
Composition, body, 7–9
Concentration, 55
Concept games, 41
Concept of Around Activity, 132
Conformity, 30–31, 163
Confucius, 12
Constructive Playthings, 238, 239
Content areas, 192
Content of movement program, 76–105
 educational gymnastic skills
  balance, 101–102
  climb, 102–103
  hang and swing, 103
  overview, 100
  roll, 100
  transfer weight, 100–101
 elements of movement
  flow, 80
  force, 79–80
  overview, 77
  rhythm, 80
  shape, 78–79
  space, 77–78
  time, 79
 locomotor skills
  crawl, 81–83
  creep, 83
  gallop, 86
  hop, 86
  jump, 84
  leap, 84
  overview, 81
  run, 84
  skip, 87
  slide, 86–87
  step-hop, 87–88
  walk, 83–84
 manipulative skills
  ball roll, 97–98
  bounce, 98–99
  catch, 99
  dribble, 99–100
  kick, 97
  lift, 96

 overview, 94
 pull, 94
 push, 95
 strike, 96
 throw, 96–97
 volley, 98
 nonlocomotor skills
  bend, 90
  dodge, 93
  fall, 93–94
  rock and sway, 92
  shake, 91
  sit, 90–91
  stretch, 89–90
  swing, 92
  turn, 91–92
  twist, 92–93
Contrasting musical elements activity, 155
Control level of skill proficiency, 89
Convergent problem solving, 164, 165
Cooperation, 10–11
Cooperative activities, 49, 57, 65–66
Cooperative Musical Chairs activity, 91
Cooperative Sports and Games Book: Challenge Without Competition, 11
Copple, C., 38
Copyright laws, 154
Corrections, creative, 176
Corso, M., 16
Coulter, D. J., 24
Counting and Movement activities, 196–197
Counting Fingers activity, *117f*
Cowboys, Cowgirls activity, 86
Crawling, 44, 81–83
Creative corrections, 176
Creative dance, 95
Creative development
 future implications, 30–32
 overview, 29–30
 role of movement, 32–33
Creative movement activities, 32–33
Creative thinking abilities, 29
Creativity, 163, 168, 176
Creativity question, 216
Creepers and Crawlers activity, 83
Creeping, 44, 83
Crescendo, 150, 151, 156
Critical-thinking skills, 56, 164
Cross-curricular movement programs
 art, 188–192
 language arts, 192–193
 mathematics, 193, 195–198
 overview, 187–188
 science, 198–202
 social studies
  families and friends, 203–204
  holidays and celebrations, 204
  multicultural education/diversity, 205
  occupations and transportation,
   204–205
  overview, 202–203
  self-concept, 203
Crossing midline activity, 41
Cross-lateral creeping, 83
Cross-lateral movements, 16
Cross Over game, 226
Cues, adult, 40
Cultural appropriateness, 38
Curiosity, 54
Curricula. *See also* Cross-curricular movement programs
 benefits of, 3
 preschool, 251
 stressing cooperation in, 10
Curtis, S. R., 131, 225

D
Dance, 42, 67
Decrescendo, 150, 151, 156
Deep breathing, 182
Demonstrations, 163, 165, *165f*
Denver Developmental Screening Test
 (DENVER II), 170
Departure transitions, 221
Developmentally appropriate movement
 programs. *See also* Preschoolers,
 developmentally appropriate movement programs
 children with special needs
  emotional disabilities, 72
  hearing impairments, 70–71
  limited understanding, 72–73
  overview, 68–69
  physical challenges, 69–70
  visual impairments, 71
 early-elementary children
  affective development, 64–66
  cognitive development, 62–64
  motor development, 66–68
  overview, 61–62
 infants
  affective development, 41–42
  cognitive development, 39–41
  motor development, 42–44
  overview, 38–39
 overview, 38
 preschoolers
  affective development, 56–58
  cognitive development, 54–56
  motor development, 58–61
  overview, 54
 toddlers
  affective development, 48–51
  cognitive development, 45–48
  motor development, 51–53
  overview, 44–45
Developmental progressions, 113–114
Diabetes, 4
Direct approach to teaching, 161–163
Directions, 46
Discovery, guided, 163–167
Disruptive behavior, 179–180
Divergent play experiences, 225
Divergent problem solving, 32, 165, 167,
 167f
Diversity, 13, 205
Dodging, 93
Do-Re-Mi activity, 156
Downhill/Uphill activity, 98
Dribbling, 99–100
Drumming, 136
Dudek, S., 29, 32–33
Dynamic balance, 101, 102

E
Early Childhood Music and Movement
 Association (ECMMA), 237
Earlychildhood NEWS publication, 238
Early Ed Watch, 238
Early-elementary children (5- to 8-year olds)
 developmentally appropriate movement
  programs
  affective development, 64–66
  cognitive development, 62–64
  motor development, 66–68
  overview, 61–62
 musical development in, 27
 overview, 61–62
EarlyStories, 238

Early Years, 238
ECMMA (Early Childhood Music and Movement Association), 237
Educational Activities, Inc., 239
Educational gymnastic skills
  balance, 101–102
  climb, 102–103
  hang and swing, 103
  overview, 100
  roll, 100
  transfer weight, 100–101
Educational Record Center, 206
Edwards, L., 156
Eel activity, 81
Egg Roll activity, 100
Electricity, 201
Elementary stage of motor learning, 88
Emotional development
  future implications, 10
  infant affective development, 42
  overview, 9
  in preschoolers, 58
  role of movement, 10–12
Emotionally disabled children, 72, 225
Emotions, 203
Encouragement, 169, 177, 179
Endurance
  cardiovascular, 5–6
  muscular, 6
Energy expenditure, 4
Energy levels, monitoring, 178
Environment activities, 200
Equipment
  balls, 131
  beanbags, 133
  hoops, 131–132
  overview, 130
  parachutes, 137–138
  playground, 234–235
  rhythm sticks, 135–136
  scarves, 134–135
  streamers, 133–134
Essa, E., 52, 179, 180, 195
Ethnicity, 205
Everyone Wins! Cooperative Games and Activities book, 11
Exercise, 5–6
Existentialist intelligence, 14
Exploration teaching method, 167–170
Exploring
  hygiene, 199
  nutrition, 199
  scientific concepts, 200–202
  senses, 199
Exploring Continuums activity, 155–156
Exploring In and Out Activity, 132
Exploring Line activity, 190
Exploring Positions Activity, 133
Exploring Straight and Round activity, *118f*
Exploring Texture activity, 190
Exploring Up and Down activity, 17, *115f, 118f*
Extending activities, 167, 168

F

"Face Has Many Roles in Life, A" song, 34
Falling, 93–94
Fall Like … activity, 94
Families, 203–204
Fantasy play, 231
Fast tempo, 149
Fauth, B., 12, 18
Fears, 57
Feeling Calm/Feeling Nervous activity, 182

Feelings, 202, 203
Field trips
  studying about occupations, 204, 206
  transitions to and from, 218
Fingerplays
  during arrival transitions, 214
  defined, 193, 209
  and language arts, 193
  for nap time, 220
  for toddlers, 47
Finger puppets, 41
Fitness, health-related
  body composition, 7–9
  cardiovascular endurance, 5–6
  flexibility, 7
  muscular endurance, 6
  muscular strength, 6
Flaghouse, Inc., 239
Flaherty, G., 12
Flat head syndrome, 43
Flemming, B. M., 214, 215
Flexibility
  in health-related fitness, 7
  lesson plan, 109, 125–126
Flow, 80
"Flying Like …" activity, 233
Folk dances, 67–68, 87
Follow the Leader activity, 53, 217
Footsie Roll activity, 100
Force, 79–80
Forming Number Shapes activity, 196
Fowler, J. S., 126
Fox and Hound activity, 86
Free flow, 80
Free times, 216, 217
French, R., 180
Friends, 203–204
Frost, J. L., 224, 234
Frostig, M., 10
Full-day programs for preschoolers, *212f–213f*
Function of Heart activity, 199
Functions of Human Body activity, 199
Furniture, playground, 235

G

Gabbard, C., 38
Gallahue, D. L., 72, 88–89, 109, 161, 180
Galloping, 86
Games. *See also* Individual activities by name
  concept, 41
    Cross Over, 226
    Mirror Game, 53, 78
    "Ring around the Rosie," 221
    sound, 41
    tossing, 53, 135
Gardening equipment, 235
Gardner, Howard, 12, 187
Gender awareness, 65
General space, 77–78
Generic levels of skill proficiency, 89
Geometric shapes, 197
Gerber, L. L., 142, 147, 148, 150, 151
"Giants and Elves" poem, 196
Giddy-Up activity, 9
Gilbert, A. G., 187, 194
Gilliom, B. C., 29–30, 126
Girls
  cooperation of, 57
  flexibility in, 7
Goff, K., 29, 32
Goleman, D., 31, 33
Gordon, A., 216, 218
Graham, G., 31, 89, 99, 165, 169, 174, 180

Gravity, 198, 200, 201
Greata, J., 25
Greenberg, P., 9
Grineski, S., 66–67
Griss, Susan, 207
Group activity schedules, *116f–117f, 125f*
Group balance activity, 66
Group size, 124, 128–129
Group time, 124, 216, 217
Gruber, J. J., 12
Gryphon House, Inc., 238
Guided discovery, 163–167
Guidelines, physical activity, 174
  body composition, 7–8
Gym-mats, 138, 139
Gymnasiums, 127
Gymnastic skills
  balance, 101–102
  climb, 102–103
  hang and swing, 103
  Olympic, 100, 101
  overview, 100
  roll, 100
  transfer weight, 100–101

H

Haines, B. J. E., 142, 147, 148, 150, 151
Half-day programs, *212f*
Halsey, E., 167
Hamilton, D. S., 214, 215
Hammering, 136
Hammett, C. T., 131, 132
Hand motions, 148, *149f*
Hanging, 103
Hannaford, C., 15–16, 18
Head, Belly, Toes activity, 47, *117f*
Health, 5
Health-related fitness
  body composition, 7–9
  cardiovascular endurance, 5–6
  flexibility, 7
  muscular endurance, 6
Hearing impaired children, 70–71, 224
Hearron, P. F, 211
Heart disease, 4
Henderson, H., 180
Hendricks, G., 187
Hendricks, K., 187
High balancing activities, 102
HighScope Educational Research Foundation, 238
Hildebrand, V., 211
Hit the Air! activity, 96
Hokey Pokey activity, 61
Holt-Hale, S., 31, 89, 91, 99, 180
Homolateral crawling, 81
Honest praise, 176–177
Hoops, 77–78, 131–132
Hopping, 86
Household sounds identification activity, 156
Human Kinetics, 73, 238

I

Identifying Household Sounds activity, 156
IEPs (Individual Education Plans), 69
"If You're Happy and You Know It" song, 51, 156, 221
Igloo activity, 138
Ignoring disruptions, 179
Imagery
  during cleanup, 219

Imagery (*continued*)
  exploring flow with, 80
  familiar, 177
Images for relaxation, 181
Imagination, 13, 31–32, 46
"Imagine That You Are …" activity, 229
Imitation, 71, 84, 161, 163
In and Out of the Hoop activity, 86
Incorporating Other Senses activity, 192
Independence, 42, 65
Indirect teaching approaches, 161, 164
Individual appropriateness, 38
Individual Education Plans (IEPs), 69
Infants (birth to 12 months)
  developmentally appropriate movement
      programs
        affective development, 41–42
        cognitive development, 51–54
        motor development, 42–44
        overview, 38–39
  interaction between, 42
  motor development in, 59
  musical development in, 26
  physical activity guidelines for, 7–8
  push/pull toys for, 95
Initial phase of skill development, 88
Initial stage of motor learning, 88
Instruments
  introducing, 156
  playing, 148
Integrated approach to literacy, 193
Intelligence, 12, 14, 18
Interaction
  between infants, 42
  between toddlers, 48
Intermediate phase of skill development, 88
Interpersonal intelligence, 14, 18
Intrapersonal intelligence, 14, 18
IPA/USA (American Association for the
    Child's Right to Play), 237
Isenberg, J. P., 18, 23, 194
It's a Dog's Life activity, 120
"It's Their World, Too" poem, 13
It Takes Two activity, 13

J

Jack Be Nimble activity, 53
Jacobsen, E., 181
Jalongo, M. R., 18, 23, 194
Jaques-Dalcroze, E., 15, 26
Jarnow, J., 146
Jewett, J., 10
Jumping, 9, 52, 84

K

Kaplan Early Learning Company, 239
Kaufman, P., 31
Keep It Bouncing! activity, 138
Kicking, 44, 97
Kimbo Educational, 239
Kindergarten plan, half-day, *213f*
Kinesthetic mode of learning, 12, 187
Kirchner, G., 88
Klein, J., 15, 164
Knowledge acquisition, modalities of, 12
Kohn, Alfie, 177–178

L

Lakeshore Learning, 238, 239
Language arts, 192–193
Language skills
  infant, 39

music in development of, 23
  primary-grade children, 63
  toddler, 46
Large muscle playground equipment, 234
Laterality, 56, 113
Lazdauskas, H., 25
Leaping, 84
Learning-disabled children, 72
Legato, 145, 151, 156
Leg movements, 135
Lesson planning
  creating plans, 109–114
  developmental progressions, 113–114
  overview, 109
  single movement themes, 117–119
  single unit themes, 119–121
  varied movement themes, 114–117
Let's Bend activity, *118f*
Let's Have a Parade activity, 232
Let's Slither activity, 66
Let's Turn activity, *116f*
Let's Walk activity, *115f*
Lifting, 96
Limited movement activities, 56
Limited understanding, children with, 72–73
Lines, activities exploring, 190
Linguistic intelligence, 12–14, 18
Listening activities, 193
Listening centers, 144
Listening skills, 23
Listening to music, 147
Literature
  art, 189–192
  mathematics, 198
  science, 201
Locomotor skills. *See also* Motor
      development
    crawl, 81–83
    creep, 83
    gallop, 86
    hop, 86
    jump, 84
    leap, 84
    overview, 81
    run, 84
    skip, 87
    slide, 86–87
    step-hop, 87–88
    walk, 83–84
Logical/mathematical intelligence, 14, 18
Log Roll activity, 100
Loovis, E. M., 72
Loud volume, 150
Low balancing activities, 102
Low pitch, 151
Lummi sticks. *See* Rhythm sticks
Lunch, transition to or from, 216–217

M

Maas, J. M., 109
Machines, 200–201
Magnets, 201
Make believe play, 56
Make Believe Striking activity, 33
Make Believe Walks activity, 33
Making Ripples activity, 138
Making Shapes activity, 34, 78, 190
Making Straight and Round activity, 190
Making Waves activity, 138
Maneuvering activity, 232
Manipulative skills
  ball roll, 97–98
  bounce, 98–99
  catch, 99

dribble, 99–100
  kick, 97
  lift, 96
  in outdoor settings, 225
  overview, 94
  in preschoolers, 58
  pull, 94
  push, 95
  strike, 96–97
  throw, 96–97
  volley, 98
Marching, 8–9
Marching Band activity, *116f–117f*
Marking boundaries, 175
Mathematics, 193, 195–198
Mature stage of motor learning, 88–89
Mayesky, M., 195
McDonald, D. T., 24
Melodic instruments, 144
Melody House, 239
Melting activity, 181
MENC (National Association for Music
    Education), 237
Mental retardation, 72
Meters, 153
"Mexican Hat Dance," 68
Midline-crossing activities, 41
Miller, D. F., 173, 177, 179, 180
Miller, K., 40, 45–46
Miller, L. G., 42
Minus signs, 198
Mirror Game, 53, 78, *116f*
MMB Music, 238
Modalities of knowledge acquisition, 12, 14
Modeling, 161, 163
Moderate to vigorous physical activity
    (MVPA), 4
Monitoring energy levels, 178
Monkeys! activity, 103
Moods, 23–24, 153
Moralizing, 177
Morris, Ann, 206
Mosston, M.
  command-style teaching, 162
  divergent problem solving, 168–170
  results of problem solving, 11
  The Slanted Rope, 165
Motor development
  early-elementary children, 66–68
  infants, 42–44
  preschoolers, 58–61
  toddlers, 51–53
Motor impairments, 70, 224
Motor skills, 3, 8
Movement elements
  flow, 80
  force, 79–80
  overview, 77
  rhythm, 80
  shape, 78–79
  space, 77–78
  time, 79
Movement in child development
  cognitive domain
    future implications, 15
    overview, 12–15
    role of movement, 15–18
  creative development
    future implications, 30–32
    overview, 29–30
    role of movement, 32–33
  musical development
    future implications, 25
    overview, 23–24
    role of movement, 25–28

overview, 3
physical domain
   body composition, 7–9
   cardiovascular endurance, 5–6
   flexibility, 7
   future implications, 5
   muscular endurance, 6
   muscular strength, 6
   overview, 3–5
social/emotional domain
   future implications, 10
   overview, 9
   role of movement, 10–12
Movement sessions
  attire, 129–130
  equipment and props
   balls, 131
   beanbags, 133
   hoops, 131–132
   overview, 130
   parachutes, 137–138
   rhythm sticks, 135–136
   scarves, 134–135
   streamers, 133–134
  group size, 128–129
  length of, 126
  overview, 124
  for preschoolers, 55
  scheduling, 124–126
  space, 126–127
  for toddlers, 45
Movement skills, 103
  categories of, 103
Movement themes
  single, 117–119
  varied, 114–117
Moving In, On, and Around the Tire activity, 230
Moving & Learning Across the Curriculum book, 119
Moving Like Animals activity, 51, 200
Moving Slow/Moving Fast activity, *117f*
MTNA (Music Teachers National Association), 237
Multicultural education, 205
Multiple intelligences, 14, 187
Murray, R. L., 88
Muscular endurance, 6
Muscular strength, 6
Music. *See also* Cross-curricular movement
  programs; Musical development;
  Musical elements; Musical experiences
  activities
   bean bag, 133
   clapping rhythms, *28*
   exploring common meters, 28
   with hearing impaired children, 71
   for infants, 44
   rhythm, 81
   rhythm stick, 137
   statues, 28
  and art, 189–192
  choosing
   nationalities, 145
   overview, 142
   periods, 143
   styles, 142–143
   textures, 145
  for galloping, 86
  and mathematics, 198
  overview, 142, 145–147
  for relaxation, 182
  in special need movement programs, 69
  in toddler movement programs, 47
  for transitions

arrival, 212–216
within classroom, 216–217
cleanup, 218–219
departure, 221
nap time, 219–220
to outside classroom, 217–218
overview, 211–212
Musical development
  future implications, 25
  overview, 23–24
  role of movement, 25–28
Musical elements
  contrast activities, 155
  crescendo and decrescendo, 151
  form, 152–153
  mood, 153
  overview, 149
  phrases, 151–152
  pitch, 151
  rhythm, 153
  staccato and legato, 151
  tempo, 149–150
  volume, 150
Musical experiences
  creating, 148
  listening, 147
  overview, 147
  playing, 148
  singing, 147–148
Musical Hoops activity, 132
Musical intelligence, 14, 18
Musical storytelling, 194
Musical versions of fingerplays, 214
Music and movement centers, 143–145
Music in Motion, 238
Music Teachers National Association (MTNA), 237

N

NAEYC (National Association for the Education of Young Children), 237
Nap time transitions, 219–220
National Association for Music Education (MENC), 237
National Association for Sport and Physical Education (NASPE), 7–8. *See also* Preschoolers, developmentally appropriate movement programs
National Association for the Education of Young Children (NAEYC), 237
National Dance Association, 95
Nationalities, music, 145
Naturalist intelligence, 14, 18
Nature activities, 13, 200
Nirschl, E., 109
No Contest: The Case Against Competition book, 11
Noise, participation with little, 175
Nonlocomotor skills
  bend, 90
  dodge, 93
  fall, 93–94
  rock and sway, 92
  shake, 91
  sit, 90–91
  stretch, 89–90
  swing, 92
  turn, 91–92
  twist, 92–93
Nonparticipants, 178–179
Notice of forthcoming cleanup sessions, 218
Numbers, forming shape of, 196
Numbers and Letters activity, 78

Nutrition
  example cross-curriculum program, 205–206
  exploring, 199

O

Obama, Barack, 4
Obama, Michelle, 4
Objectives, 109–110, 113
Object permanence, 39, 41
Observational assessment, 170
Observation cues, 110
Obstacle courses
  and language arts, 193–194
  for toddlers, 48
Occupations, 13, 119, 204–205
Olds, A. R., 193
Olympic gymnastics, 100, 101
One-Ball Activity, 131
One Step at a Time album, 64
Onlooker behavior, 49
Outdoor movement education
  balance beams, 228–229
  climbing structures, 227–228
  overview, 224–226
  platforms, 229–230
  playground as place of learning, 234–235
  playground space, 226–227
  riding toys, 231–232
  sand, 231
  slides, 232, 233
  swings, 232
  tires, 230–231
  tunnels, 229
Outer space, 200
Over the Rope activity, 86

P

Palm to palm activities, 66
Parachutes, 137–138
Parallel play, 49
Parker, M., 31, 89, 180
Parten, M., 49
Participation
  with little noise, rules regarding, 175
Partner Activity, 131
Partner-based activities, 61
Pass a Beat activity, 66
Pass a Face activity, 66
Pass a Movement activity, 66
Passing Overhead Activity, 131
Passing the Parachute activity, 138
Pathways Around the Body activity, 134
Pathways Through the Air activity, 134
Pattern of development, *52f*
Patty-cake, 42
Peekaboo, 42, 135
Peer relationships, 10, *11f*
Percussion, body, 47
Percussion instruments, 144, 145, 152
Percussive movement, 82
Periods, music, 143
Personality traits, 29
Personal space, 77–78, 113
Personal space activities, 174
Personal Space activity, 230
Pets theme, *120f*
Phrases
  creativity-fostering, 33
  musical, 151–152
Physical activity guidelines, 7–8

Physical domain of child development
  body composition, 7–9
  cardiovascular endurance, 5–6
  flexibility, 7
  muscular endurance, 6
  muscular strength, 6
  overview, 3–5
Physical education classes, 4
Physical fitness, 5
Physically challenged children, 69–70
Pica, R., 200, 204, 207
Pitch, 151
Platforms, 229–230
Plato, 25
Playgrounds
  as place of learning, 234
  space, 226–227
  static, 225
Play leaders, 224
Play with a Purpose, 239
Plus signs, 198
"Pop Goes the Weasel" activity, 9
Porter, L., 167
Positional concepts, 196
Positive challenges, 176
Positive learning environment
  disruptive behavior, 179–180
  nonparticipants, 178–179
  overview, 173
  role of relaxation, 181–182
  teaching tips
    being flexible, 178
    establishing boundaries, 175–176
    establishing rules, 174–175
    honest praise and positive reinforcement, 176–177
    making corrections creatively, 176
    monitoring energy levels, 178
    overview, 173–174
    using familiar imagery, 177
    using positive challenges, 176
    using voice as a tool, 177
Positive reinforcement, 176–177
Praise, 176–177
Praise addicts, 176
Precontrol level of skill proficiency, 89
Premobile period, 43
Preschoolers (3- to 5-year olds)
  developmentally appropriate movement programs
    affective development, 56–58
    cognitive development, 54–56
    motor development, 58–61
    overview, 54
  full-day programs for, *212f–213f*
  motor development in, 59–60
  musical development in, 26–27
  physical activity guidelines for, 8
  sample early childhood curriculum, *188f*
Pretending to Be … activity, 227
Pretend play, 56, 114, *114f*
Pretend to Dodge activity, 93
Pretend to Lift activity, 96
Primary Colors activity, 190
Primary theme, 110
Problem solving
  during classroom transitions, 216
  when transitioning to outside of classroom, 217
Proficiency level of skill, 89
Props
  balls, 131
  beanbags, 133
  hoops, 131–132
  overview, 130

  parachutes, 137–138
  rhythm sticks, 135–136
  scarves, 134–135
  streamers, 133–134
Psychosocial development, 9
Pulling, 44, 94
Punchinello activity, 221
Punished by Rewards: The Trouble with Gold Stars, Incentive Plans, A's, Praise, and Other Bribes book, 177–178
Pushing, 44, 95

Q

Quality, music, 142
Quantitative ideas, 195
Questions, 163, 164, 167
Quiet Moves, 136
Quiet transitions, 218

R

Rabbits and 'Roos activity, 9
Raines, S. C., 193, 194
Ramsey, M. E., 69–70
Rapping, rhythm stick, 136
Ray, M., 31
Reaching activities, 44
Reaction, 200, 201
Reading-readiness activities, 194
Recesses, 15
Recordings, fingerplay, 214
Reiff, J. C., 12, 14
Reinforcement, positive, 176–177
Relationships, peer, 10, *11f*
Relaxation
  nap time, 219–220
  in positive learning environment, 181–182
Repetition, 50, 73, 146, 147
Resistance training, 6
Rhythm, 80–81, 153, 193
Rhythm Band Instruments, 238
Rhythm sticks, 135–137
Ribbon sticks, 130, 133–134
Riding a … activity, 232
Riding toys, 231–232
"Ring around the Rosie" activity, 48, 87, 221
Robots and Astronauts activity, 27, 79
Rocking, 92
Rolling, 100
Rolling a Ball activity, 53
"Roll Over" song, 198
Round, exploring concept of, 190
"Row, Row, Row Your Boat" song, 152
Rowen, B., 194, 201
Rules, 56–58, 174–175
Running, 9, 52, 84
Running as Though … activity, 84

S

Safety
  of equipment, 139
  of infants, 44
  in movement session area, 127
  of toddlers, 52
Samuelson, E., 68
Sand, 231
Sanders, S. W., 130
Scarves, 134–135
Scheduling
  movement sessions, 124–126
  sample of, *212f*

Schirrmacher, R., 30, 32
Scholastic Early Childhood Today publication, 238
Scholastic Instructor publication, 238
Science, 198–202, 231
Scraping, rhythm stick, 136
Sedentary behaviors, 3–5
See My Face activity, 51
Self-concept, 48, 50, 68
Self-confidence, 3, 11, 42
Self-consciousness, 130
Self-control, 72
Self-expression, 30–31, 33–34, 189
Self-responsibility, 164
Senses, exploring, 199
Sensory experiences, 43
Separation anxiety, 41
Seven Kinds of Smart book, 187
Sex-role barriers, 66
Shake Like … activity, 91
Shaking, 91
Shapes
  art activities, 190
  as element of movement, 78–79
  forming number, 196
  geometric, 197
Shapes and Colors activity, 190
Shared space, 77
Shipley, D., 224, 226, 232
Shyness, 179
Silliman, L., 180
Silly Moves activity, 57
Simons, G. M., 24
Simon Says activity, 47, *115f, 117f, 121f*
Sinclair, C. B., 54, 84, 126
Singing, 147–148
Single movement themes, 117–119
Single unit themes, 119–121
Sitting, 90–91
Skill-related fitness, 5
Skinny Paths activity, 227
Skipping, 66, 87
Sky theme, *121f*
Slanted Rope, 165
Slides, 232
Sliding, 86–87
Snack-time, transition to or from, 216–217
Social appropriateness, 38
Social development
  future implications, 10
  overview, 9
  role of movement, 10–12
Social play, 49
Social studies
  families and friends, 203–204
  holidays and celebrations, 204
  multicultural education/diversity, 205
  occupations and transportation, 204–205
  overview, 202–203
  self-concept, 203
Soft movements, 79
Soft volume, 150
Solar System activity, *121f*
Solitary play, 49
Song picture books, 259
Songs. *See also* Music; Individual songs by name
  during cleanup, 219
  to encourage movement, 8–9
  and language arts, 194
  for nap time, 220
  for transitions, 216, 217
Sound games, 41
Sound identification activities, 193

Space
    as element of movement, 77–78
    movement sessions, 126–127
    personal, 77–78, 113
Space Songs for Children project, 200
Spatial awareness activities, 64
Spatial concepts, 55, 56
Spatial intelligence, 14, 18
Special needs children
    developmentally appropriate movement
        programs
        emotional disabilities, 72
        hearing impairments, 70–71
        limited understanding, 72–73
        overview, 68–69
        physical challenges, 69–70
        visual impairments, 71
Spectrum of Teaching Styles model, 165
Speech development
    infant, 39
    preschooler, 54
    primary-grade children, 63
    for toddlers, 45
Speed of movement, 79
Staccato, 151
Stages, platforms as, 230
Stamina, 6
Static playgrounds, 225
Static stretching, 7
Statues activity, 28, 80, 155
Statues and Rag Dolls activity, 79
Step-hopping, 68, 87–88
Stick Sounds Activity, 136
Stinson, S., 95, 126, 129
Story S-t-r-e-t-c-h-e-r-s books, 194
Storytelling, musical, 194
Story time, transition to or from, 217
Straight, activity exploring concept of, 190
Stranger anxiety, 41
Streamers, 133–134
Strength, muscular, 6
Stretching, 7, 89–90
Striking, 96–97, 99
Strong movements, 79
Styles, music, 142–143
Subtracting activities, 198
Success, 53, 65
Successive approximations, 179
Sullivan, M., 94, 126, 129, 176, 178
Sunrise/Sunset activity, *121f*
Suspended movement, 82
Sustained movement, 82
Swaying, 92
Swaying and Rocking activity, 92
Swinging, 82, 92, 103
Swinging in Different Ways activity, 233
Swing Like ... activity, 93
Swings, 232

T

Tactile modality of knowledge acquisition, 12
Taking turns, 211
Tapping to a Beat Activity, 137
Target Practice activity, 97
Teachers
    communication
        with hearing impaired children, 70–71
    in-classroom activities, 8–9
    including physical activity in classrooms, 7

promotion of communication skills by, 63
promotion of problem-solving skills by, 63
promotion of social development by,
    11–12
role in physical activity of children, 5
Teaching methods
    direct, 161–163
    exploration, 167–170
    guided discovery, 163–167
    overview, 161
Teaching tips
    being flexible, 178
    establishing boundaries, 175–176
    establishing rules, 174–175
    honest praise and positive reinforcement,
        176–177
    making corrections creatively, 176
    monitoring energy levels, 178
    overview, 173–174
    using familiar imagery, 177
    using positive challenges, 176
    using voice as a tool, 177
Teach Preschool, 238
Television viewing, 4
Tempo, 149–150
"Ten Little Children" activity, 87
Ten Seconds activity, 64
Test of Gross Motor Development, 2nd
    edition (TGMD-2), 170
Textures
    exploring concept of, 190
    music, 145
Themes
    single movement, 117–119
    single unit, 119–121
    varied movement, 114–117
This Is My Friend activity, 215
Throwing, 96–97
Tightrope activity, *115f*
Time as element of movement, 79
Time-outs, 180
Tips, teaching. *See* Teaching tips
Tiredness, *62f*
Tires, 230–231
Toddlers (12 to 36 months)
    developmentally appropriate movement
        programs
        affective development, 48–51
        cognitive development, 45–48
        motor development, 51–53
        overview, 44–45
    half-day programs for, *212f*
    motor development in, 51–53, 59
    musical development in, 26
    physical activity guidelines for, 8
Torrance, E. P., 29, 32
Tossing games, 53, 135
Track Meet activity, 9
Traffic safety, 204
Trampolines, 234
Transferring weight, 100–101
Transitions, 211
    arrival, 212–216
    within classroom, 216–217
    cleanup, 218–219
    departure, 221
    nap time, 219–220
    to outside classroom, 217–218
    overview, 211–212
Transportation, 204–205

Traveling Along the Beam activity, 228
Travel Like This ... activity, 229
Tummy time, 44
Tunnels, *83f*, 229
Turning, 91–92
Turns, taking, 211
Turtles activity, 120
Twisting, 92–93
Twist Like ... activity, 93
Two-Hand/One-Hand Volley activity, 98
Type 2 diabetes, 4

U

Understanding Words activity, 194
Uniformity, 163
Unit themes, single, 119–121
Unoccupied behavior, 49
Unrestrictive clothing, 129
Up and Down activity, 47–48
Using a Tire: The Many Imaginative
    Possibilities activity, 230
Using the Ladder activity, 233
Using the Slide activity, 233
Utilization level of skill proficiency, 89

V

Varied movement themes, 114–117
Variety, music, 142, 143, 153
Vehicles, playground, 234
Verbalization, 165, 166
Vibratory movement, 82
Visually impaired children, 71, 224
Visual modality of knowledge acquisition, 12
Visual signals, 175
Voice, using as tool, 177
Volleying, 98
Volume, 150

W

Walking, 43, 83–84
Walking a Tightrope activity, 102
Warnings
    about disruptive behavior, 180
    of forthcoming cleanup sessions, 218
Water equipment, 235
Weather activities, 13
Weight
    body, 7
    transferring, 100–101
Weightlessness, 200
Weight training, 6
Weiler, V. B., 109
Weimer, T. E., 200
Welcoming children to class, 212, 215
Wet Noodle activity, 94
"Wheels on the Bus" song, 216
Where Is Thumbkin? activity, 47, *116f, 117f*
"Whistle While You Work" song, 219
Whole child, 188, 202. *See also* Cross-
    curricular movement programs
Witkin, K., 30

Y

Young children. *See* Preschoolers